Basque Nationalism and the Spanish State

The Basque Series

ANDRÉ LECOURS

Basque Nationalism and the Spanish State

University of Nevada Press   Reno   Las Vegas

The Basque Series

Copyright © 2007 by University

of Nevada Press

All rights reserved

Manufactured in the United States

of America

The paper used in this book is a recycled

stock made from 50 percent post-consumer

waste materials and meets the requirements

of American National Standard for Infor-

mation Sciences—Permanence of Paper

for Printed Library Materials,

ANSI/NISO Z39.48-1992 (R2002). Binding

materials were selected for strength

and durability.

16 15 14 13 12 11 10 09 08 07

5 4 3 2 1

Library of Congress

Cataloging-in Publication Data

Lecours, André, 1972–

Basque nationalism and the Spanish state /

Andre Lecours.

p. cm. — (The Basque series)

Includes bibliographical references

and index.

ISBN 978-0-87417-722-0 (hardcover :

alk. paper)

1. Nationalism—Spain—País Vasco.

2. País Vasco (Spain)—Politics and govern-

ment. 3. Spain—Politics and government.

I. Title.

DP302.B55L43 2007

320.540946'6—dc22

2007004973

For Natasha, Elizabeth, and Charles

Contents

Figures and Tables

Preface

Nationalism is a tricky research subject, because it is difficult to write about it without being categorized as either a "sympathizer" or a "critic." This tendency to place tags on writers is understandable, because much of the literature on particular cases is outright political, in the sense of representing explicit support for the cause of a nationalist movement or clear denunciations of their activity, even existence. I found that this propensity for labeling authors as "nationalist" or "antinationalist" was particularly important in the Basque Country. This is hardly surprising considering the intensity of the conflict and the polarization of society over the political status of the Basque Country. In the study of Basque nationalism, as in nationalism studies in general, the line between politics and scholarship can be easily blurred. Some would say this is unavoidable and that a neutral treatment of nationalism and nationalist conflict is impossible. From this perspective, research on nationalism is always underpinned by a concern for either the plight of a "stateless nation" or for the integrity of the state and the unity of the nation it projects.

I think that this issue of normative positioning can be largely avoided if one focuses on explaining the emergence and subsequent dynamics of nationalist movements. This is what I have tried to do in the first half of this book. I have used the tools of comparative politics, more specifically historical institutionalism, to present a state-centered argument about the development of Basque nationalism. The primary purpose of this book, therefore, is not to put forward a normative judgement about Basque nationalism or to engage in a political debate about the merits of its claims. Rather, the idea is to make a theoretical contribution to the study of nationalism by using the Basque case.

At the same time, I did not want to pass up the opportunity to analyze important political developments in the Basque Country such as the development by the Basque government of international relations (paradiplomacy), the presentation by Basque lehendakari Juan José Ibarretxe of a proposal for the restructuring of the relationship between the Basque Country and the Spanish state, and the announcement by ETA in 2006 of a permanent cease-fire. Since this task involves delving into the intricacies of Basque politics, one could argue that it is more difficult to be neutral and objective. Still, my objective in discussing these processes and events is to be analytical rather than polemical, that is, to provide a fair assessment of their causes, meaning, and potential consequence. This is where, I think, being an "outsider" can be useful, because I have no emotional attachment to one side or the other, nor do I have a stake of any kind in political outcomes.

Finally, I also take a chapter in this book to place Basque nationalism in comparative perspective. Here again, my objective is not to show that the Basque nationalist movement is better or worse than others in Western societies. Rather, I am looking to demystify nationalism in the Basque Country and make the point that the presence of political violence for most of the democratic period does not mean that Basque nationalism is fundamentally different from Catalan, Scottish, Quebecois, or Flemish nationalism. There is a pattern to the politics of substate nationalism in Western societies (in terms of structure, claims, discourse, arguments, and so forth) that seems to cut across the specifics of a case.

In sum, I hope this book represents a contribution to the field of nationalism studies that combines a theoretical purpose with the rich analysis of a fascinating case.

Acknowledgments

Research for this book was conducted in the Basque Country as well as in the Basque Studies Library at the University of Nevada, Reno. I would like to thank Noé Cornago Prieto, in the Basque Country, for his help and William A. Douglass, in Reno, for informative conversations. I want to thank Claire Delisle and Peter Nasr for their research assistance and the two anonymous reviewers for their useful advice. Special thanks to Luis Moreno for having commented on the manuscript.

I drew much inspiration in thinking about the relationship between state and substate nationalism from my work in the Research Group on Plurinational Societies led by Alain-G. Gagnon at Université du Québec à Montréal.

Basque Nationalism and the Spanish State

Introduction

Substate Nationalism, Historical Institutionalism, and the Basque Country

"Es la realidad del País." This is a statement I heard more than once when conducting research on Basque nationalism in the Basque Country. It conveys a sense of resignation about the deep polarization of Basque politics and society that has accompanied the expression of Basque nationalism in the democratic period. Basque nationalism questions with tremendous strength and pugnacity the legitimacy of the Spanish state's rule in the Basque Country and the idea of a Spanish nation. This is most obvious in the politics of the radical stream of Basque nationalism whose flagship organization ETA (Euskadi ta Askatasuna) was, until its declaration of a permanent cease-fire in March 2006, committed to using violence in an attempt to achieve the independence of the Basque Country. The moderate nationalists of the PNV (Partido Nacionalista Vasco) have challenged the Spanish state in their own way while staying clear of formally supporting political violence. The PNV has been consistent in claiming that the Basques have a right to self-determination. This right would suppose that the Basque population alone can decide if the Basque Country remains part of Spain, becomes independent, or adopts some other type of political status. In this spirit, Basque *lehendakari* Juan José Ibarretxe put forward a proposal for a "Statute of Free Association" between the Basque Country and Spain.

The position of the central government toward Basque nationalism was uncompromising during the second mandate of the Partido Popular (PP) (2000–2004). After the 2000 elections, when it won an absolute majority in the Congress of Deputies, the PP took a hard line toward both radical and moderate Basque nationalists. It pursued a policing rather than a political strategy toward ETA, whose violence it considered a form of criminality. For example, the PP supported 2002 and 2003 court orders to outlaw Batasuna, the radical nationalist party with close links with ETA, and shut down the Basque-language daily *Egunkaria*. In reaction to the Ibarretxe proposal of a free association, the PP government made it illegal to hold referendums that could compromise the political and territorial integrity of Spain.[1]

1

The consequence of all these decisions was to aggravate the polarization between Basque nationalists, who typically seek more autonomy or independence for the Basque Country, and non-Basque nationalists, who defend the status quo.[2] Between 2000 and 2004, the political climate in the Basque Country was the most volatile and tense it had been since the end of the dictatorship. The election of the Partido Socialista Obrero Español (PSOE) in the spring of 2004 improved the atmosphere, as the new socialist government stated it was open to a dialogue with the Basque government about political and institutional reform.[3] ETA's declaration of a permanent cease-fire in 2006 opened up more opportunities for change.

The contemporary political situation in the Basque Country is the product of a process, the development of Basque nationalism, that has been unfolding for a century but whose structural roots are much older. How did Basque nationalism emerge? How did it gain such significant popular support? Why does it feature a radical stream, which until recently tolerated violence? Why is contemporary Basque politics permeated by the national question? In other words, why is Basque politics to a large extent nationalist politics? These are questions guiding this book as it develops, in chapters 1–4, a historical institutionalist perspective on Basque nationalism. There is a considerable literature on Basque nationalism, some of which examines these types of questions. Authors have insisted on many different factors when analyzing Basque nationalism: culture, political economy, elite behavior, foral autonomy, state centralization, dictatorial rule, and others. This study does not have the pretension to invoke brand new explanatory factors for Basque nationalism; rather, it seeks to develop a historical state-centric perspective that considers the rise of nationalism in the Basque Country to be inextricably linked to the development of Spanish nationalism. The main argument is that Basque nationalism should be understood in relation to state- and nation-building in the Iberian Peninsula. The book suggests that Basque nationalism is the product of a historical trajectory that saw the Spanish state assume four different forms in its relation with the Basque provinces/Country: confederal-like (up to the nineteenth century); centralizing (in the late nineteenth and early twentieth centuries); authoritarian (the Primo de Rivera and Franco dictatorships); and democratic with the Estado de las Autonomías (since 1978).

The specific argument is the following. The Spanish state did not engage in nation-building until very late in the nineteenth century, which allowed for the crystallization of non-Spanish identities in the Basque provinces. When some efforts at "national integration" were made in the late 1800s, they were half-hearted and ultimately unsuccessful because the state, although centralizing, was too weak and sending conflicting images of the Spanish nation. This failure to "nationalize the masses" as well as the traditional landholding elites in the Basque provinces meant that attachment to nations other than Spain could be engineered. This is what happened when the traditional elite of the Basque province of Bizkaia challenged state centralization by spearheading a Basque nationalist movement. In the context of the twentieth-century authoritarian state, Spanish nationalism was discredited by the brutal policies of Franco, while Basque nationalism became associated with freedom and democracy. The structures of the democratic state allowed for the political expression of Basque nationalism while also rehabilitating, for a substantial segment of Basque society, the idea of a Spanish nation. This duality of national attachments explains nationalist conflicts in the Basque Country.

The argument for a state-centric perspective on Basque nationalism is made drawing from historical institutionalism. This approach offers a historical quality to political analysis that, combined with the theoretical importance given to political institutions, brings a focus to the temporal articulation of state forms and its effect on agency, preferences, strategies, identities, and the overall organization of politics. From a historical institutionalist perspective, the various historical forms of the Spanish state represent critical junctures for Basque nationalism insofar as the succession of these forms narrowed to nationalist conflict the developmental pathway of Basque politics through specific patterns of interaction with (depending on the historical period) Basque elites, political parties, ETA, and the larger civil society.

This book uses the historical institutionalist framework to conduct a single case study of nationalism, the Basque Country. In this context, it is difficult to put forward generalizations, especially since the Spanish state, with its multiple and clearly delineated state forms, lends itself particularly well to a historical institutionalist analysis and its preferred methodological strategy of periodization. Nevertheless, the Basque Country serves as a case that can hint at the usefulness of historical institutionalism for shedding light on substate nationalism. The analysis of Basque nationalism presented in this study may not offer an exact template for conducting other case studies (the historical trajectories of states and their nations being too different from one to another), but it is intended to suggest historical institutionalism as a framework for thinking about the development of nationalist movements.

In addition to examining Basque nationalism through a historical institutionalist framework, this book offers analytical and comparative perspectives on the Basque nationalist movement. The last three substantive chapters proceed with a logic different from the first four insofar as they focus on specific political dynamics stemming from Basque nationalism. First, nationalism has meant that Basque governments have aggressively pursued networks, strategies, and policies of international action. The substantial and multidimensional paradiplomacy found in the Basque Country is not exclusive to this case, and a strong argument can be made that substate nationalism is functionally related to nationalism. Also, the existence of the Basque nationalist movement has required the democratic Spanish state to devise political and institutional management approaches and strategies. Its system of autonomous communities that decentralized power following a federal logic became the centerpiece of an accommodation strategy, while the deployment of a liberal, democratic, and constitutionally grounded Spanish nationalism was aimed at gaining the loyalty of the Basques. The recent proposal of Basque lehendakari Ibarretxe suggests a redesign of the political and institutional arrangements of 1978. Finally, Basque nationalism is a differentiated phenomenon, featuring various and contrasted ideologies, that has been engaged by the processes of globalization, including continental integration. These political dynamics are not unique to the Basque case and can be compared to those of other nationalist movements in Western societies.

These contributions seek to fill gaps in the literature on Basque nationalism. Basque paradiplomacy has not been significantly documented and analyzed in English. Discussions about the management of Basque nationalism are typically limited to a description of the Estado de las Autonomías. They usually ignore Spanish nationalism as a central process aimed at solving the Basque "problem," and treatments of the Ibarretxe proposal in English are rare. Finally, comparative works featuring the Basque case are also fairly rare despite the fact that, apart from political violence, nationalist politics in the Basque Country have much in common with nationalist politics in Cataluña, Quebec, Scotland, and Flanders.

Basque Nationalism: A Literature Overview

There is a substantial literature on Basque nationalism, especially if one considers studies on Basque culture, tradition, language, and literature that generally fall under the heading of "Basque studies."[4] The focus of this section is on works specifically on nationalism rather than on culture in the broader sense, or on the diaspora.[5] The objective is not to offer a comprehensive review of the literature, but rather to provide an assessment of how this literature is structured and where the present contribution fits in.

A first type of work on Basque nationalism is the historical narrative. Its focus is on recounting in great detail the history of the Basques, the rise of Basque nationalism, and its struggle during the Franco dictatorship. Many of these books give great attention to the role of Sabino Arana in articulating Basque nationalism.[6] Others focus on post-Arana periods.[7] The degree of analysis contained in these types of monographs varies greatly: a particularly good author is José Luis de la Granja Sainz, whose *El nacionalismo vasco: Un siglo de historia* provides a most insightful examination of the development of Basque nationalism.[8] The perspective also varies. Some authors offer nationalist accounts of Basque nationalism insofar as they present the Basque nation more or less as an organic reality that has persisted throughout history, most often in hostile conditions.[9] Others have told the story without the Basque nationalist slant, or as some have said, from an antinationalist perspective.[10] The Spanish state is always there somewhere in these histories. In the writing of Basque nationalists, it is typically portrayed as a source of oppression and therefore largely negatively. For scholars adopting a Spanish perspective, substate nationalism is negatively perceived because it prevents the complete integration of Spain. In none of these literatures are the macroprocesses of state- and nation-building at the center of a coherent theoretical explanation for the development of Basque nationalism. In fact, these historical studies are not informed by explicit theoretical frameworks; they are meant to be detailed narratives, rather than parsimonious explanations or "thick descriptions" of Basque nationalism.

A second focus for scholars working on Basque nationalism has been ETA and political violence. Many authors have detailed the birth of ETA, its ideological struggles, tactical dilemmas, and so on.[11] Others, such as Robert P. Clark and Ludger Mees, have tackled ETA and political violence from a conflict resolution perspective.[12] Another research angle has been to look at the counteroffensive of the Spanish and French states.[13] From a more anthropological perspective, scholars such as Joseba Zulaika and Begoña Aretxaga have written about the various meanings and social consequences of violence stemming from ETA or the radical Basque youths involved in "street fighting" (*kale borroka*).[14] The focus on political violence has also led to very insightful research about the broader radical nationalist community.[15] Indeed, current work on ETA is considerably enhancing our understanding of Basque nationalism by investigating the social foundations of violence.

Another research focus has been the politics of Basque nationalism during the transition and the construction of the Basque Statute of Autonomy.[16] In his *Conflicto en Euskadi*, published in 1986, Juan Linz predicted that the PNV's ambiguous position toward the new constitution and the Estado de las Autonomías meant that the Spanish state would remain a contested presence in the Basque Country.[17] Many other good studies have tied the history of Basque nationalism to contemporary manifestations while making specific arguments about the peculiarity of Basque nationalism. For example, Barbara Loyer has emphasized the great diversity of positions toward Spain within the Basque Country, while Cyrus Zirakzadeh has provided an account of Basque nationalist politics in reference to class and economic structures.[18] Basque nationalism has also been discussed in the larger context of territorial and nationalist politics in Spain. Let us mention here the work of Luis Moreno on the federalization of the Spanish state.[19]

Some of the most interesting and theoretically informed work on Basque nationalism has featured comparisons with other nationalist movements. Cataluña has been a favorite case.[20] Daniele Conversi has put forth the intriguing argument that violence is a feature of Basque nationalism because Basque society lacks the functional common language found in Cataluña.[21] Juan Díez Medrano has suggested that different patterns of economic development are at the heart of the distinct development processes of Basque and Catalan nationalism.[22] Another case used quite often to structure comparisons with the Basque Country is Northern Ireland.[23] Here, an interesting contribution comes from Cynthia Irvin, who has looked to explain, using interviews with Sinn Féin and Batasuna militants, why radical nationalists sometimes accept to play the game of electoral politics.[24] A slightly different approach is taken by Jan Mansvelt Beck who is one of the rare scholars of Basque nationalism sensitive to explaining the strength in Spain and weakness in France.[25] Finally, there are also larger comparative works that include discussions of the Basque Country. For example, Michael Keating has argued that nationalist movements in the West typically adopt a post-sovereignty view of the world; they do not look for straight secession but rather attempt to secure a political status that would provide their community with extensive autonomy while retaining links with the central state.[26]

To reiterate, this comment on the literature is not meant to provide a comprehensive review of everything written on Basque nationalism,[27] but rather to get a sense of what types of contributions have been made. Discussions and analyses of Basque nationalism typically involve some mention of the Spanish state. This book seeks to go further by developing a state-centric perspective on Basque nationalism that explicitly takes the historical articulation of the various forms of the Spanish state and their particular expressions (or lack thereof) of a Spanish nation as central theoretical determinants. Before considering historical institutionalism as the most adequate framework for such a task, I now examine different theories and understandings of nationalism.

Theories of Nationalism

The central debate in the field of nationalism has arguably been between modernist and primordialist (or perennialist) understandings of the phenomenon.[28] These positions used to be quite crudely laid out. Modernists argued that the nation was a European invention created by processes of modernization and state centralization during the seventeenth and eighteenth centuries. They suggested that the emergence of nationalism was a functional necessity since industrial capitalist societies could only operate in the context of cultural homogeneity.[29] In other words, modernity required political, institutional, economic, and cultural integration and, therefore, the construction of genuine nation-states. From this perspective, nations do not have "ancient histories." In fact, all history before the seventeenth century is irrelevant for understanding nations and nationalism, as well as all non-European history before the nation-state model was exported by colonial powers. A key modernist idea is that nations do not have an organic nature but rather are constructed. From this perspective, nationalism creates nations, not the other way around.[30]

Primordialists, as they were called in the 1970s and the 1980s, argued that nations were naturally occurring sociocultural groups whose members felt a bond with one another stronger than any other type of ties they could experience. Some primordialist scholars sought to make the link between nationalism and genetics,[31] but most suggested that nations were the inevitable consequence of cultural diversity. Cultural markers, sometimes referred to as "basic ties,"[32] were said to be powerful "in and of themselves."[33] These markers were seen as constitutive of a type of group identity, that is, national or ethnic identity, more fundamental and more *primordial* than identities deriving from class, gender, or other cleavages. Primordialism gave a sense of naturalness to the nation that derived not from functional but rather psychological needs. It held that nations were very ancient communities, not necessarily European in origins or nature, whose existence was buried in history. From this angle, nations generate nationalism.[34]

In the last fifteen years, there has been a considerable rapprochement between the modernist and primordialist positions. Sharp criticisms, from both sides, have hit the mark. Perhaps most obvious is the change in discourse from those closest to the primordialist tradition as well as a change of name: virtually no scholar of nationalism accepts the tag of "primordialist" today, even if their research focuses on the impact of culture on national identity and mobilization. The preferred label is "perennialist" or "ethno-symbolist." Both perennialists and ethno-symbolists readily speak of nations as constructs.[35] Gone are the ideas that nations are "givens" of social existence and that their foremost characteristic is some form of mystic primordialism. Perennialists and ethno-symbolists acknowledge the importance of state-building for nations, although they do not agree with the modernist idea that nations were built from scratch by modernizing states. Instead, they suggest that state modernization represents an important, if not decisive, process in the development of nations. They do maintain, however, that this development usually began before the modernization process or, in other words, that the genesis of nations typically precedes industrialization as well as political and institutional integration. Ethno-symbolists stress most particularly the importance of the construction of narratives and symbols in explaining the power of nationalism.

Modernists have also had to respond to difficult objections to their theory of nationalism. Critics argued that the modernist paradigm could not capture the emotional and volatile character of nationalism. Modernists responded to this criticism by saying that they were well aware of the power of symbols and myths; however, there seems to be little room in their approach for incorporating this type of factor. Perhaps most important were charges of Eurocentrism and ahistoricalness. Modernists, drawing primarily from European empirical material, denied much of the history of non-European societies or, at least, could not make room for the possibility that there existed national identities or communities before contact with the Europeans. For instance, responses to strongly voiced claims that aboriginal populations in the Americas adopted nationlike forms of organization before colonization can only play on the issue of scale, that is, on the idea that nations are communities where most members never have face-to-face relations. Other troublesome cases, such as ancient Greece, Armenia, or Israel, have been thrown at the modernists, who have tended to remain more steadfast in their argument than perennialists. Nevertheless, it is clear that the perennialist critique has had its effect on the literature on nationalism. Whereas in the 1980s modernists seemed to have won the battle of paradigms, the 1990s featured a renaissance of much-lauded perennialist work.[36] And that is without counting an abundance of poststructuralist and feminist works that do not fit very well within the modernist paradigm.[37]

In short, there seems to have been a fruitful dialogue among specialists of nationalism, although there certainly has not been a synthesis of the modernist and perennialist paradigms. Ethno-symbolism has become, to an extent, the meeting point of these two traditions in nationalism studies. Placing a specific tag on the conception of nationalism informing this study of the Basque case is not easy. However, my understanding of nationalism is closer to the modernist perspective: it stresses the state, does not place decisive importance on cultural variables, and believes in the construction of nations in the most profound and theoretically meaningful sense. I do, however, take exception to the ahistorical character of the modernist perspective. It is one thing to argue that nations did not exist before the seventeenth century, but quite another to say that nothing that happened previously mattered for the construction of nations. This book makes the claim that a genuine historical approach is important and that such an approach must pay close attention to the process of state development. The modernist and perennialist perspectives have often been erected as polar opposites, and, as a consequence, the state and history have, strangely enough, often been viewed as antithetical in the study of nationalism: modernists focused on the state but began their investigation in the seventeenth century, whereas perennialists made greater use of history while marginalizing the state. The approach taken in this book is that the history *of* the state is of foremost importance for understanding nationalism, and that in many cases the genesis of state construction, which often goes back several centuries, is central to explaining contemporary nationalism even if its emergence is relatively recent.

Above and beyond the debate over the broader nature of nationalism, there are also disagreements about which specific factors are most important in its development. There are a variety of ways to categorize theories of nationalism. For the purpose of the current review, I adopt a fairly conventional typology and distinguish between cultural, economic, political, and macrostructural approaches.

Cultural theories focus on the formative role of cultural markers such as language or religion in the development of national identities and communities. From this perspective, there is not much emphasis on nationalist politics in the sense of mobilization and competition. Rather, the identities stemming from cultural markers are viewed more or less as naturally permeating the political realm. This was very much the position of the early primordialists.[38] In this tradition, the link between culture and nationalism is very straightforward: cultural markers unite and divide human populations; they delineate groups and forge the most basic and fundamental ties of collective identity.

Another group of scholars that has developed cultural theories of nationalism comes from political philosophy. Charles Taylor, Will Kymlicka, and others have sought to develop an alternative view to classical liberal theory that, they argue, conceptualizes human beings in isolation from their sociocultural environment.[39] These scholars suggest that human agency is always informed by cultural considerations. They argue that culture, and more specifically language, has a natural subjective meaning and that it generates collective identities that fulfill a need to belong. From this angle, these identities are bound to have political consequences in the form of claims for recognition, autonomy, or independence. This type of cultural perspective on nationalism suggests that most societies are permeated by an irreducible diversity. It typically informs the writings of nationalist scholars[40] as well as researchers who are pessimistic about the long-term survival of multi-ethnic and multinational states and the peaceful coexistence of their populations.[41] To this group, we could also add consociational theorists who put a positive spin on cultural diversity and argue that political leaders should not look to transcend it, but rather use it to build stable democracies.[42]

These cultural approaches lack the historical perspective necessary to understand long-term processes such as identity construction and the building up of nationalist mobilization. In fact, I would argue that these approaches consider identities and mobilization largely as "givens," and that their existence does not seem to be the product of a process. Here, culture is overwhelming, and nationalism is, at the constitutive level, almost apolitical and asocial.[43] As a consequence, the state does not factor into the explanation for nationalism; rather, it is seen exclusively as a reflection of a society's cultural composition, or as an instrument that can be used for the management of diversity and nationalist conflict.

Perennialism and ethno-symbolism can also be considered cultural theories of nationalism insofar as they locate the origins of nations in premodern cultures.[44] These perspectives are historical and not limited to cultural considerations; they view the emergence of nations as a process involving cultural, social, political, ideological, technological, and other forces. The state is present here, but mostly in its centralizing and modernizing seventeenth- and eighteenth-century forms; this is a point taken from the modernist perspective. Perennialism and ethno-symbolism are certainly richer approaches than the old primordialism, but they still give theoretical primacy to cultural factors.[45] Cultural theories are not the best suited for explaining Basque nationalism. After all, there is a similar Basque culture in both Spain and France, but only in the former is there a strong nationalist movement.[46] Of course, it is not unimportant that the Basques are a population with unique cultural, linguistic, and, some have even said, physical characteristics; however, these cultural features are relevant for an understanding of Basque nationalism only insofar as they are connected to political and institutional considerations. For example, the early structure of the Spanish state fostered among the Basque population, or at least its elites, collective self-perceptions of exceptionalism that, following the transformation of the state in the nineteenth century, were rearticulated into powerful nationalist narratives.

If cultural theories have evolved from primordialism to perennialism over the last couple of decades, the economic perspective has switched from a focus on uneven development to globalization. The traditional economic theory of nationalism held that the territorial cleavages created by the capitalist economy produced feelings of frustration and resentment on the part of inhabitants of both underdeveloped and overdeveloped regions; in turn, these feelings led to the development of identities and nationalist (or regionalist) claims.[47] The Marxist version of this theory, the internal colonialism thesis, viewed the state as creating and sustaining these economic discrepancies for the purpose of exploiting peripheral regions for the benefit of the dominant class.[48] These theories posited the theoretical primacy of economic factors insofar as cultural differences were not a necessary condition for the emergence of nationalism; from this type of perspective, some scholars even suggested subsuming nationalism within a theory of political cleavages.[49]

These types of hard-core economic theories of nationalism have been subjected to harsh criticism and have lost much of their popularity. Walker Connor, in particular, has effectively questioned the emphasis on economics.[50] The internal colonialism thesis was attacked from every angle, and its main proponent, Michael Hechter, although still defending it in principle, has gone on to adopt different approaches.[51] At the end of the day, identifying under- and overdeveloped regions is problematic; however, even if there were agreement on specific cases, the causality implied by economic theories would remain unclear. For example, substate nationalism emerged, if one accepts the following classifications, in relatively underdeveloped (Scotland and Wales) as well as overdeveloped regions (Cataluña and the Basque Country). There are also nationalist movements in regions that are neither truly under- or overdeveloped (Quebec), while in other cases (Flanders) nationalism emerged in the context of relative poverty but remained, and even thrived, in a situation of relative wealth.

More recently, scholars have sought to link substate nationalism with globalization.[52] At first, there were suggestions that globalization would have a homogenizing effect on states and that the political salience of their cultural diversity would be considerably reduced or completely eliminated. However, this is no longer the dominant academic wisdom. Rather, most scholars now contend that free trade, regional integration, and global interconnectedness through new technologies weaken the state and therefore loosen its subjective ties with citizens.[53] As a result, regions have a new impetus to protect their own cultural and economic interests, and to claim the political power they feel is necessary to act efficiently in an autonomous manner. Some writers have argued that globalization reduces the benefits of staying together and lessens the potential costs of secession.[54] Overall, scholars who bring globalization into explanations for nationalism do not have it replacing cultural, political, and social factors. Rather, globalization is seen as exacerbating whatever forces are already at work. Indeed, globalization in itself cannot account for substate nationalism. For one thing, many nationalist movements emerged in the nineteenth century when globalization was, at the very least, qualitatively different. With respect to the Basque case, globalization can no more than culture explain why there is a strong nationalist movement in Spain but not in France. This being said, incorporating globalization into a discussion of Basque nationalism can be illuminating; for example, Manuel Castells has argued that new technologies give the Basques an importunity to promote their identity.[55] In many ways, discussions on the relationship between globalization and substate nationalism come down to the state. The state is being transformed by globalization, and, ultimately, the new state form (if one believes it exists) changes the dynamics of nationalist movements. This is especially clear when regional integration in Europe is mentioned as part of globalization; certainly, the European Union (EU) is about much more than economics. It involves a transformation in the role, capability, and perhaps even the nature of the state, a process that in turn can affect its territorial structuring.

Political theories conceive of nationalism as a form of politics. From this angle, nationalism is not primarily about culture or economics but rather power. The processes of identity construction and nationalist mobilization are seen as political in nature; they are embedded in power relationships. Typically, the ontological focus of these theories is on political elites. Scholars using these theories suggest that elites play a central role in providing objective cultural markers with subjective meaning and politicizing identities. They also argue that elites will tend to define group interests in a manner coherent with their own.[56] Some elite-centered theories present nationalism almost as an unintended consequence of elite power struggles. From this angle, political elites competing for power may adopt a nationalist language as they try to outbid their political adversaries. A slightly different version, often referred to as "instrumentalism," views elites as "ethnic entrepreneurs,"[57] that is, manipulative, and most often highly strategic actors,[58] who exploit fear and security dilemmas to maintain or gain political power.

At the broadest level, this study of Basque nationalism takes nationalism to be a political rather than a cultural or an economic phenomenon. Indeed, nationalist claims are political, and they take form in the context of a political process. There is also much to be said for considering the role of elites in constructing identities and stimulating nationalist forms of mobilization. After all, nationalist movements are like social movements; they have leaders and militants who play to a certain audience with the objective of shaping political preferences and identities. However, elite-centered approaches tend to marginalize the state so that elites appear to be operating in an institutional vacuum. This characterization may lead theorists to exaggerate the voluntarist quality of identity construction and nationalist mobilization. There is no doubt that elites, sometimes a single person as is the case with Sabino Arana for Basque nationalism, play a central role in the development of nationalist movements through the construction of narratives, symbols, and myths. However, their agency, and the extent to which the larger targeted population will give credence to the nationalist doctrine is heavily conditioned by the structure of the state and, more specifically, the pattern of its historical development. Not only does the historical developmental pathway of the state provide constraints to, and opportunities for, elites, but it also structures patterns of relationships (among elites, groups, parties, and so on) in ways that affect the likelihood of politics being transformed into nationalist politics.

At first glance, theoretical insight into the relationship between historical processes of state development and substate nationalism could be found in the macrostructural modernist theory. After all, Gellner argued that nations were created by the modern centralized state through the imposition of a "high culture."[59] In a similar type of argument, John Breuilly suggested that nationalism was the result of a reorganization of politics: only with the breakdown of privileges and the beginning of state intervention did the state become the focal point of political activity and produce claims for legitimacy framed in nationalist terms.[60] There are a few problems with drawing insight from these theories for building a historical and state-centric approach to substate nationalism. First, these theories are squarely focused on the historical period corresponding to the construction and centralization of the modern state; they ignore any previous history and significantly marginalize subsequent ones. As such, they concentrate on one particular state form and therefore fail to capture the *process* of state development, that is, the articulation of various state forms over a long period. Second, one could argue that the macrostructural modernization theory is more functionalist than institutionalist. Of course, the state is viewed as playing the central role in national integration, although, to a certain extent, it is only responding to broader structural conditions such as industrialization and capitalism. Finally, this theory focuses on state nationalism. It fails to see the variety of possible outcomes stemming from processes of state development, assuming rather that the modern centralized state leads societies into a nearly teleological path toward national integration. After all, modern states have so many tools (for example, national education systems and all kinds of symbolic outputs such as flags, anthems, and so on) to achieve cultural homogenization that peripheral resistance is not foreseen as being very effective. In other words, this literature assumes that state-building always leads to successful nation-building, an assumption invalidated by the Spanish case. Therefore, substate nationalism is not supposed to exist, a conclusion that clearly clashes with contemporary politics.[61]

At this point, it is useful to recall once again that there is no strong Basque nationalist movement in France as there is in Spain. Therefore, it is most likely that differences between the historical developments of the two states have something to do with the distinct outcomes. In other words, Basque nationalism emerged in Spain as a consequence of the specific historical trajectory of the Spanish state. The present study therefore adopts a political but state-centric approach to nationalism that focuses more particularly on the historical articulation of the various forms taken by the Spanish state and its influence on the agency of Basque elites, organizations, parties, and the larger civil society. To flesh out such an approach, this study draws from historical institutionalism.

Historical Institutionalism and Substate Nationalism

New institutionalism is no longer new, and the story of its emergence has been told many times.[62] In short, the development of new institutionalism has to be understood in the context of the trajectory of American political science.[63] Before the 1950s, the discipline in the United States (as elsewhere) concentrated on the study of formal-legal institutions: constitutions, parliaments, executives, and so on. This approach came under heavy criticism for being too descriptive, atheoretical, and parochial.[64] Formal-legal scholarship was challenged by behavioralism, which became the dominant approach in the United States starting in the 1960s. Behavioralists were interested in producing general theories of politics using quantitative analysis. From this angle, political institutions were judged superfluous to their research. Not only did political institutions represent an obstacle for such grand theorizing because they differed from state to state, but they were also burdened by the stigma of description and parochialism. In the 1980s, some scholars began to argue that the behavioral revolution had gone too far and that the state should be brought back into the study of politics.[65] Scholars such as Theda Skocpol and James March and Johan Olsen arguably became the first "new institutionalists."[66]

The central argument of new institutionalism is that institutions should be given theoretical importance because they have an independent effect on sociopolitical outcomes.[67] In other words, new institutionalists suggest that scholars have greater analytical leverage if they conduct their analyses starting with the state rather than society.[68] New institutionalism did not develop as a unified theoretical school.

Rather, three streams emerged in relative isolation from each other: sociological, rational choice, and historical. The differences between the three streams have often been discussed, so I will summarize them only briefly.[69] It is important to note that scholars are increasingly looking for meeting points between the three streams,[70] which have typically been presented as very different, if not mutually exclusive.

Sociological institutionalism developed out of organizational theory. It defines institutions in normative and cognitive terms, that is, as norms, values, culture, and ideas.[71] The central argument of sociological institutionalism is that institutions are internalized by actors or, in other words, that human agency is embedded in the institutional context.[72] From this perspective, agency often follows a "logic of appropriateness" where the preferences of actors are highly conditioned by the need to conform.[73] Even institutions themselves will often come to resemble one another, a process usually called "isomorphism."[74]

Rational choice institutionalism is an extension of rational choice theory; as such it is committed to methodological individualism and assumptions of strategic rationality.[75] This approach typically defines institutions as "rules of the game" and has been used mostly to study legislatures and political parties. Its central argument is that institutions provide opportunities for, and pose constraint to, actors who must factor them into their strategic calculations.[76] From this perspective, institutional change occurs when a specific institutional framework yields suboptimal results: at this point, actors make the conscious decision to remodel institutions.

This study chooses to adopt historical institutionalism. I will explain in the next few paragraphs why this approach is the most appropriate for tackling substate nationalism. Historical institutionalism is the stream of new institutionalism that most explicitly developed as a reaction to behavioralism. It is also the type of new institutionalism most closely associated with the movement to "bring the state back in."[77] As such, historical institutionalism most often adopts a materialist definition of political institutions. In the macrohistorical style, such as the one used in this study, political institutions are taken into consideration through the concept of the state. Other studies focus on particular state structures: bureaucracies, the executive, federalism, and so on. Increasingly, historical institutionalists are also incorporating ideas into their frameworks.[78] Whatever the conceptualization of institutions they adopt, historical institutionalists share a common interest in tackling the "big issues" of political science:[79] transitions toward democracy, social movements, the welfare state, and so on.[80] Nationalism is arguably one of political science's big issues, but historical institutionalism, or any other version of new institutionalism, has rarely been used to study it.[81] This study of Basque nationalism therefore seeks to make a contribution to the historical institutionalist literature.

Historical institutionalists also tend to share research strategies. Typically, they start with an empirical puzzle. This often takes the form of cross-national differences. For example, historical institutionalists have asked why different types of public policy (social, environmental, and so on) take distinct forms across states.[82] In cases of public policy as in other instances of cross-national differences, the theoretical focus of historical institutionalists is on variations of institutional structures between states. Historical institutionalism can also be applied to single case studies. Here, the research question may concern the particular timing of an outcome, or simply the very occurrence of this outcome. For this study, the guiding question is the existence of Basque nationalism in Spain. Why does such a movement exist? The answer to this question is not self-evident. After all, some countries are culturally diverse without featuring substate nationalism (for example, Switzerland). In other words, not all culturally distinct populations develop nationalism. Other research questions informing this study include the timing, strength, as well as the ideological and programmatic nature of Basque nationalism. In other words, why was Basque nationalism formally articulated in the late nineteenth century? Why does it include a violent radical stream? Why is nationalism so pervasive in Basque politics? Following the insight of historical institutionalism, this study develops an explanatory argument about Basque nationalism that stresses the historical trajectory of the Spanish state and its projection of a Spanish nation.

Historical institutionalism presents two key strengths as an approach to substate nationalism. First, it gives theoretical importance to political institutions. As I have already discussed, there are limitations to placing theoretical stress on culture, economic conditions, or even elites. The cultural makeup of a society is not unimportant when considering the emergence of a nationalist movement; indeed, substate nationalism rarely emerges without some measure of cultural distinctiveness. However, such distinctiveness is never a sufficient condition for substate nationalism. Uneven economic development and the forces of globalization do not create nationalist movements, although they can factor in its strength and development. Elites may forge, politicize, and mobilize identities through the creation and manipulation of symbols, myths, and narratives, but they do so as a result of a specific institutional process. Substate nationalism needs to be understood in light of this process. This does not mean that other factors should be completely discarded. Virtually no historical institutionalist argues that institutions are the sole explanatory factor for sociopolitical process; the claim of the approach is simply that the theoretical focus should be on the state rather than society. A historical institutionalism perspective on substate nationalism can highlight the multidimensional impacts of institutional development on processes of identity formation and nationalist mobilization while being sensitive to social, cultural, and other conditions. Most importantly, it can connect institutions to agency in a way that allows for a conceptualization of the mechanisms leading to sociopolitical outcomes as neither strictly voluntarist nor overwhelmingly structural.

Political institutions are of crucial importance for the development of substate nationalism in at least three ways. First, institutions can launch and sustain a process of identity construction quite independently of agency. For example, arrangements of territorial division of power, through federal or other decentralized structures, have inherent identity-generating potential; after all, they establish boundaries between groups, including some people and excluding others. The creation of a "region" with an autonomous executive and legislature, as well as a distinct political class, gives a new territorial focus to politics. The development of an identity may soon follow the creation of the regional unit, even if politicians do not actively promote it, because the establishment of a new center of representative and democratic government typically lays the foundations for the emergence of a political community. Spain provides a striking example of this phenomenon as surveys show the presence of regional identities in autonomous communities such as Madrid and Cantabria that lacked any historical foundations.[83] Another similar type of example is Belgium, where a regional identity can also be noticed in the equally "artificial" region of Brussels-Capital.[84] This type of process is strongly captured by historical institutionalism, which puts great emphasis on the idea of unintended consequences. Institutions may be created with a specific purpose in mind but lead to a wide range of unforeseen or, at least, unintended outcomes. For example, the creation of decentralized structures may have for objectives the fostering of democracy (as in Spain) or the stimulation of regional economic development (as in France), but end up transforming the identity landscape of the country.

Second, certain institutional configurations generate patterns of elite relationships that favor nationalist politics. In these situations, the proximate forces molding substate nationalism are agency related, but the behavior of political elites is strongly conditioned by the institutional dynamic. It is not that these elites deliberately and cunningly choose to create or exploit nationalist sentiments, but rather that they are encouraged and pushed to practice a particular type of politics by the institutional framework in which they operate. This type of view on structure and agency is strongly articulated by historical institutionalism: to put it simply, action is strongly conditioned by structural forces, many of which are institutional in nature. This is very apparent in Belgium, where the schism of political parties along linguistic lines during the 1970s has left the country with only Flemish and Francophone parties. As a consequence, politicians from one linguistic community do not have to appeal to voters from the other, which removes incentives to behave moderately and favors nationalist discourses. It is therefore hardly surprising that Belgian politics remains deeply permeated by the *question communautaire*. Institutions also shape elite relationships in a way that favors nationalist politics after regional units are created. Not only do political parties (and other actors) adopt regional perspectives on politics, but they often attempt to outbid each other in terms of who is the best protector of their community's interests and identity. Quebec is a good example of such a dynamic, as the Parti Libéral du Québec (PLQ) is keen on presenting itself as aggressive a guardian of Quebec's interests as the more nationalist Parti Québécois (PQ). The focus of this struggle is most often Quebec-Ottawa relations. Indeed, decentralized systems create patterns of relationships between elites from different levels of government that often prove conflictual. This context can provide a spark, or at least sustain nationalist politics. Of course, none of these institutional contexts and the patterns of elite relationship triggered by them necessarily lead to substate nationalism. This is where it becomes important to consider institutional forms and the political dynamic they generate as part of the larger historical sequence of state development, and in relation to noninstitutional factors peculiar to the region.

Third, certain institutional environments provide actors with special incentives to adopt nationalism as a form of politics. In other words, when political actors are faced with an institutional situation that highlights the benefits of identity-building and nationalist mobilization, they are likely to make the conscious and calculated decision to spearhead these processes. This strategic dimension is central to rational choice institutionalism but also present in the historical stream. Historical institutionalists do not deny that agency sometimes has a strategic quality where institutions are an important variable; it is only that they emphasize more the contingent character of structure-agent relationships and situate strategic decision-making within a historical sequence where other types of dynamics are at play. In the Basque case, the authoritarian state certainly provided an incentive for the adoption of violence as a political strategy and the rearticulation of the nationalist discourse along third-world revolutionary lines, but the political dynamic generated through previous contacts between the Spanish state and the Basque elites cannot be ignored; after all, political violence has never been a major issue in Cataluña where the Franco dictatorship was equally as repressive as in the Basque Country.

In addition to giving theoretical importance to political institutions, historical institutionalism, viewed as an approach to substate nationalism, also presents the advantages of offering a genuine historical perspective. At the broadest level, this means viewing history as a contingent process. This is a useful philosophical starting point for scholars of nationalism since it can help avoid the reification of culture or economics. Historical institutionalism also suggests using history as a theory. Researchers of various theoretical persuasions can make the claim that they use history in their work; indeed, many do since it tends to be seen as problematic to be completely ahistorical in the contemporary study of politics. However, there are many ways of using history in political science. Most often, scholars use history to provide context or illustrations. Having history as context means writing a historical narrative that has little to do with developing an argument. Having history as illustrations involves using historical snapshots to support a previously made argument about causality. Historical institutionalism proposes taking history as a causal mechanism. Hence, timing and sequence become crucial: *when* things happen is equally as crucial as what these things are.[85] More specifically, historical institutionalists argue that minor events occurring early in a sequence can have a greater impact on sociopolitical outcomes than major ones taking place later on.[86] From this perspective, sociopolitical outcomes are not simply the product of discrete events. Nor are they the result of a combination of factors at play at one particular point in time, or even of a series of time-specific, temporally unarticulated processes. Rather, they are viewed as the consequence of an inextricably linked chain of processes where both muted, unremarkable reinforcing feedback and highly visible, sometimes spectacular transformations affect every next step, and whose importance is therefore carried over the long term.

Historical institutionalist research on slow-moving macrohistorical processes tends to rely on the analytical tools of path dependency[87] (or developmental pathways) and critical junctures.[88] These are also tools employed in this study. The concept of path dependency is closely linked to the argument about the theoretical importance of institutions. It refers to the idea that a specific institutional framework produces patterns of politics from which deviation becomes increasingly unlikely as time goes on. The processes generated are self-reinforcing and sustained by the institutional framework in existence. Paul Pierson has put it in the following words: "the claims in path dependent arguments are that previously viable options may be foreclosed in the aftermath of a sustained period of positive feedback, and that cumulative commitments on the existing path will often make change difficult and will condition the form in which new branching will occur."[89] Path dependency is a continuity argument. Substate nationalism such as Basque, Catalan, and Flemish nationalism are resilient processes. They have existed for over a century, albeit with periods of strengths and weaknesses. From a historical institutionalist perspective, this continuity does not have to be viewed in primordialist terms. Rather, it suggests that substate nationalism is a path-dependent process: if early institutional structures favor the creation and strengthening of a common identity among a population and the practice of nationalist politics, a logic of appropriateness about this identity and type of politics sets in. This makes nationalism resilient.

Despite its focus on explaining resilience and continuity, historical institutionalism has needed to deal with the reality that change does occur in politics. To tackle change, historical institutionalists most often use the concept of critical junctures. Critical junctures represent moments where the institutional landscape is transformed and, along with it, the patterns of agency it supports. They are "choice points that put countries (or other units) onto paths of development that track certain outcomes—as opposed to others—and that cannot be easily broken or reversed."[90] Historical institutionalists often portray critical junctures as exogenous shocks, which has brought the criticism of being unable to provide an institutionalist explanation for institutional change. This is certainly an area where historical institutionalism needs to make progress.[91] However, this study is interested in putting forward a perspective on Basque nationalism using the various historical forms of the Spanish state as critical junctures, rather than explaining these institutional transformations. This means, for example, that I am not attempting to explain the emergence of the authoritarian state under Franco, although I consider it a critical juncture that served to narrow the developmental pathway of Basque politics.

Summary of the Argument and Methodology

This book makes the claim that the successive dimensions of the Spanish state shaped a developmental process that turned Basque politics into nationalist politics. The four historical forms of the Spanish state are considered critical junctures for the development of Basque nationalism insofar as they are linked with specific choices of territorial governance and articulations of Spanish nationalism that created openings for Basque nationalism. Hence, the approach to territorial governance of the early Spanish state (that is, the lack of early political centralization) made the later emergence of nationalism in the Basque provinces more likely because it allowed for the continued development of substate identities around the *fueros*. The decision to attempt centralization in the late nineteenth century involved challenging the well-established foral autonomy and therefore triggered the rise of Basque nationalism. The Franco policy of repression enhanced the legitimacy of Basque nationalism, creating a situation where identification with, and loyalty to, the Spanish state and nation in the Basque Country was problematic from that moment on. The choice of establishing a system of autonomous communities meant that Basque nationalism was certain to survive and thrive as it secured institutional grounding. In other words, the early Spanish state prepared Basque nationalism by forging and nesting a Basque identity; the centralizing state precipitated nationalism by further elaborating, promoting, and politicizing this identity; the authoritarian state legitimized and transformed nationalism by repressing it; and the democratic state not only gave Basque nationalism the opportunity to be expressed, but stimulated this movement by generating several different competitive and conflictual patterns of relationships.

The argument is not that one particular juncture created Basque nationalism, but rather that the developmental process of Basque nationalism should be understood in terms of a larger historical sequence of junctures and pathways. In this respect, this study presents a slightly different approach to critical junctures from most historical institutionalist scholarship that focuses on *one* such juncture, which separates the before and after.[92] It suggests that a developmental pathway (here, substate nationalism) may be forged by a *series* of critical junctures that have for consequence the narrowing of that path. This approach helps to spell out the mechanisms unleashed by an initial critical juncture by showing not only the immediate subsequent choices it conditioned but also how these choices shaped a subsequent one. In our case, for example, there is great insight in saying that the loose territorial structure of the early Spanish state represented the critical juncture for explaining the subsequent emergence of Basque nationalism. However, this structure as such still allowed for a different outcome, that is, the absence of substate nationalism (this was the case in Switzerland, for example). Therefore, subsequent choices (in our case, half-hearted centralization and repression) were crucial in maintaining and even narrowing the path. The logic behind the use of the concept of critical juncture is preserved in this perspective since it involves the idea that, with a juncture, a reversal (in our case, an absence of Basque nationalism) becomes much less likely.

The central argument of this book is that Basque nationalism is a product of the historical development of the Spanish state and of Spanish nationalism, which forged a developmental process in the Basque Country whereby each successive pathway further narrowed politics to nationalist conflict. From its creation in the fifteenth century to the nineteenth century, the Spanish state had a confederal-like structure and did not actively work to create a Spanish nation. If anything, Spain was defined by internal pluralism and territorial autonomy. As a consequence, the Basque provinces developed as autonomous political communities in relative isolation from the Spanish state. This history of political autonomy for the Basque provinces rendered the late-nineteenth-century process of state centralization problematic, especially because throughout the nineteenth and in the early twentieth centuries efforts at Spanish *nation-building* were sporadic and unsuccessful. The Spanish state was unable to "make Spaniards" out of all of its populations, including many in the Basque provinces. The reasons were many. The Spanish state could not rely on an effective education system. Political, cultural, and economic centers did not overlap. Politics revolved around clientelism rather than mass mobilization, and the political elite was reluctant to change this comfortable situation. Also, the essence of the Spanish nation was never clear since there were Catholic and Liberal projects, and the attraction of the Spanish "brand" was in rapid decline with the end of the empire. As a consequence, state centralization met with opposition in the Basque provinces as traditional elites formally articulated Basque nationalism. When the Spanish state morphed into authoritarianism toward the middle of the twentieth century, it expressed a clear idea of the Spanish nation as a conservative and Catholic community but did so through violence. As such, the authoritarian state, through its emphasis on centralism and the unity of Spain and its repression of cultural distinctiveness, had the unintended consequence of delegitimizing Spanish nationalism and legitimizing a fairly weak Basque nationalism. The repressive approach of the Franco dictatorship, combined with the legacy of its traditionalist founding fathers, also served to radicalize the Basque nationalist movement. Finally, the Estado de las Autonomías of the democratic state consecrated, sustained, and bolstered nationalism as the dominant form of politics in the Basque Country while also rehabilitating Spanish nationalism as a political option. The political projects stemming from the different variants of both Basque and Spanish nationalism have been institutionalized in a series of conflictual/competitive patterns of political relationships supported by the federal-like structure of the democratic Spanish state.

How can one link these various historical manifestations of the Spanish state and their expressions of Spanish nationhood to provide a coherent perspective on the development of Basque nationalism? Here again, I draw insight from historical institutionalism and use a methodology of process-tracing, or systematic process analysis.[93] Typically, historical institutionalists look at the outcome to be explained as a historical process that should be understood in relation to another historical process institutional in nature. From this angle, they can go back and correlate crucial stages in the unfolding of the process to be explained with specific outlooks in an institutional landscape. This is often done using a strategy of periodization whereby the development of processes is divided into "historical slices."[94] This study combines process-tracing and periodization as it puts forward a perspective on Basque nationalism by focusing on four historical forms assumed by the Spanish state. The historical processes of Spanish state- and nation-building are used to understand the development of Basque nationalism. This being said, state-centric perspectives do not imply that agency (purposive action) as well as societal conditions are unimportant. Few historical institutionalists, for example, would argue that institutions are the only relevant factors in political analysis.[95] Rather, the idea is to make the theoretical choice of starting with the state, understood as a set of potentially autonomous institutions.[96] From there, the analysis can proceed toward society by exploring how the state shapes the behavior of social and political actors. For example, the transformation of a state triggers responses from regional elites[97] whose status, power, and/or influence may become threatened or enhanced.

This study relies primarily on secondary sources about Basque nationalism and politics as well as the history and contemporary politics of Spain. The idea is not to uncover new facts but to place them in a state-centric framework. The theoretical focus and methodology of historical institutionalism come with certain epistemological positions. Historical institutionalists are satisfied with putting forward middle-range theories—theories that are bound by place and/or time—since spatial and temporal variations in institutional structures typically defy general explanations. This caveat about the possibility of generalizing fully applies to this study. Not only is the historical trajectory of the Spanish state obviously unique, so are the patterns of relationships that connect it historically to various actors in Basque politics and society. Moreover, the political and institutional presence of the Spanish state varied, for most historical periods, across regions. In fact, the relationship between the state and the Basque provinces/Country is particularly distinctive, which makes generalizations even to other Spanish regions where there are nationalist movements such as Cataluña or Galicia difficult. While this study cannot offer ready-made explanations for cases other than the Basque one, it does provide a broad research suggestion: historical institutionalism is a promising approach for studying substate nationalism.

Outline of the Book

The next four chapters (chaps. 1–4) of the book develop the historical institutionalist perspective on Basque nationalism. Chapter 1 focuses on the early Spanish state and its territorial management. Here, the point of departure is the idea that Basque nationalism has its roots in the early territorial structuring of the Iberian Peninsula that began with the Reconquista and led to the creation of the three Basque provinces that eventually fell under the authority of the Crown of Castile and later of the Spanish state. The crucial point here is that the Spanish state remained, even several centuries after its formal creation, a patchwork of semiautonomous entities. It adopted a political institutional configuration that favored the preservation of diversity. This is the first critical juncture for Basque nationalism, although the Basque nationalist movement was to emerge only in the late nineteenth century. Partly as a result of a governing philosophy that favored accommodation over forced integration and assimilation, and partly because its focus was on the empire rather than on the "domestic" scene, the Spanish state structured its relationship with the Basque provinces through fueros (autonomous laws) rather than seeking national integration through homogenization and the diffusion of a Spanish nationalism. This foral autonomy, which would last longer in the Basque provinces than anywhere else in Spain, further molded the idea of Basque exceptionalism and made the centralization process of the nineteenth century conflictual.

Chapter 2 argues that the formal articulation of Basque nationalism at the end of the nineteenth century was the consequence of a fundamental transformation in the nature of the Spanish state. In the nineteenth century, a new governing philosophy brought by the influence of the French Revolution and the perceived need to strengthen a faltering empire through a more efficient state structure and additional financial resources led to spurts of centralization, liberalization, and secularization. This liberal project of nation-building was far from hegemonic, however, and conflicts over the nature of the Spanish nation as well as the incapacity of the Spanish state to effectively "nationalize the masses" meant that inhabitants of the Basques provinces were not unequivocally transformed into Spaniards at that time. Nevertheless, the experiments of the Spanish state with liberal and secular ideas and its elimination of the territorial autonomy of the Basque provinces represent a second critical juncture in the development of Basque nationalism since

Basque traditional elites (for example, Sabino Arana), who stood to lose from these political and institutional changes, articulated Basque nationalism as a means of resistance. The chapter argues for the importance of timing and the connection with earlier history in the development of the Spanish state when analyzing the emergence of Basque nationalism. The strong opposition to centralization in the Basque provinces needs to be understood in light of centuries of foral autonomy. Likewise, in crafting nationalist narrative and symbols, Arana was able to draw from, and interpret, historical patterns of relationships between the Spanish state and the Basque provinces.

Chapter 3 suggests that the authoritarian state represented a critical juncture in the development of Basque nationalism because it provided this nationalism with great legitimacy and assured its wide diffusion to civil society. Differently put, the authoritarian state made Spanish nationalism unpalatable to most Basques. The Franco dictatorship had the unintended consequence of equating (substate) nationalist politics with democracy because its authoritarian rule was based on opposition to the ideas of cultural differences and territorial autonomy. Hence, the developmental pathway of the Basque Country became that of Basque nationalism. The timing of Franco's dictatorial rule was important because it came on the heels of Spain's most ambitious democratic and, to a certain extent, decentralized experiment, the Second Republic, and seemingly destroyed a progressive and tolerant variant of Spanish nationalism. This Republican regime produced the first Basque government above and beyond the provinces, thereby giving a first institutional reference to the idea of a Basque nation. This chapter also argues that the authoritarian state was a critical juncture insofar as it led to the emergence of a radical stream of Basque nationalism that was informed by Third World liberation movement ideologies and strategies. The rise of ETA and its use of political violence gave a new twist to Basque nationalism that would shape this movement and the larger Spanish politics into the democratic era.

Chapter 4 looks at this era and argues that the establishment of the Estado de las Autonomías represented a critical juncture for Basque nationalism because it allowed for all the nationalist sentiments that had built up from Arana through the dictatorship to be expressed democratically and in the open while returning credibility to Spanish nationalism. The federal-like democratic state created patterns of political relationships involving primarily the many variants of both Basque and Spanish nationalisms. The chapter identifies four such patterns: a first one involving the Basque and the Spanish governments, which is mostly confrontational but also features the former being able to draw concessions from the latter in situations of minority government; a second between the Basque Country and other autonomous communities—especially historical nationalities—that is very often competitive but sometimes cooperative in the sense that regional leaders attempt to forge an alliance to redefine Spain; a third, mostly conflictual pattern, featuring

Basque nationalist and non-Basque nationalist parties within the Basque political system; and an ambiguous relationship involving moderate and radical Basque nationalists. This chapter will explain how these various patterns of political relationships are materialized through, among other things, negotiations with ETA, the outlawing of Batasuna, and the proposal of lehendakari Ibarretxe for a Statute of Free Association between Spain and the Basque Country.

In the latter chapters, the book makes three other contributions to the study of Basque nationalism. Chapter 5 analyzes the international relations of the autonomous community of the Basque Country. The Basque Country is a rare case of paradiplomacy not simply oriented toward economic gain but featuring strong cultural and, above all, political dimensions. Basque paradiplomacy, I argue, is the product of nationalism. For the Basque government, the development of an international personality serves to build, express, and promote the Basque identity and assert the notion of self-determination in its relationship with the central government. The chapter shows how paradiplomacy in the Basque Country is linked to processes of identity-building and nationalist mobilization by discussing its main axes: European affairs, aid to development, support of Basque communities abroad, and transborder cooperation (with the French Basque Country).

Chapter 6 analyzes Spain's strategy for managing Basque nationalism in the democratic period. The chapter begins with a theoretical discussion of the various approaches democratic states use for dealing with nationalist movements. It distinguishes three approaches: providing the minority group with a voice within central institutions through, for example, consociational arrangements or special representation; recognition of a distinct status; and territorial autonomy through federalism or other types of decentralized structures. Spain, I argue, has not favored the first approach but rather has relied on a limited form of recognition and a fairly extensive degree of political autonomy.

Chapter 7 compares Basque nationalism with other nationalist movements in Western liberal democracies, namely Cataluña, Flanders, Scotland, and Quebec. This chapter argues that, with the exception of political violence, which brings about a distinct political dynamic in the Basque Country, Basque nationalism is very similar to other cases of substate nationalism in the West. It seeks to dispel the notion that Basque nationalism is totally exceptional among cases of substate nationalism in the West. This is true if one focuses uniquely on ETA, but appears more problematic if the Basque case is considered more broadly.

Finally, the last chapter presents some ideas for the future of scholarship on nationalism. It suggests looking at the literature of comparative politics on the state and state-society relations to further theoretical advances.

Chapter One

The Early Spanish State

Basque nationalism can be understood only in the context of a particular historical process: the construction, transformation, and evolution of the Spanish state and its relationship with Spanish nation-building. The erection of the Spanish state began in the fifteenth century with the dynastic alliance leading to the creation of Spain, although the roots of the territorial structuring of the Iberian Peninsula date back to the Reconquista that unfolded in the previous seven hundred years or so. The crucial consideration here is that the creation of the Spanish state was not followed by efforts at nation-building. Differently put, the timing of the erection of the Spanish state (in the sixteenth century) in relation to the first nation-building efforts (in the nineteenth century) is very important for understanding the emergence of Basque nationalism. Juan Linz has argued that part of the explanation for the fact that Spain is "not a nation for important minorities" is that "Spanish state-building went on before the age of nationalism."[1]

Explaining the development of Basque nationalism necessitates an appreciation for early forms of political and territorial organization in the Iberian Peninsula. The seeds of the Basque identity underpinning contemporary nationalist politics were planted during this period by institutional arrangements that formalized the existence of Basque territories and gave certain qualities to their populations. There was a strong path-dependency effect to the relationship between the early Spanish state and the political status of the three Basque provinces of Araba, Bizkaia, and Gipuzkoa: the longer the Spanish state allowed these provinces to remain relatively self-governing, the more autonomy became a central feature of their politics. As a result, integrating the Basque provinces within a centralized Spanish state was an option that grew to present very high political costs and that would be favored only when circumstances left little choice.

At the broadest level, the beginning of this path-dependency process of identity construction was the Reconquista by Christian forces of Iberian territories controlled by the Moors. The Reconquista led to the creation of various kingdoms whose integrity was guaranteed by a series of political arrangements that fostered traditions of autonomy and exceptionalism. It therefore represents the historical basis for Spain's contemporary plurality of identity. More crucial is the fact that Spain remained a loose arrangement of semiautonomous territories several centuries after it was created because the state was, at times, unwilling and, at others, unable to alter this status quo. Spain was, in other words, a confederal-like state. Historian José Ortega y Gasset put it best when he said that particularism had historically been at the center of the Spanish state and constituted a universal feature of Spain.[2] The approach to territorial management of the early Spanish state emphasizing autonomy and asymmetry, and the state's later failure to impose a different model, represents the first critical juncture in the development of Basque nationalism. However, all states have been built from a variety of territories; what is important for their contemporary territorial politics is their subsequent approach to territorial management. In Spain, it was the continuing use of autonomy and other accommodation strategies toward the Basque provinces that set up the formal articulation of nationalism later on.

From this perspective, this critical juncture precedes the outcome to be explained. Indeed, nationalism actually takes form in the Basque Country during the late nineteenth century. The argument, however, is that the structure of the early Spanish state is central to the later emergence and continued strength of Basque nationalism insofar as the building of the Spanish state was not accompanied by a comprehensive effort to build a Spanish nation that would include all of the Crown's subjects in the Iberian Peninsula. The complex political makeup of the territories of present-day Spain before unification discouraged the imposition of centralized and symmetrical structures, and made difficult an effective integration of all the kingdoms. The practice of the fueros used by the early Spanish state in lieu of such an integration served as a unifying force for the three Basque provinces. Still today, these fueros underpin Basque identity (as well as the individuality of the provinces) and claims for self-determination. The early choices made by the governing dynasties of Spain do indeed loom large in contemporary Spanish politics.

This chapter explains how the territorial configuration generated by the Reconquista was maintained following unification by practices that constructed a tradition of Basque autonomy above and beyond provincial borders. It delves into medieval and early modern Spanish history because, in the words of Ortega y Gasset: "The secrets of Spain's great problems are to be found in the Middle Ages."[3] It is important to notice that the chapter does not focus exclusively on the Basque provinces: what is central to this period for understanding contemporary Basque nationalism is the development of the Spanish state and the (non)development of a Spanish nation.

As mentioned in the previous chapter, the historical nature of the inquiry strategy should not be misunderstood as meaning that nationalism and national identity are ancient. This is clearly not the case for Basque nationalism and the Basque identity, as will be demonstrated in the next chapters. Nevertheless, premodern and early modern history must be taken seriously in the Basque case because the construction of the Spanish state is grounded in these periods.[4] History is not merely context for the emergence of Basque nationalism; rather, it represents a causal chain for its development.

The Reconquest and Territorial Structuring in the Iberian Peninsula

The roots of Spain's plurality of identities may be traced back to the efforts of Christian principalities to regain the territories taken by the Moors in the eighth century.[5] This event, known as the Reconquista, lasted almost eight centuries and targeted the whole of the Iberian Peninsula. At the broadest level, the Reconquista was a struggle whose objective was not only to destroy Arabo-Muslim power in the Iberian Peninsula, but also to unify its territory under Christianity. The wars of the Reconquista were not coherent and integrated military actions, nor did they occur simultaneously. They were launched from different regions that had escaped the invasion, mostly in the north. These offensives followed different patterns in different areas, and experienced various degrees of success. They also generated a territorial restructuring in the Iberian Peninsula. The political units created during the Reconquista had little to do with the Roman and Visigoth influence that dominated before the Arabo-Muslim presence. Because the waves of the Reconquista were asynchronic and differentiated, the territorial organization of the peninsula came to feature multiple independent kingdoms.[6] Many of these kingdoms, albeit often in altered forms, have been an enduring feature of Spanish history. They constituted the political landscape that future Spanish kings had to confront.

In the northeast, for example, the Moors were chased in the early 800s, leaving the territories of present-day Cataluña isolated from the rest of the peninsula and exposed to European-Mediterranean influences. These territories gradually came under the influence of Barcelona and its powerful counts. Ramón Berenguer I was the central figure in their eleventh-century unification. He developed the Codi dels Usatges, a codified set of rules surrounding the exercise of political power, which underpins much of the Catalan tradition of autonomy. Other kingdoms created during this period include Asturias (739), León (866), Navarre (905), Aragón (1035), Castile (1037), and Galicia (1065).[7]

The scenario played out differently in the territories of the present-day Basque Country, which were inhabited by a population later assumed to have distinct social, cultural, and even biological characteristics. In early Roman times, the Basque population was limited to the modern province of Navarre as well as parts of Araba and Gipuzkoa, but an expansion around the sixth century led to Basques populating Bizkaia and the southwestern corner of what is now France.

The Basques have long intrigued various types of scholars and experts. Linguists have puzzled over the origins of a language, Basque (or Euskara), which does not resemble any Indo-European tongues. The Basque language has been often presumed to have some type of connection to the languages of the Caucasus, but linguists are overall skeptical toward this hypothesis. Another link has been established with Aquitaine, although this language might simply have been an early form of Basque.[8] Basque may also be close to Iberian, a pre-Christian-era language. Specialists have also highlighted the difficult syntax and morphology of the Basque language. In popular culture, these intricacies have translated into various narratives denoting Basque exceptionalism. In one story, for example, the devil came to the Basque country to learn the language but could get no further than *bai* (yes) and *ez* (no) and therefore had to leave.[9]

Physical anthropologists have found that type O blood is much more common among the Basques than among any other population, that the A and B types are almost nonexistent, and that the Rh-negative factor is unusually high.[10] Starting in the nineteenth century, attention was also paid to the skulls of the Basques, which were said by some to be "built like that of no other men" and by others to resemble either those of Turks, Tartars, Magyars, Germans, or Laplanders.[11]

From a cultural point of view, the Basques were historically known as expert whalers. Whale hunting was central to Basque commercial activity starting in the seventh century as whale meat became an alternative to "red-blooded" meat forbidden by the Catholic church on holy days.[12] Whaling as a socioeconomic activity can be situated within a larger picture of maritime culture. Throughout the centuries, and perhaps starting as early as the ninth century, the Basques became known for shipbuilding. As seamen, there is a good case to be made that they reached North America, more specifically what is now the Canadian province of Newfoundland and Labrador, before the better-known European explorers.

There is no doubt that the peculiarities of the Basques as put forward by sociologists, linguists, anthropologists, and cultural studies specialists have been central to the construction of a Basque sense of nationhood a posteriori.[13] Perhaps most importantly, the Basque language has served to establish the boundaries of the nation. Territories considered Basque are those where Euskara is spoken: Bizkaia, Araba, Gipuzkoa, Navarre (in Spain); Lapurdi, Nafarroa Beherea, and Zuberoa (in France). This is the spatial conceptualization of the Basque nation underpinning Basque nationalism, and the territories that radical Basque nationalists seek to unite politically. Language has also been central to narratives that have contributed to the construction of Basque exceptionalism. Euskara was conceived by some intellectuals of the eighteenth and nineteenth centuries, most famously the Jesuit Manuel de Larramendi, as being a language of the Tower of Babel. Still today, the Basque language is central to the deeply engrained belief that the Basques are, much like the aboriginal populations of the Americas, an "original people." Together with notions of physical and cultural distinctiveness, the uniqueness of the Basque language feeds the powerful idea that the Basques were the first Europeans. In turn, these images suggest homogeneity and unity among the Basques. However, the extent to which the common language, as well as other cultural and socioeconomic markers, created a common Basque identity in the Middle Ages (or before) is a matter of debate. For some, there is a social, cultural, and, at least in the loosest sense, political unity to the Basque Country that has existed from time immemorial.[14] For others, there is no such thing as a historical Basque civilization.[15]

What is certain is that there was never a Basque kingdom, but rather three provinces in the territories of present-day Spain: Araba, Bizkaia, and Gipuzkoa. The historical record is sketchy with respect to when and how these provinces were formed. Araba was the first province to be created, most likely in the 700s; its name is mentioned in several texts written in eighth century.[16] Bizkaia first appeared in the early ninth century. The first written reference to Bizkaia came in a text (*Crónica de Alfonso III*) written in 900.[17] The territories of present-day Gipuzkoa were partly included in Bizkaia until the eleventh century when the province was formed.[18] The Kingdom of Pamplona, which later evolved into the Kingdom of Navarre, was well established as a political entity in the ninth century. The status of Navarre as a Basque kingdom has always been ambiguous; Navarre was more exposed to population movements than the three provinces, which made its ethnic composition less clearly Basque.[19]

The Basques largely avoided being subjugated and assimilated by powerful groups such as the Romans, the Visigoths, and the Moors. Indeed, the Arabo-Muslim invasion of Spain did not fully extend to the territories of the present-day Basque Country. The Moors made no serious attempt to establish their authority over this area, and only a small fraction of the Basque population fell under Moorish control. This is significant for the later construction of the Basque nation because it fed the idea of a pure people untarnished by multiple waves of invasion in the Iberian Peninsula. This type of logic was not peculiar to the Basque provinces. Spain as a whole, especially its religious and clerical element, was very much preoccupied with the issue of "blood purity" in the sixteenth century.[20] There were two categories of Spaniards: pure-blooded old Christians and new Christians whose blood had been tarnished by the Moors (or the Jews).[21] The Basques fell in the first category. In addition to theologians, everybody from writers to physical anthropologists held to the notion of the Basque as a pure race, perhaps the original European race, whose physical features and spiritual character remained unchanged and unblemished in virtue of centuries of isolation. As a consequence, the Basques were often considered the purest of Spaniards.

The Reconquista had no direct effect on the northeastern area of the peninsula. The Basque provinces were never merged into a single Basque entity, not even during the construction of the Spanish state. This serves to highlight that there is no ancestor to the Basque Country formed as an autonomous community in democratic Spain that can be found buried in the ancient history of the Iberian

Peninsula. The three Basque provinces were indirectly affected by the Reconquista because they became targets for more powerful kingdoms. These provinces moved back and forth between autonomy and control by a major kingdom between the eighth and the fourteenth century. One of those kingdoms was Navarre, which was one of the most powerful Christian entities of the peninsula during the eleventh century. Navarre controlled Gipuzkoa for nearly two hundred years, and also included Araba and Bizkaia after they broke away from Asturias.[22] The Basque provinces in present-day France also came under Navarrese control. During this period, Bizkaia developed a distinct form of political organization, the *señorio* (seigniory), and the Bizkaian *señor* became the interlocutor for whatever kingdom held sway in the province at any particular time. Only for a few years in the eleventh century were the three provinces controlled by Navarre. Therefore, the linkage made by some Basque nationalists between the three provinces currently forming the Autonomous Community of the Basque Country and Navarre has virtually no historical foundations, at least from a political and institutional perspective. Still from this point of view, the three provinces never formed a Basque Country in the Middle Ages. There was, of course, a population sharing a common language whose exact origins are unknown, but no formal unity.

The notion of a Basque political unit stretching into the territories of present-day France (more specifically in Aquitaine) has even weaker historical foundations. The Basques emigrated north of the Pyrenees starting in the sixth century until roughly the tenth century; the international border between France and Spain would therefore make any political relationship between the Basques from the south and the north very difficult. The Basque territories of France also came to be divided in provinces: Zuberoa and Lapurdi were created in the eleventh century, and Nafarroa Beherea was formed in the twelfth century.[23] Even between these three provinces, there was little unity. Zuberoa and Lapurdi came under English rule in the twelfth century, while Nafarroa Beherea, geographically situated between the two other entities, was part of the kingdom of Navarre. Zuberoa and Lapurdi were formally integrated into France in the fifteenth century. Nafarroa Beherea came under French rule in the late sixteenth century.[24] The Basques provinces of the north kept their autonomy and privileges (*fors*) for some time after having been incorporated into France, but the Revolution's Jacobin doctrine swept away their special status.[25]

In sum, for all the cultural and linguistic links between the various Basque territories, individuality, heterogeneity, and asymmetry best characterize their historical political relationship and institutional situation. Or, in the words of Salvador de Madariaga: "The Basque country itself as a unit is a modern creation for history and knows only three provinces: Alava, Guipúzcoa, and Biscay; and a kingdom: Navarre; as well as three linguistically connected regions over the French border—La Basse Navarre, La Soule, and Le Labourd."[26]

The institutional environment of the Basque provinces was affected by the process of territorial consolidation that unfolded before, and culminated with, the formal creation of Spain. Most significantly, two kingdoms became particularly prominent: Aragón and Castile.[27] Aragón added the territories of present-day Cataluña through a dynastic union in 1137. In the thirteenth century, it added new territories (Valencia and the Balearic Islands), often under the leadership of Cataluña.[28] Castile, which united with León in 1230, incorporated Gipuzkoa (1200), Araba (1332), and Bizkaia (1379). The terms of these unions are a matter of debate. Some authors speak of conquest, but the reality is in all likelihood more complex and different depending on the province.[29] This consolidation did not drastically reduce the political autonomy of the kingdoms that had been integrated. Aragón, for example, really worked as a confederation of two independent units where Cataluña was the dominant power.

The Basque provinces exercised no such leadership role within Castile, but they were allowed to preserve much of their political autonomy. This was done through the fueros. The fueros were agreements between local authorities (typically towns or villages) and a Crown that gave the former the right to retain their system of laws. This was a common practice in medieval western Europe, but in the Basque case the fueros took a slightly different form because they were conferred upon larger territorial units than towns or villages: the province. This is not insignificant; the provincial fueros served to strengthen provincial autonomy while limiting political fragmentation to the local level. The fueros in Spain had their roots in the Reconquista since they "originated in legal statuses awarded . . . by monarchs as rewards for services rendered in the struggles against the Muslims."[30] The exact timing of their development is unclear and a matter of debate partly because they featured customary and formal legal aspects that probably developed asynchronically.[31] Fueros were akin to constitutions in the sense that they were codes that defined the political relationship between the Crown and the local authority involved. These codes were presented to the monarch for securing an understanding of the treatment and position of a territory's population within a larger political ensemble. The fueros were also intended to protect specific customs that could be threatened by the change in ruler. It could be therefore said that they were really "special rights";[32] at least, this is how they have been interpreted by Basque nationalists from the late nineteenth century to this day.[33] The Basque fueros predate the creation of the Spanish state, but proved an enduring feature of postunification Spain.

Territorial Autonomy in Early Modern Spain

The process of unification triggered by the Reconquista took a giant step in 1469 with the marriage of the heirs to the Kingdoms of Castile and Aragón, Isabel and

Ferdinand. This event marks the formal creation of the Spanish state. The dynastic union put most of the territories of present-day Spain under a single political rule. From the northwest, the Kingdom of Castile had already taken control of neighboring kingdoms, including Galicia in 1071. Its military victories in the southern region of Andalucía in the thirteenth century all but chased the Moors from the Iberian Peninsula.[34] Only Granada (1492), the Canary Islands (1477), and Navarre (1512) were added after 1469.

The formal unification of the Christian kingdoms (with the exception of Portugal) did not lead to effective state centralization and even less to nation-building.[35] One scholar has described Spain in this period as featuring "internal separatism and differentiation."[36] He goes on to say:

> There are, in the first place, innumerable lines of cleavage between the two great component parts of Spain—between Castile on the west, and the realms of the Crown of Aragon on the east. In their aims and ideals, in the character and aspirations of their inhabitants, in their social, institutional, and economic life, the two kingdoms were utterly divergent. Then again, within each of the two realms the process of differentiation continues, until the student finds himself confronted with a vast number of apparently unrelated petty units—social, geographical, institutional, and economic.[37]

The early Spanish state maintained most of the old structures and practices that meant the union of Castile and Aragón had virtually no immediate consequences for the political and legal status of most of their component territories. Typical of the logic behind the process of unification were the assurances by Ferdinand to the Navarrese that nothing would change with the incorporation of the kingdom within Spain save for the name of the king.[38] There was a path-dependency effect at play here: from the perspective of the center, there was no reason why practices of territorial management that had been central to the constitution of the Kingdoms of Castile and Aragón should be discarded. This was especially true since the new state initially functioned as something akin to a confederation of its main units; only with the rise of the Empire in the sixteenth and seventeenth century did the Mediterranean-oriented Aragón decline, leaving Castile to assume the leading role in running Spain.

The institutional configuration of the early Spanish state favored the preservation and development of multiple identities. Navarre, which was incorporated late within Spain, was arguably the most autonomous of all component territories since it was treated more like a kingdom than a province or principality.[39] In the Crown of Aragón, Cataluña, Valencia, the Balearic Islands, as well as Sicily and Sardinia all had their own parliaments.[40] Castile was more centralized, with a single parliament representing most territories, except Galicia and the Basque provinces. These provinces successfully preserved their fueros, which were grounded in provincial assemblies (*juntas generales*) and involved a right not to implement and enforce royal decisions (*pase foral*). Each new monarch throughout the sixteenth century swore to abide by these agreements, but kept formal authority over the Basque provinces and used an agent (*corregidor*) for the administrative management of the relationship.[41] It is also from the late fifteenth to the seventeenth century that the fueros were formalized in written form to be presented to the monarchical authority; it happened first in Araba (1463), then in Bizkaia (1526), and finally in Gipuzkoa (1696).[42] These fueros were justified largely using the mythology of the Basques as a pure race. In the case of Gipuzkoa, Miguel de Aramburu stated:

> There is no specific mention in the sacred scriptures regarding the place in which descendants of the Patriarch Noah founded, for the first time, their settlement and domicile in the initial populating of Spain after the universal flood; however, there is very specific information . . . that Tubal, fifth son of Japhet, and grandson of the second father of humankind, was the first to come to this region from Armenia with his family and companions after the confusion of tongues in Babylon, and that his first stop and settlement was in the lands situated between the Ebro River and the Cantabrian Ocean. . . . Witness to Tubal's presence is the Basque language itself, legacy of the resulting confusion when God created seventy-two languages at the destruction of the tower of Babel. Basque was the language of Tubal and his followers, and they were the ones to introduce it into Spain, where it became the original tongue of this kingdom.[43]

At the most basic level, the fueros served a similar purpose in all the territories; they established a special relationship with the state that allowed for political autonomy. In the context of the new state, the Basque fueros had a particularly important strategic dimension. Spain's border with France was viewed as the most sensitive, and through the fueros the Basque provinces committed to its defense in exchange for an exemption from military conscription. The fueros also meant that the Basques were exempt from taxation. This was also particularly significant in the postunification period because of the Empire; the Spanish state was then constantly looking for sources of revenues to finance its multiple wars and colonial ventures. It is important to note that the development of the Basque fueros followed distinct patterns depending on the province. Also, attachment to the fueros was uneven among Basque provinces, as was the degree of institutionalization. Bizkaia was the most autonomous province and the one with the most developed fueros. As a consequence, it is in Bizkaia that the fueros were most fiercely guarded and where they acquired the greatest symbolic meaning.

A second practice used by the early Spanish state to secure the loyalty of the Basques was collective nobility.[44] This practice, which had few parallels in western Europe, consisted in granting anyone able to prove Basque descent the status of nobles. For the Basque provinces, collective nobility served as a further justification, if not legal basis, for foral autonomy. It also transformed the three provinces (particularly Bizkaia) into *social* as well as historical, political, and ethnic categories. The Basques approximated, in a formal sense, a social class.[45] For the Spanish monarchs, the granting of this collective privilege served a crucial military function since it meant transforming the Basques into guardians of its northeastern territories. The Spanish monarchs had to resort to this type of strategy because they were at the helm of a state characterized by important internal political differentiation that was more preoccupied with imperial expansion than domestic territorial consolidation. However, the official reason for the Basque collective nobility was that this population had never been "contaminated" by the Moorish invasion of the Iberian Peninsula.[46]

The territorial structure of the early Spanish state, especially how it accommodated the Basque provinces through the fueros and collective nobility, is central to understanding the development of the Basque identity in all its ambiguity. The fueros united the Basque provinces in the face of the Spanish state while at the same time maintaining a distance between them. They are also the starting point for explaining the nature of political mobilization in the late nineteenth and twentieth centuries as the Spanish state evolved. Collective nobility brought a sense of moral exceptionalism to the Basques as a population, or a "race," untarnished by outside influences. More specifically, it fed a tradition of egalitarianism, or at least a self-perception of the Basques as forming an egalitarian community since all Basques were nobles. Collective nobility was linked to descent and therefore functioned as a mechanism of exclusion. For example, a sixteenth-century ordinance stated that "no one who is not of noble status can be admitted to the villages of this province of Guipúzcoa."[47] In the case of Navarre, its status as a "kingdom within a kingdom" led to a particularly weak sense of political community with the rest of Spain.[48]

Another institutional feature of Spain in the sixteenth century is significant for understanding the sociological basis of the Basque nationalist movement that would emerge in the late nineteenth century: the colonial nature of the state. Spain may have been, during this period, a confederal-like state, but it was also an emerging empire. The Basque bourgeoisie was strongly connected to this empire. Ties to the state were not only economic but political; Basque nobles and industrialists "developed political connections and networks of relationships that probably strengthened their commitment to Spain."[49] In sum, the Basque bourgeoisie came to participate actively in Spain's political and economic affairs. It is therefore unsurprising that the Basque nationalist movement that emerged in the late nineteenth century was spearheaded by preindustrial conservative elites rather than the bourgeoisie.[50]

In the case of the Basque provinces, the imperial nature of the Spanish state had consequences for the practice of the fueros since the political influence of the

Basque bourgeoisie and nobles in Madrid made it easier for the three provinces (and Navarre) to resist the centralizing tendencies of the Spanish state during the seventeenth and eighteenth century.[51] We now turn to the political dynamic emerging between the state and the Basque provinces during this period.

Early Centralization and Resistance

Prior to the seventeenth century, the Spanish state had made no serious attempt to centralize power and do away with the fueros and other similar practices that conferred autonomy on many different territories. This approach is often said to have reflected the particular governing philosophy of the Habsburg dynasty;[52] indeed, the central political figure of the sixteenth century, King Philip II, chose to maintain the existing institutional order.[53] Spanish monarchs during this period never considered the "unification" of Spain insofar as uniting involved cultural homogenization and "nationalization." The territorial governance of Spain featured autonomy in much the same way as did the management of imperial possessions such as the Low Countries, Sicily, and Sardinia. In other words, territories such as the Basque provinces were considered by the Castile-oriented rulers as fitting into the larger framework of the Empire.[54] This philosophy did not per se change in the seventeenth century, but circumstances did. The Spanish state experienced serious financial problems resulting from a combination of costly wars, imperial expansions, and a weak fiscal basis.[55] It also sought to bolster its army. There was therefore little choice but to turn toward the territories of Spain proper.

The effort to increase the revenues of the Spanish state and to add to the number of soldiers meant departing from the traditional Habsburg mode of territorial accommodation in favor of more state centralization. In the seventeenth century, the change was dictated by power imperatives rather than underpinned by an alternate philosophy aimed at the creation of a unified and coherent Spanish nation. State centralization nevertheless involved some measure of homogenization because all territories were asked to contribute financially and to send men to the military.[56] This was opposed most forcefully in Cataluña, where it triggered the so-called revolt of the Catalans in 1640, and in the Basque province of Bizkaia. There, it was a new tax on salt that led to a rebellion (El Motín de la Sal) in 1632. This rebellion was a popular one, but, contrary to what happened in Cataluña, it received little support from the province's nobility, who benefited from imperial expansion and was therefore close to the Spanish state. The state was eventually successful in imposing the new tax, albeit not without some concessions, but its model of territorial organization remained largely unchanged. The Basque provinces still retained their fueros, and, if anything, the attempt at levying new taxes showed the difficulty in challenging a status by then well engrained. Territorial autonomy produced positive feedback and reinforcing effects. This being said, there were consequences to the seventeenth-century attempt at centralization since the resistance considerably strained the relationship between the Spanish state and many of its constituent territories.

In the case of the Basque provinces, this episode of centralization only increased the political and symbolic importance of the fueros. It spurred the articulation of a long-standing position of nurturing and protecting these special rights and statuses into a political and ideological movement known as foralism (*fuerismo*). Foralism revolved around the defense of provincial autonomy. Its central idea was historical continuity in the face of a changing state. Foralism appeared in the works of many Basque writers starting in the fifteenth century; the fueros served to affirm the distinctiveness of the Basques alongside the mysterious origins of this population and their language.[57] There was a definite construction of history to this movement that would continue through the romantic foral literature (*literatura fuerista*) of the nineteenth century. As a political force, foralism matured into the late nineteenth century when its key ideas of political autonomy and distinct status were rearticulated as nationalism. This being said, foralism was not nationalism. It did not employ ideas of nationhood and self-determination. Nor did it seek the congruence of the political and the cultural unit; indeed, the fueros were provincial privileges and, as such, foralism effectively prevented a pattern of political mobilization along the lines of a unified Basque culture.

The War of Succession (1700–1713) ushered in a new era for the Spanish state. The succession meant a transition from the Habsburg dynasty, comfortable with ruling a patchwork of territories over which they could exercise only partial and uneven control, to the Bourbon dynasty, which aspired to a more centralized and tightly integrated state. The full consequences of this transition would be felt only in the nineteenth century, but already in the early 1700s the outlook of Spain's territorial arrangement had changed. The state had stripped most of its component territories of their autonomy, including Cataluña's in 1716. Only the Basque provinces and Navarre managed to preserve their distinct status of autonomy. The Basque business community and nobility, always close to the state, played the right card by supporting Philip V in his struggle against the Archduke Charles, and the fueros were preserved.[58] Still, with the exception of the Basque and Navarrese fueros, the War of Succession paved the way for exercises in state-building and political modernization such as the imposition of new taxes on property and income.[59] It also set up the nineteenth-century nation-building project insofar as the Kingdom of Castile assumed the effective political leadership of the country. Or, in the words of Richard Herr, the government of Castile became that of Spain.[60]

Understanding the Origins of Basque Nationalism
in the Context of the History of the Spanish State

A recent characterization of current debates about political science pits rational choice theorists against historical institutionalists.[61] While this view is American-centric and oversimplifies the diversity of competing traditions in political science, it nevertheless identifies two fairly different types of approaches to research on politics. One central element of this difference, albeit it not the only one, is the place of history in political science. For rational choice advocates, history represents at most context for the strategic calculations of individuals. Historical institutionalists argue that "history matters" and make it the center of their causal explanation.

As discussed in the previous chapter, the claim that "history matters" can prove deceptive for nationalism studies. Most scholars of nationalism invoke history in one way or another, but often without being historical in the sense of conceptualizing history as a process involving inherent causal mechanisms. Perennialists may insist on the importance of history, but only to find the proto-form of current communities. Modernists start their history with European modernization.

This chapter has shown that understanding contemporary Basque nationalism involves an appreciation of medieval and early modern Spanish history. This does not mean that Basque nationalism is a medieval or even an early modern phenomenon; in fact, it is not. Neither does this statement mean that the origins of Basque nationalism are to be found in this period per se, but rather that its structural roots are the early Spanish state. From this perspective, understanding Basque nationalism requires a focus on the construction of the Spanish state.

The first historical critical juncture for Basque nationalism was the maintenance by the early Spanish state of the territorial structuring inherited at the time of formal unification. From the fifteenth to the seventeenth centuries, the territorial organization of the Spanish state closely resembled the preunification situation, with Aragón and Castile granting autonomy to many of their incorporated territories. The developmental pathway that had begun during the Reconquista was therefore allowed to unfold; indeed, it was bolstered because the Habsburgian Spanish state based its legitimacy in part on territorial autonomy as a mode of governance and elected not to develop nation-building strategies guided by cultural homogenization and a tight control of populations by the state.

In the specific case of the Basque provinces, the most significant aspect of the construction of the Spanish state was its practice of the fueros.[62] At the formative, or nesting, stage of the Basque identity, the fueros provided a common political status for the Basques. However, their unifying consequences were mitigated by the fact that they also fostered provincial distinctiveness. In this context, the fueros are important for explaining not only the political strength of the Basque identity, but also its territorial nuances reflected in the federal-like structure of the Autonomous Community of the Basque Country. Moreover, the fueros are crucial for explaining the construction of the Basque identity because they have continually been used to support claims for autonomy and distinctiveness, and have served as the basis for the Basque statutes of autonomy created in the twentieth century. The fueros are also central to the nationalist mobilization of the contemporary era because foralism, the movement that developed for their defense, led to nationalism.

Debates over the exact nature of the fueros are inherently political. For example, in the preamble to the Ibarretxe proposal seeking to redefine the relationship between the Basque Country and the Spanish state (further discussed in chap. 7), it is said that "the citizens of the existing Autonomous Community of the Basque Country . . . , in respect of our democratic will and *in virtue of the respect and actualization of our historical rights recognized in the Statute of Guernica and the Spanish constitution,* declare our intent to formalize a new political pact of peaceful coexistence."[63] Here, the fueros are rights, which supposes that their development is a historical process endogenous to the Basque provinces.[64] From this perspective, the sovereignty of the Basque provinces was never voluntarily relinquished, but rather deposited in fueros that predate the Spanish state. Consequently, the right to autonomy naturally leads to another right, that of self-determination. The historical Basque fueros are therefore said to involve a freedom for the Basque Country to choose its political future independently of the preferences of the Spanish state.

The "Spanish" parties operating in the Basque Country have a different understanding of the fueros and their consequences. There exists at least two different views among non-Basque nationalists. The first considers the fueros to be a privilege. From this perspective, the fueros have no inherent legitimacy and can be removed at any time. They do not involve a right to self-determination, that is, the prerogative to unilaterally change the political status of the Basque Country. The second view broadly accepts the idea of the fueros as a right but dissociates them from any notion of self-determination. Similar debates over the nature of the fueros are also at the center of the controversial historiography of the Basque Country.[65] Those holding the rights view of the fueros often defend the position that this provincial autonomy served as the context for early democratic practices.[66] On the contrary, those who view the fueros as privileges suggest that they correspond to a conservative, even reactionary political order.[67] The existence of these debates about the fueros highlights the significance of medieval and early modern Spanish history for understanding contemporary Basque nationalism.

In conclusion, this chapter has suggested that the structure of the early Spanish state as a loose collection of semiautonomous territories, rather than the agency of particular actors, fostered a plurality of identity during the medieval and early modern period. In other words, the sheer weight of institutions and related accommodation practices gave meaning to what it meant to be Basque. This being said, one specific pattern of agency was crucial in mediating the effect of the Spanish state on the Basque identity and its political consequences: the close connection between Basque elites and the Spanish state. On the one hand, this relationship contributed to the maintenance of the Basque fueros until the nineteenth century, and therefore to the long-term building of a Basque identity. On the other hand, it reduced the intensity of mobilization against the Spanish state and kept the Basque identity compatible with Spain. This was to change in the late nineteenth century when a conservative elite led a challenge to the emerging centralizing liberal state and laid the foundations for the development of Basque nationalism.

Chapter Two

The Centralizing State

If the structures of the early Spanish state favored the construction of a Basque identity through foral autonomy, they were not immediately conducive to Basque nationalism for at least two reasons. First, the fueros maintained the individuality of the Basque provinces, which rendered problematic the mobilization of the Basque population above and beyond provincial borders. Second, political mobilization on the basis of the idea of a Basque nation defined in opposition to Spain was unlikely as long as foral autonomy was a mutually acceptable approach for the Spanish state to conduct its relations with the Basque provinces. In other words, the early Spanish state did not deploy a comprehensive nation-building project in the Iberian Peninsula, which means that the Basque provinces were in a situation of indirect rule unfavorable to the development of substate nationalism.[1] Indeed, their fueros, although periodically challenged and gradually weakened, kept them at a distance from the Spanish state. There were therefore few opportunities for a sustained opposition to the state and for the articulation of Basque interests different from the Spanish ones. This was particularly true because the links between the Basque elite and the Spanish state created a situation where there was no leadership for launching a nationalist movement.

In the nineteenth century, the Spanish state underwent a transition from confederal structures toward more centralization in its relationship with the Basque provinces. At the same time, the state's efforts at crafting a Spanish nation were half-hearted and ineffective as a result of institutional weakness, the existence of conflicting national projects, and the lack of political willingness on the part of the political elite running the country in the last half of the century. Therefore, explaining the rise of Basque nationalism requires an emphasis not only on state centralization (which is found in much of the literature on nationalism in the Basque Country), but also on the *absence* of a corresponding process of Spanish nation-building (which is most often overlooked). Spain's decentralized structures that had satisfied Basques elites transformed into the basis for opposition precisely because integration into the Spanish state was unmatched by a Spanish national project perceived as legitimate. In the words of Ortega y Gasset: "Castile made Spain and unmade it."[2]

Substate nationalism emerged in Spain during the late nineteenth and early twentieth centuries. Basque and Catalan nationalism, most often discussed in the rest of Spain during this period in terms of *separatismo,* led to a more negative evaluation of Spain. For example, for Spanish nationalists deploring the lack of nation-building, Spain was said to be "spineless" and to suffer from a "serious illness."[3] The centralizing Spanish state is the second historical critical juncture in the development of the Basque nationalist movements. It is, indeed, the crucial one for prompting the formal articulation of Basque nationalism since there was no political movement seeking the independence, or even the autonomy, of the Basque population as a whole before the nineteenth century. Centralization put the Spanish state and the Basque provinces on a collision course because it challenged the Basque foral tradition. The centralizing Spanish state steered the Basques from foralism toward Basque nationalism. This pathway involved the formal articulation of a Basque nation above and beyond provincial and international borders, the definition of Basque interests as different from Spanish ones, and the presentation of the Basque identity as distinct from, and incompatible with, Spain. The centralizing state triggered a transformation from a crystallization of a Basque identity through the fueros and foralism to its politicization, mobilization, and articulation as a national identity.

Contrary to the early Spanish state, the centralizing state did not establish the type of structures that nurtured the development of a Basque identity. It did, however, change the politics of Spain's traditional elites into a position of challenge and confrontation. In this context, the mechanisms of identity construction and nationalist mobilization were triggered by the reaction of these elites who saw their status and interests threatened by state centralization. In other words, the institutional change brought by centralization led to a transformation in agency patterns that triggered Basque nationalism. Therefore, Basque nationalism validates, at least partially, the modernist view since its emergence is undeniably tied to the modernization, or more exactly, the centralization of the Spanish state. It also vindicates modernists of the instrumentalist variety in regard to the particularly important role of elites in generating symbols and creating a nationalist narrative. Indeed, few nationalist movements owe as much to one individual as Basque nationalism does to its "founder" Sabino Arana.

Centralization and Liberalism

The Spanish state underwent a transformation starting in the seventeenth century. Initially structured around territorial autonomy and internally differentiated, it gradually became more centralized and less tolerant of distinct statuses. In the seventeenth and even in the eighteenth century, the reasons for the change in territorial management were more practical than philosophical: the state needed additional financial and military resources, and it could no longer afford to have some of its territories remain at the margin of the political framework. The movement toward centralization in the nineteenth century was different because it was, albeit sporadically, underpinned by new values and a new vision of the nature of the state. This was to be immensely consequential for the Basque provinces, which still enjoyed their fueros in the eighteenth century, because this most recent centralist impulse meant that no exception would be made for them.

The switch in governing philosophy can be explained by two external shocks. The first is the end of the Empire. Already in the early eighteenth century, Spain had ceased to be a major power in Europe, but with the loss of its colonies in the Americas the decline appeared more clearly. This loss of power and prestige was linked to the perceived ills of the Spanish state, most notably a general lack of efficiency and the incapacity to generate the necessary revenues to sustain a great power politics. In other words, the collapse of the Spanish Empire suggested that there was something fundamentally flawed with the Spanish state. So did a second major international event, the Napoleonic wars and France's occupation of Spain.

Arguably, Spain's occupation by a foreign power further pointed toward the weakness of the state and made its elites more receptive to alternate modes of governance. Perhaps more important, however, is the fact that the occupying power itself was promoting, and indeed imposing, a different type of state model. From the French Jacobin perspective, the internal differentiation of Spain meant backwardness and inefficiency. In other words, there had to be a modernization and rationalization of Spain. From a socioeconomic perspective, this project consisted in turning Spain's largely rural economy and population into an industrial and free-trading society. From a political, institutional, and cultural perspective, modernization and rationalization involved two related dimensions. The first was state centralization and the removal of territorial autonomy and special territorial statuses. The second was cultural homogenization. The implementation of these two processes was meant to achieve a larger objective: the creation of a nation, one and indivisible. Nationhood was associated with modernity, progress, and enlightenment. Still from the French Jacobin perspective, the nation represented a necessary framework for the flourishing of liberal values and priorities such as the universal equality of rights, secularism, and industrial development. Hence, the territorial and political aspects of the French liberal project intersected at the nation. A liberal version of Spanish nationalism was crystallized by the French occupation and the ensuing struggle.[4] In the words of José Álvarez Junco: "Modern times, liberal revolutions, and the 'Age of Nationalism,' entered Spain with the Napoleonic army."[5]

The war against Napoleonic France was not unlike the Reconquista: the various territories of Spain all fought against French troops but largely in an uncoordinated fashion. This pattern of resistance reflected the territorial nature of the Spanish state. The offensives against French troops were also led by groups that embodied different visions of Spain: traditionalists fought for religion and the monarchy, while Liberals saw in the revolt an opportunity to dismantle the Old Regime.[6] Significantly, this conflict was later dubbed the "War of Independence" and featured prominently in the emerging discourse of Spanish nationalism.[7]

Despite the multifaceted opposition to the French armies, the Liberals dominated the many different provincial juntas heading the war and, subsequently, the *junta central* established to organize the resistance. The end of the French occupation would therefore not signify a return to the status quo ante; in fact, it provided an opportunity for Liberals to put forward a different form of political and territorial organization in Spain. As one historian put it: "The collapse of the Bourbon dynasty under the combined strength and perfidy of Napoleon meant more than a mere regime change for Spain. It meant a revolution in her outlook."[8]

In concrete terms, Spain's new outlook was embodied by the Cádiz constitution of 1812 and a few other legislative measures adopted around that time. These documents were drafted by an extraordinary assembly (Cortes) created from the junta central. Not surprisingly, they were liberal in nature. The decree of August 6, 1811, formally dismantled the social structure of the Old Regime by abolishing privileges.[9] The Cadiz constitution divided power between the Cortes and the monarch (article 15) and guaranteed Spaniards the freedom to write, print, and publish their ideas (article 371).[10] It also placed sovereignty in the nation (article 3), although suffrage was limited to propertied males. The Spanish nation is arguably the central theme of the Cádiz constitution; many of its first articles speak of the nation. The Spanish nation is said to be composed of all Spaniards (article 1); to have only one religion, Catholicism (article 12); and to be both the basis for, and focus of, government (articles 13 and 14). Its conceptualization is as an undifferentiated and indivisible community united by religion in a new liberal framework. At the helm of this nation is a strong and centralized state. The decree of 1811 states that all the "seigniories," for example, Bizkaia, must be incorporated within the nation. The Cádiz constitution sought to make sure that the Spanish state had adequate fiscal resources by making it a responsibility of all Spaniards to contribute to the public treasury (article 8).

This constitution, which was the work of a small minority of bourgeois liberals, was endorsed by representatives of the Basque provinces.[11] The representative from Navarre, on the contrary, fiercely resisted the change in constitutional structures.[12] The support of the Basque bourgeoisie for the project of a liberal Spain clearly positioned it within a Spanish political framework rather than a provincial or Basque one. This alignment, which is to some extent an extension of the close connection between the Basque bourgeoisie and the state at the time of the empire, is important for explaining why Basque nationalism, unlike Catalan nationalism, was not spearheaded by the bourgeoisie but rather by preindustrial conservative elites.

The Cadiz constitution was short-lived; when French troops left Spain in 1814, Ferdinand VII returned to the throne and reestablished absolutist rule after a brief liberal period. However, the constitution's principles served as the foundations for Spain's approach to territorial management in the nineteenth century.[13] For the express purpose of eradicating attachment to substate political communities, the Liberals created new administrative units modeled on the French *départements*, provinces, whose boundaries did not for the most part coincide with the old autonomous territories. They also created the position of governor, who, much like a French prefect, was appointed to represent the state in the province and held sway over their assemblies. In the Jacobin spirit, this centralization of state structures was meant to eliminate intermediate levels of political authority between state and citizen, but also to reengineer Spain as a united and indivisible nation.

The exercise of articulating a new vision of Spain through the Cádiz constitution was the easy part for the Liberals. More difficult were the implementation of the new political and institutional model, and the construction of a coherent and homogeneous Spanish nation. Such objectives necessitated a strong ruling class, something that Spain did not have at the time. The legacy of Spain's internal structures also weighed heavily on the liberal project. Of course, it would be overly deterministic to suggest that Spain's past rendered any genuine transformation of the state and of the sense of nationhood impossible in the nineteenth century. Nevertheless, the granting of political autonomy to various territories and their recognition as distinct communities within Spain for centuries represented a developmental pathway from which any attempt to deviate would be difficult. The practices of autonomy and recognition strengthened attachment to substate territories, most importantly Cataluña and the Basque provinces, and bolstered the identity they embodied. They explain in part the difficulty in forging a Spanish nation "one and indivisible" in the late nineteenth and early twentieth centuries.

Spanish Nation-Building: A Problematic Process

To explain the rise of Basque nationalism in Spain involves understanding the failure of the Spanish state to generate feelings of Spanishness in the population of the Basque provinces. Probably no other case illustrates the connection between substate nationalism and nation-building by the state as clearly as the Basque Country. Indeed, the strength, scope, and legitimacy of state nationalism is the only variable for explaining the different levels of nationalist mobilization among the Basque populations of France and Spain.[14] Of course, this does not imply that there was no credible projection of a Spanish nation in the nineteenth century. Many authors, such as Álvarez Junco, have argued convincingly that by the mid-1800s, "there was such a thing as a Spanish identity, a Spanish character, a Spanish 'soul' or 'essence.'"[15] This Spanish identity, however, was strongest in its heartland of Castile, and it failed to become hegemonic, or even dominant, in many other parts of Spain, including the Basque provinces. A few reasons explain this outcome.

First, politicians running Spain only sporadically sought to vigorously promote the Spanish identity among the masses. At the end of the nineteenth century, such an exercise involved a level of popular politicization that threatened the comfortable position of the Conservative and Liberal parties, which alternated in power. "Politicians from the two governing parties had a practical interest in maintaining the status quo" because their fate was predictable.[16] In addition, Spanish politics during the second half of the nineteenth century and the first quarter of the twentieth was characterized by *caciquismo*, a system of clientelism that saw politicians rely confidently on local bosses (caciques) to secure electoral victory in districts. Caciquismo linked political participation with personal benefits rather than a sense of national purpose, and made it difficult to have an emphasis on the Spanish national state associated mainly with unpleasant obligations such as paying taxes or military service.[17] For some, these clientelistic networks that formed such a central part of Spanish politics and society at the turn of the twentieth century were the consequence of the extension of suffrage on a still largely rural and "backward" society.[18]

To say that there was no attempt at nation-building in Spain during the nineteenth century and early twentieth would be an exaggeration. More accurately, one could say that divisions about the nature of the Spanish nation hindered its diffusion. Contrary to France where republicanism was becoming dominant at that time, Spanish nationalism was fragmented between two highly antagonistic positions: traditional-Catholic and liberal-secular.[19] Even without these two broad categories, there were different movements. The liberal-secular view of Spain was carried by a first group seeking the reproduction of the French Jacobin model for Spain, and a second, spearheaded by Catalans, who aimed at modernizing the Spanish state but on the basis of regional autonomy.[20] The traditional-Catholic idea of Spain was predominantly linked to the defense of the Old Regime; it was the view of a profoundly Catholic Spain of the monarchy, privileges, and territorial autonomy. In the early twentieth century emerged a military-authoritarian stream of Spanish nationalism looking to "reconcile the needs of modernization and traditional nationalism."[21] This version of Spanish nationalism sought to go beyond the structures of the Old Regime while emphasizing the organic unity of Spain founded in Catholicism. The struggles between these competing visions of Spain were played out in the politics of nineteenth- and early-twentieth-century Spain to produce a choppy sequence of regime changes punctuated by civil wars and military takeovers that hindered the projection of a coherent national model.

Spain's nation-building process was also rendered problematic by the incapacity of the state to penetrate society all over Spanish territory. For example, two key mechanisms for making "peasants into Frenchmen," the education system and military service, did not work nearly as well in Spain as they did in France.[22] There was no mass public education in Spain before the 1930s, whereas it was established in France during the 1870s.[23] As a consequence, illiteracy in Spain was very high in 1900, approximately 56 percent (compared to 17 percent in France).[24] These high rates of illiteracy made the "nationalization of the masses" difficult since the written word is a prime medium for communicating ideas about the nation. Another such medium, one's experience in the (national) army, was fairly ineffective in Spain. Not only were the wealthy able to buy their way out of military service, but the Spanish army had relatively low prestige: it was primarily engaged in civil wars, lacked a defining external enemy, and, after the loss of the remaining colonies in 1898, lacked a formal purpose.[25] The Spanish state was also deficient in its symbolic output. Spain had no national flag until 1843 and no national anthem until 1898.[26] Few monuments or statues were built, and national celebrations were also few.[27]

From this perspective, Spain was a "weak" state insofar as it was ineffective at penetrating society to "nationalize the masses." There were many causes to this weakness, including a large debt stemming from wars and the struggles between various strands of Spanish nationalism. There was also a deep structural condition at play: political aspirations of Spanish nation-building and economic power did not coincide in one center. At the end of the nineteenth century, Cataluña was the most prosperous region of Spain, and the Basque provinces were undergoing industrialization while most of the country remained poor and rural.

In the end, the lack of comprehensive nation-building in Spain is an issue of timing. At a time when there was semblance of a desire to unite all of the populations of Spain, the country seemed past its prime and Spanishness was a tough sell in regions such as the Basque provinces. This was true especially after the "disaster" of 1898 that saw Spain lose its last colonial possessions: Cuba, Puerto Rico, and the Philippines. The loss of Cuba, viewed as prized colony, was to be considered particularly tragic: a foreign minister had declared in 1848 that Spaniards "sooner than see the island transferred to any power . . . would prefer seeing it sunk in the ocean."[28] The end of the Empire confirmed the descent of Spain from the elite group of major powers. Juan Linz summed this up neatly: "Spain in the nineteenth century lost an empire, rather than dreaming with one . . . ; its economic and scientific revolutions had been frustrated or failed; its cultural golden age was of the past; and its state was not a new creation arousing hope but a discredited inefficient machine."[29]

From Carlism to Nationalism

The liberal vision of Spain was opposed, in the Basque provinces and elsewhere in the country, by Traditionalists who sought to maintain the political order in existence before the French occupation. More specifically, Traditionalists opposed the liberalization of Spain on four grounds. First, they were absolutists and therefore rejected the political system sketched out in the Cádiz constitution where power was shared between the monarch and a Cortes representative of popular sovereignty. Second, they stood for religion and a confessional state, and saw the new constitution, despite its proclamation of Spain as a Catholic nation, as an exercise in secularism. Third, they opposed the liberal support for capitalism and industrialization, which they saw as leading to the destruction of a morally superior agrarian economy and rural lifestyle. Fourth, they defended local autonomy and consequently resisted the centralizing surge of the state.

In the Basque provinces, this blend of absolutism, religion, anticapitalism, and local autonomy took a distinctive character and came to underpin a particularly strong movement. The reason for this distinctiveness was the fueros, which gave an additional meaning to the Traditionalists' attachment to territorial autonomy. By the early nineteenth century, the Basque provinces (and Navarre) were the only units of Spain to still enjoy such autonomy. The struggle of the Traditionalists did not merely involve some potential return to a status quo ante; it was about *preserving* existing structures. Moreover, in the case of the Basque provinces, the fueros had become entangled with a sense of exceptionalism since they unfolded as an uninterrupted historical process featuring bilateral relationships with the Spanish state and were combined with other special privileges such as collective nobility.

The push for a return to absolutism in the Basque provinces also has to be understood, at least in part, in light of the foral tradition. For the Basque provinces, absolutism was somewhat of a misnomer since it had historically coexisted with territorial autonomy.[30] On the contrary, liberalism and constitutionalism were explicitly against the fueros. The defense of religion was also linked to the fueros since autonomy was presented as a way to insulate the morally superior Basque society from the contagion of foreign ideas such as secularism.[31]

> The position of Navarra toward the centralizing and liberalizing Spanish state was similar to reactions in the three Basque provinces.
>
> The predominantly conservative residents of Navarra felt particularly menaced by the encroachment of liberalism, republicanism, and anti-clericalism, the new ideas that had penetrated Spain. . . . Navarra, perhaps more than any other part of Spain, exemplified and championed the old ways now challenged.
>
> But most unwelcome and dangerous was dictation from a remote Madrid where the contractual nature of Navarra's ties with her king was ignored or disdained.[32]

Traditionalist resistance to processes of state centralization and secularization was commonplace across Europe. In Spain, it took the form of a movement known as Carlism. The immediate context for the emergence of the Carlist movement was the death of Ferdinand VII and the ensuing struggle for succession between his brother Carlos and his wife María Cristina.[33] This conflict unfolded over fifty years through a series of wars. These Carlist wars were more than simply about succession. They were played out as a struggle between two broad forces: liberalism and traditionalism. "The issue . . . was the continuation of traditional Spanish institutions—governmental, social, and religious—or their replacement by centralized parliamentary constitutional monarchy and an individualistic, capitalistic society."[34]

Carlism was articulated as a Spanish doctrine: it corresponded to a Catholic-Traditionalist stream of Spanish nationalism. Carlists celebrated Spain, but a different Spain than the one projected by the Liberals. The Carlist Spain was the Spain of absolutism, territorial autonomy, and privileges. Above all, it was a profoundly religious Spain. Carlists believed they embodied a form of Catholicism morally superior to others, and saw their struggles against Liberals as a religious crusade. For example, they claimed that "God was the first Carlist, Lucifer was the first liberal, and the Carlists were the elect of Christ."[35] This religious zeal came with a push for a return to a golden past characterized by a rural way of life. In sum, "For members of the Carlist elite, religious unity, Spanish patriotism, and some form of right-wing politics all went together. To criticize Catholicism was to subvert conservative ideals and to question the very nature of Spain itself. To import foreign ideas was to strike at church, country, and way of life simultaneously."[36]

Although Carlism's ideological content anchored it solidly in a Spain-wide framework, support for the Carlist movement was uneven across Spain.[37] Most notably, it was stronger in the Basque provinces than anywhere else in Spain. This can be explained by at least two factors. First are the fueros whose existence in the nineteenth century was unique to the Basque provinces. This meant that the liberal plans for centralization would be particularly controversial in these provinces. The foral tradition of the Basque provinces (and Navarre) helps us understand why Carlism was so strong from the moment it emerged as a political movement. Second is the fact that the Basque provinces were rapidly industrializing in the late nineteenth century, whereas the rest of Spain, with the exception of Cataluña, remained largely agrarian. Processes of sociopolitical change, such as urbanization and the development of a working class, unfolded particularly quickly in the Basque provinces. Of particular importance was the movement of population from the rest of Spain to the Basque Country, created by industrialization, which clashed with the Basque sense of purity and exceptionalism. Therefore, the socioeconomic transformations brought by industrialization may have contributed to the strength of Carlism in the Basque provinces at the end of the nineteenth century and during the first decades of the twentieth century.

There were two Carlist wars in the nineteenth century.[38] The first war started in

1833 with the first effective change to Spain's territorial structuring along the lines of the Jacobin state model, the creation of fifty-one provinces administered from Madrid via a governor. This move was followed in 1834 by a royal decree abolishing the fueros, but foral autonomy was reestablished as a compromise for the end of the conflict in 1839.[39] Hostilities during this first Carlist war raged throughout most of Spain, but were particularly ferocious in the Basque provinces and Navarre given the greater support for Carlism there. In this context, the liberalizing Spanish state appeared, at least to Basque Carlists, as a force determined to crush the political, institutional, social, and economic organization of the Basque provinces.

Carlism in the Basque provinces was reignited when the Spanish state radicalized its liberalization. In 1868, Isabel II was chased from the throne, and one year later a new constitution was enacted. Much like the document drafted in Cádiz fifty years earlier, this constitution established a constitutional monarchy based on the principles of popular sovereignty, universal manhood suffrage, and individual rights.[40] On the religious question, the document specified that Catholicism would be protected but that other faiths would be allowed. This treatment of the religious question offered by the constitution was particularly difficult to accept for Carlists. Carlism did not per se provoke the 1873 demise of the constitutional monarchy in the sense that there was no real insurrection or uprising that year. However, much of the opposition toward the constitutional monarchy emanated from traditionalist currents such as Carlism, which remained strong in a country still very much agrarian in its economy, way of life, and social structure. Indeed, only in Cataluña, a well-industrialized region with strong liberal and left-wing politics, was the new regime received with great enthusiasm.

The failure of the constitutional monarchy opened the door for another group left unsatisfied by the 1869 constitution: the republicans. Although republicans did not enjoy more support than constitutional monarchists and were divided between unitarists and federalists, they were able to present their model as the only remaining liberal alternative to Carlism.[41] It is in this context that the First Republic was proclaimed in 1873.

This republic was federal, but, for Carlists, its decentralist features were overshadowed by its anticlericalism. The creation of the new republican regime was widely interpreted in traditionalist circles as a frontal attack against religious principles. Once again, two visions of Spain came to clash, since the new regime was the trigger for a second Carlist war. This conflict took a different configuration from the first one as a result of the evolution of Carlism itself. By the early 1870s, the Carlist movement was more squarely focused on religion than ever before and somewhat less preoccupied with preserving foral autonomy in its historical forms. In the words of Stanley Payne: "Many of the leading figures of Carlism . . . had little interest in foralism. Increasingly they stressed the doctrinaire principles of religious unity and national union under authoritarian and corporative monarchy.

The idea of semi-autonomous provinces and town government based on corporative organization began to replace foralism."[42] Moreover, support for foralism had declined in much of Spain, but remained steady in the Basque provinces and Navarre. In fact, only in these four territories was support for Carlism still substantial.[43] The Second Carlist War took the form of a conflict between the Spanish state and the Basque provinces. This is why the centralizing state of the late nineteenth century had a particularly strong impact on the Basque provinces. Basque Traditionalists, who were struggling to retain the fueros and to keep a liberal and secular regime from extending to their society, had singled out the Spanish state as the enemy but found themselves alone in defending the provinces' social order, religious basis, and "purity" against constitutionalism and industrialization. This marks the beginning of a pattern of relationship where a substantial segment of Basque leadership viewed the Spanish state with great suspicion and sought disengagement from Spain as a whole.

It is not only the configuration of the conflict that rendered it so important for the political future of the Basque provinces but also the outcome: the Carlists lost the war, and the Basque fueros were abolished in 1876. The abolition of the fueros represented a watershed moment for the Basque provinces considering that they had been the centerpiece of the provinces' relationship with the Spanish state since its creation. It also meant that Basque politics would, from this moment on, feature claims for the reestablishment of the fueros in one way or another. As early as 1878 the three provinces negotiated an arrangement of fiscal autonomy with the Spanish state. These *conciertos económicos,* which represented a re-creation of the fiscal privileges inherent in the fueros, were to constitute a crucial institutional yardstick when determining the status of the Basque Country during Spain's democratic transition. The Second Carlist War had somewhat different consequences for Navarre, which managed to retain its fiscal and administrative autonomy despite having been a stronghold of Carlism.[44] This outcome added to Navarre's distinctive historical trajectory and its complex relationship with the three provinces.

As a process stemming from the transformation of the Spanish state during the nineteenth century, the struggles, the evolution, and, eventually, the downfall of Carlism led to nationalism in the Basque Country. The transition from Carlism to nationalism was the product of strategic calculations on the part of Basque traditional elites, especially in Bizkaia. Within a centralizing and liberalizing Spanish state, these elites had initially counted on Carlism to defend the political, institutional, and social orders that corresponded to their values and made them prominent, if not powerful, members of their societies. In the last third of the nineteenth century, Carlism no longer appeared to some Basque Traditionalists as a prime option for brushing back the new Spanish state and the accompanying processes of modernization, for at least three reasons.

First, they saw the institutional arrangements favored by the later forms of Carlism as insufficient for the Basque provinces. In an essay published in 1897, Sabino Arana, the father of Basque nationalism and an early Carlist himself, had these harsh words for Carlism: "The foral doctrine of the Carlist Party can be summarized by the following formula: political centralization, administrative decentralization."[45] He added: "The originality and absolute independence preserved by the Basque people during this century is abandoned by the Carlist party."[46] For Arana, the Basque fueros were laws emanating from the Basque people rather than privileges granted by the Spanish state, and any change in the contractual nature of this relationship represented an unacceptable diminishing of the status of the Basque provinces.

Second, Traditionalists in the Basque provinces were of the opinion that liberal and secular ideas had made such substantial inroads elsewhere in Spain that it was no longer possible to rescue Spain from the evils of modernization. In other words, the spirit of Carlism remained only in the Basque provinces.

Third, Carlism was failing as a political movement of resistance against centralization, liberalization, and secularization. There was little support remaining for the Carlist movement outside the Basque provinces after the abolition of the fueros. In the context of electoral politics, the concentration of Carlist support in the Basque provinces meant that Carlism no longer represented an effective vehicle for brushing back the Spanish state and its ideological underpinnings. As a consequence, Traditionalists in the Basque provinces made the transition from Carlism to nationalism.

The leader of this transition or, as he liked to call it, this "conversion," was Sabino Arana. Arana came from a Carlist family of landowners and shipbuilders that had struggled to make the adjustment to a capitalist society where new technologies were changing many industries. Arana's father, Santiago, was a lifelong Carlist who had to flee to France in the aftermath of the Second Carlist War. Sabino Arana had, as a youngster, an early identification with Carlism manifested in an attachment to the fueros and, above all, to religion and a traditional way of life. He has said that he was a Carlist by accident: "I was a Carlist until the 1870s because my father had been a Carlist."[47] Arana's loyalty was never to Carlism as a Spanish movement but rather to what it represented. An often-repeated story suggests that Sabino Arana's transformation from a Carlist to a nationalist occurred as a result of a conversation with his brother Luis.[48] Luis Arana was on a train ride to Galicia when he was asked by a fellow passenger, reading a pro-fueros slogan on Arana's lapel, why he would claim a privilege that other Spaniards did not enjoy. It is at this moment, the story goes, that Luis Arana realized that the Basques were not Spaniards, a conclusion that he shared with his brother. Sabino Arana reflected on the conversation in these terms:

After a long debate in which we attacked each other and defended ourselves with the objective of reaching the truth, and in which he presented so much historical and political evidence to convince me that Bizkaia was not Spain and made such efforts to demonstrate that Carlism was an unnecessary, inconvenient, and counterproductive means to obtain absolute autonomy or break our ties with Spain, or even recuperate the seignorial tradition, my mind, understanding that my brother knew history better than I and was incapable of lying to me, began to doubt and I decided to start studying with serene vigor the history of Bizkaia and to adhere firmly to the truth.[49]

Therefore, Basque nationalism was first articulated because it represented for Basque Traditionalists, most importantly for Sabino Arana, a more effective instrument for defending their ideas. These ideas were, of course, those of Carlism. The switch from Carlism to nationalism did not entail much sacrifice with respect to content. As Arturo Campión put in 1906: "We called ourselves "Fueristas" with pride in times more dangerous than today's. But now there is a new term, more graphic and more intense . . . which means the same. I shall now, without renouncing my past, taking up new ideas or adopting new attitudes, and while being true to my own modest history, renounce the old name and call myself a nationalist."[50]

Sabino Arana and Early Basque Nationalism

Sabino Arana created much of the institutional and symbolic foundations for contemporary Basque nationalism. He founded the Partido Nacionalista Vasco (PNV) in 1895. Of course, the ideology of the PNV evolved after Arana, but the party very much survived as the main voice for Basque nationalism. The PNV went on to become the leading political force in the Basque provinces during the Second Republic; it controlled the Basque government in exile during the dictatorship; and it has dominated electoral politics in the Autonomous Community of the Basque Country in the democratic period. Arana coined the name "Euskadi" for the Basque Country.[51] He composed what is now the official anthem of the Autonomous Community of the Basque Country, "Gora ta Gora." He designed the red and green flag that became the official flag of the Basque Country in 1936 following the model of the British Union Jack. Finally, the Basque national holiday Aberri Eguna remembers Arana's conversion to nationalism on an Easter Sunday.

Arana did more than create symbols and a party for Basque nationalism; he also conceptualized the Basque nation and provided it with a narrative. Arana articulated the idea of a Basque Country composed of seven units: the three provinces of Araba, Bizkaia, and Gipuzkoa; Navarre; and the three French departments of Lapurdi, Nafarroa Beherea, and Zuberoa. He advocated independence for Bizkaia, as clearly stated in his *Bizcaya por su independencia* (1892). In respecting the foral tradition, Arana constructed his nationalist program for Bizkaia while presuming that his plea would find sympathetic ears in all Basque territories. He hoped for the creation of a confederation of Basque states.[52] References to the Basque territories of France were sporadic in Arana's discourse, so it is unclear to what extent he truly saw their political future tied to the future of the three provinces in Spain. Navarre was more clearly in Arana's sight, and contacts were established. For example, in 1894 Arana and some fellow nationalists went to a banquet for the Navarese *diputación* in Pamplona and brought a message that concluded with "¡Viva Navarra! ¡Viva Euskeria Unida!"[53] Despite these efforts, Arana's nationalism, which advocated independence, found little support in a Navarre looking to restore foral autonomy. There were prominent Navarrese who became Basque nationalists (for example, Arturo Campión), but most who found the idea of secession attractive favored the independence of Navarre at the expense of a Basque Country made up of four (or seven) provinces.[54]

Arana's optimism with respect to the political union of all Basque territories stemmed from his vision of a Basque nation determined by race. Arana had a primordialist view of nationhood; for him, the essence of the Basque nation was race. For example, he invented the term "Euskadi" in part because he disliked the term "Euskal Herria," which refers to a community of Basque speakers.[55] For Arana, languages came and went but race stayed. The racial and exclusivist character of early Basque nationalism as shaped by Arana was influenced by the important socioeconomic transformations experienced by Bizkaia at the end of the nineteenth century. Industrialization was bringing a flow of migrants from other parts of Spain. For Arana, these *maketos* were introducing immoral habits and values into Bizkaia[56] and threatening the purity of the Basques. Migration into the Basque provinces contributed to the racializing of Basque nationalism since it exposed, at least in the eyes of Arana and like-minded Traditionalists, the fundamental differences between Basques and Spaniards. In turn, Arana's primordialist, race-based articulation of the Basque nation served to isolate the Basques from a variety of perceived social and moral evils.

Race was not all that characterized the Basque nation as defined by Arana. The Basques, for Arana, were the purest of Catholics and therefore morally superior to Spaniards who had strayed toward liberalism, capitalism, and secularism. Arana's incorporation of this religious element within Basque nationalism gave the quest for independence mystical qualities: the independence of the Basque Country is discussed in terms of a relationship with God. Or, in Arana's words: "My patriotism is not rooted in human motives, nor is it directed toward material ends. My patriotism is rooted and every day is more rooted in my love for God, and its aim is to connect God to my blood relatives, to my great family, the Basque Country."[57] Arana also said: "Ideologically speaking, before the existence of the homeland there is God; but in practical temporal life, here in Bizkaia province, in order to love God it is necessary to be a patriot, and in order to be a patriot it is necessary to love God; this is the meaning of fatherland."[58] From Arana's own words, there is a sense that religion was so important that it trumped the idea of the Basques as a historical, social, and cultural category: "I proclaim Catholicism for my nation (*patria*) because its tradition, and its political and social character, is essentially Catholic. If it was not, I would still proclaim it, but if my people were to resist, I would disown my race."[59]

Along with the religious fundamentalism of early Basque nationalism came a strong opposition to capitalism. Arana had great contempt for Basque industrialists, whom he found greedy, and he was equally intolerant of workers seeking a solution in socialism.[60] Arana deplored capitalist industrialization both for the "immoral" values it fostered and for the breakdown in social order it provoked. In reaction, to the process of industrialization and capitalist development unfolding in Bizkaia at the end of the nineteenth century, Arana spoke of a Basque precapitalist golden age. He presented the "true" Bizkaia as traditional and, in line with the collective self-perception generated by collective nobility, as egalitarian.

Arana's glorification of a traditional social structure, way of life, and economy is part of a pattern of reinterpreting and using history for political purposes.[61] Arana was very critical of Basque historiography; he thought that all of it ended up justifying the inclusion of the Basque provinces within a Spanish nation. For Arana, the value of works on Basque history should not be judged for their accuracy but rather for their contribution to the Basque nation. For example, commenting on the research of Labayru, historian of Bizkaia, Arana argued that "he was not guided by patriotism but by a love for historical studies. Consequently, his work does not represent a gift to the nation (*patria*); it is only a contribution to universal history."[62] In contrast, Arana's objective as a politically engaged historian was clear: to make a case for the existence of a Basque nation, which was free from time immemorial until the nineteenth century.[63] Arana was particularly preoccupied with tracing the historical evolution of the fueros in a way that highlighted the unrelinquished sovereignty of the Basque people. The eternity of the fueros, along with the sanctity of Catholicism, provided the content for Arana's articulation of Basque nationalism; this was summed up in his nationalist slogan "Jaungoika eta Lagi-Zara" (God and Old Laws). José Luis de la Granja Sainz has described Arana's vision of Basque history in these terms:

> The Basque Country has been, since the remotest of times, a series of free and independent states where people lived happily without knowing social inequalities . . . and by governing themselves democratically. . . . The Basque states lost their freedom only recently, in the contemporary period, with the bourgeois and liberal revolution (centralist and anti-foral), through con-

quest and domination brought by revolutionary France in 1789 on the three regions of continental Euskadi, and in 1839—at the end of the First Carlist War—from Isabel's Spain on the four historical territories of peninsular Euskadi, converting them into simple provinces of the Spanish state.[64]

Early Basque nationalism as articulated by Arana was profoundly anti-Spanish. Arana interpreted history in a way that supported the continued polar opposition between Spain and Bizkaia. For example, *Bizcaya por su independencia* is a narrative of four battles[65] that pitted Bizkaia against León or Castile. The book's conclusion reads like this:

Yesterday.—Bizkaya, Confederation of independent republics, struggled against Spain which pretended to conquer her, and came victorious at Arrigórriaga (888), remaining free. Bizcaya, Republic seignorial independent . . . struggled against Spain which pretended to conquer her, and came victorious at Gordexola y Otxandiano (1355), remaining free. Bizcaya, Republic seignorial independent . . . struggled against Spain which pretended to conquer her, and came victorious at Mungia (1470), remaining free.

Today.—Province of Spain.

Tomorrow—?. . . . ? The future depends upon the conduct of nineteenth-century Bizcayans.[66]

The book's message is clear: Bizkaia never surrendered its original sovereignty to the Spanish state. In Arana's words: "Bizcaya, free and completely sovereign in its actions, instituted, for convenience, the seigniory. Later, this Bizcaya had it within its prerogative to abolish this institution when it was no longer considered conducive to the good of the state."[67] Arana's anti-Spanishness was further expressed in his famed 1893 discourse of Larazábal as he highlighted the Basque history of resistance against foreign invaders and deplored that Bizkaia was "already in the eighteenth century, intoxicated by the virus of Spanishness (*españolista*)" and, in the nineteenth century, humiliated by "Spain, this miserable nation."[68] In a similar vein, Arana contrasted Bizkaians and Spaniards in these terms:

The physiognomy of the Bizkaian is intelligent and noble; that of the Spaniard is inexpressive and gloomy. The Bizkaian walks upright and manly; the Spaniard . . . has a feminine air. . . . The Bizkaians is energetic and agile; the Spaniard lax and dull. . . . The Bizkaian's character degenerates through contact with the outsider; the Spaniard needs from time to time a foreign invasion to civilize him.[69]

Interestingly, Arana tended to see the whole of Spain outside the Basque provinces as essentially homogeneous. This was in large part the result of his emphasis on race: for Arana, the mysterious origins of the Basques made them fundamentally different from all Spaniards who were themselves all alike. This included Catalans, for Arana saw Cataluña as a mere region of Spain rather than a nation like the Basque.

> Catalonia is Spanish in its origins, in its political nature, in its race, in its language, in its character, in its habits. If there are anthropological differences, or differences of character and habits, between Catalans and other Spaniards, they are not more important differences than those existing between brothers.[70]

In the first issue of his publication *Bizkaitarra*, Arana described himself as, among other things, anti-Carlist, anticonservative, and antirepublican; or, "in one word, anti-liberal and anti-Spanish."[71] To a large extent, the feelings of disdain for Spain expressed by Arana and like-minded nationalists stemmed from the view that the Spanish state, by taking the route of liberalism and secularism, was rendering Spaniards morally bankrupt. "The Spanish domination," wrote Arana, "is for our race source of profound and extensive lack of religiosity as well as advanced amorality . . . Bizcaya, dependent upon Spain, cannot go toward God and cannot be Catholic in practice."[72] Basque nationalism was imbued with a strong sense of Basque moral superiority, which translated into the use of racial categories and the objective of independence. In other words, Arana's preference for the Basque provinces leaving Spain should be understood primarily as a strategy for avoiding moral and social "contamination."

This articulation of Basque nationalism did not go unchallenged. There was also a liberal strand to Basque nationalism that was spearheaded by businessman and industrialist, Ramón de la Sota. De la Sota favored autonomy rather than independence, and emphasized the Basque language instead of the "race." His nationalism was secular, and he embraced capitalist development. If Sabino Arana's "conversion" to nationalism was the direct product of Carlism's political weakness, the political and socioeconomic forces behind the emergence of liberal nationalism are less clear. This is especially true since the leaders of this strand were members of the Basque business elite that had strong ties with the Spanish state. Some authors have speculated that de la Sota's group included many foreign-born businessmen who had not developed this type of relationship with the state. Others have argued that de la Sota and some other Basque businessmen took a nationalist stand because they were pursuing divergent economic interests from other Basque bourgeois.[73] Support for Basque liberal nationalism remained limited since the bulk of the Basque bourgeoisie favored Spanish unity. In this context, it was overshadowed by Arana's traditionalist nationalism.

Arana himself took somewhat of a different approach to the political status of the Basque provinces in the last few years of his life (around 1898) as he shied away from the project of creating an independent Basque state in favor of pursuing a strategy of "maximal autonomy." This move, announced in his paper *La Patria* in 1902, is known as Arana's "Spanish evolution." This change of heart went beyond abandoning the idea of independence; it also involved dropping nationalism as political vehicle altogether. Arana even suggested dropping the PNV in favor of a new party, Liga de Vascos Españolistas.[74] It is unclear how far Arana would have gone in this new direction since he died in 1903. What is certain is that the party created by Arana survived its founder's death and never fully took this autonomist turn. Indeed, despite the presence of *sotistas* (members of de la Sota's group), the PNV preferred following Arana's earlier and more radical writings.

Electoral success came slowly to the PNV and occurred primarily in Bizkaia. The nationalists won municipal elections in Bilbao and elections to the Bizkaia diputación. Despite the fact that supporters of Arana held a tight grip over the party's program and ideology, it was primarily the sotistas who drew support for the PNV. The most significant electoral gains made by the PNV occurred during the 1918 Spanish elections when the party won seven out of the twenty seats in the Basque provinces: six in Bizkaia and one in Gipuzkoa. Support for the PNV in Araba and Navarre was much weaker. In the case of Navarre, Carlism still dominated the conservative political landscape. Therefore, Basque nationalism in the early twentieth century was a significant political force only in Arana's province of reference, Bizkaia. Moreover, the PNV was plagued by rivalries between radicals and moderates that led to the creation in 1921 of a moderate Basque nationalist party, the Comunión Nacionalista Vasca (CNV). This split left Arana's faithful in complete control of the PNV.

Arana's Legacy

Basque nationalism has evolved since the late nineteenth and early twentieth centuries, but it still bears the marks of its founder Sabino Arana in its position on the political future of the Basque Country and in its attitude toward Spain. Generally speaking, Basque nationalists want to have as little to do with Spain as possible; differently put, they do not articulate an alternate vision of Spain to the extent of, for example, Catalan nationalists.[75] The secessionist position was articulated by Batasuna, which until recently represented the political arm of ETA.[76] The stance of radical Basque nationalists on the political future of the Basque Country is clear: they seek its secession from Spain. Radical nationalist politics also comes with strong anti-Spanish feelings: the Spanish state is denounced for its oppression, and Spain is identified as the problem in the political conflict in the Basque Country. This is all very much in line with Arana's early thinking except for the rhetoric: Arana criticized the Spanish state for its liberalism and secularism, whereas contemporary radical nationalists call it fascist. Another departure from Arana in the politics of radical Basque nationalism is the use of violence as a strategy for achieving independence. For ETA and its supporters, the right to life can be subordinated to the cause of Basque independence. No comparable views can be found in the writings of the very religious Arana. These different positions on the issue of violence stem partly from the ideological turn of radical Basque nationalism toward revolutionary left-wing ideologies under Franco.[77] It could be argued, however, that the virulent anti-Spanish discourse of Arana and of early Basque nationalism is the precursor to ETA's violence.

Contemporary Basque nationalists also take from Arana a conceptualization of Euskadi as including not only the Basque provinces of Spain but also Navarre and the three French departments of Zuberoa, Nafarroa Beherea, and Lapurdi. They see the international border between Spain and France as the artificial division of a nation; there are Basques from the south (Spain) and Basques from the north (France). The Basque state that radical nationalists would like to see created would include all of these territories. The formidable obstacles standing in the way of the realization of such a project makes the resolution of the political conflict particularly difficult.

Placing the PNV, and to a lesser extent its breakaway party Eusko Alkartasuna (EA), within an Aranist framework calls for more nuances. The PNV's politics is a mixture of Arana's early radical ideas and his later more pragmatic "Spanish evolution." The PNV presents an ambiguous position toward the possibility of independence and typically limits the involvement of Basque governments in Spanish-wide affairs, preferring to deal with the Spanish state through bilateral relationships. This being said, the PNV has exhibited a fair amount of pragmatism in its dealings with other political actors in Spain. It has cooperated with other nationalist and regionalist parties to promote the idea of Spain as a multinational state. It has also provided support to minority governments with the objective of furthering decentralization in Spain. The PNV's attitude toward the radicalism of ETA was ambiguous during the first decade of the democratic period, distancing itself from violence but typically explaining it to be the result of a political conflict instigated by the Spanish state. Starting with the 1988 Pact of Ajuria-Enea condemning ETA violence, to which it was a signatory, the PNV began to denounce violence more categorically. Ambiguities did remain, however, until the late 1990s, as exemplified by the political alignment of all nationalist parties, including Herri Batasuna, at that time. Moderate nationalists are also uncomfortable with the Marxist discourse of the radicals. In keeping with Arana's emphasis on religion, the PNV became a Christian-Democratic party in the 1940s (it was one of the founding parties of the Christian Democratic International), and moderate Basque nationalism is still very close to the Roman Catholic Church.

The importance of Arana's legacy for Basque nationalism becomes particularly illuminating when it is compared to Catalan nationalism.[78] Overall, nationalism in the Basque Country seeks more fundamental constitutional and institutional rearrangement than in Cataluña, when not outright secession.[79] Moreover, there is little history of political violence in Cataluña when compared to the Basque Country. These differences represent a challenging puzzle for social scientists because the two movements developed within the same state. Juan Díez Medrano has explained the persistence of two nationalist movements with different natures and programs by the existence of different patterns of development and political competition.[80] Daniele Conversi's original thesis for explaining political violence in the Basque Country suggests that the lack of a common cultural marker such as language makes violence useful, if not necessary, for the reproduction of Basque identity and nationalism. On the contrary, the presence in Cataluña of a common language distinct from Castilian means that there are natural ties that bind Catalans and that violence would therefore serve no purpose. The elements brought up by these two authors are certainly relevant. However, it is necessary to highlight a crucial political difference between the two cases: the nature of the elites who first articulated nationalism in the two regions. This point is discussed by both Medrano and Conversi as well as by other authors such as Luis Moreno, but it needs to be made more central in any comparison between Cataluña and the Basque Country.[81]

The nineteenth-century processes of state- and nation-building in Spain triggered different political dynamics in Cataluña and the Basque Country. In the Basque provinces, these processes were opposed by traditional elites who adopted nationalism as a political instrument to brush back the forces of liberalization and secularization. As we have seen, these elites gave Basque nationalism a radical and secessionist twist that can still be felt today. In Cataluña, political centralization was opposed by a bourgeoisie for whom the Spanish state represented a fallen power as well as a largely agricultural and backward society. Contrary to in the Basque provinces, the bourgeoisie in Cataluña had always conducted its business with little or no help from the state and, consequently, feared the implications of state centralization for their activities. It was therefore the bourgeois segment of Catalan society, not its traditionalist elements, that struggled against the centralization of the Spanish state through nationalism. At the same time, the Catalan bourgeoisie looked for alliances with central elites for the purpose of protecting their goods from external competition in the Spanish market. Catalan nationalism was constructed as a liberal and procapitalist movement favoring autonomy for Cataluña but without seeking independence from Spain with which it felt a sense of solidarity. In stark contrast with Arana's discourse, Valentí Almirall, one of the father figures of Catalan nationalism who advocated a federal model for Spain, found that "from Cataluña's long-standing cohabitation with other peoples, derives a certain element of unity, of community, which these peoples ought to preserve and consolidate."[82] This view is still dominant in contemporary Catalan politics. The longtime Catalan nationalist leader Jordi Pujol always insisted on maintaining political links with Spain. His political party, Convergència Democràtica de Cataluña (CDC), which is part of the larger electoral federation Convergència i Unió (CiU), describes its project of developing Cataluña as a country as involving political action in Cataluña, Spain, and Europe.[83]

Basque Nationalism: Macroprocess and Microbehavior

As a state-centered approach to politics, historical institutionalism focuses on macroprocesses. It explores how the state and its various structures were created and transformed, and examines the consequences of these processes on political, social, cultural, and economic outcomes. In certain situations, the weight of state-making processes can be related to some outcomes without much agency. This was the case for the creation of the Basque identity through the various territorial management strategies of the early Spanish state, most notably the fueros and collective nobility. In other circumstances, institutions shape politics because they condition the behavior of actors, favoring some choices at the expense of others. In this context, group, or even individual, behavior needs to be understood in terms of the overarching institutional architecture that makes an institutionalist approach still appropriate. Despite its macrolevel nature, historical institutionalist analysis can take into account microlevel behavior. From an institutionalist perspective, agency can serve as the link between macroprocesses and outcomes.

This chapter's analysis of the creation of Basque nationalism in the late nineteenth century illustrates how historical institutionalism can integrate macro and micro dimensions in a causal explanation. This explanation starts with processes of state centralization and nation-building and ends with Sabino Arana as the immediate creator of Basque nationalism. Basque nationalism would not have emerged, at least in the form it took, had it not been from the fundamental transformation of the Spanish state in the nineteenth century and its failure to generate and diffuse to the masses a coherent national project. This represents the most critical juncture for nationalism in the Basque Country, since it eventually led to Sabino Arana inventing the idea of the Basque nation. It involved not only the transition from a state whose basic philosophy was to let many of its constituent territories have some degree of political autonomy to one functioning along the lines of the Jacobin model. It also featured confrontation between different visions of Spain that impeded Spanish nation-building.

A large part of the reason why these processes eventually led to Basque nationalism is institutional in nature. The Spanish state had developed in such a way that centralization and liberalization would be particularly unwelcome in the Basque provinces. The tradition of political autonomy deriving from the historical trajectory of the Spanish state, combined with endogenous social characteristics such as strong religious practice, led to politics in the Basque provinces being dominated by opposition movements and ideologies such as foralism and Carlism for most of the nineteenth century.

Neither foralism nor Carlism was nationalism. To explain the emergence of nationalism, agency needs to be introduced into the analysis. Opposition to the centralizing and liberalizing state came primarily from conservative elites. Not only did they have a lot to lose, in terms of political and social power and influence, from the transformation of Spain engineered by Liberal reformers, but the values and principles underpinning this transformation were completely contrary to their own. These elites, most importantly Sabino Arana, made the strategic decision to frame their political discourse of opposition in nationalist terms. They created the symbols necessary for the production and reproduction of Basque nationalism and brought into it the ideological content of Carlism. The symbolic and ideological dimensions of Basque nationalism have proven to be quite enduring legacies. Above all, Arana and like-minded elites pushed politics in the Basque provinces in the developmental pathway of nationalism, which was later on narrowed by the Spanish authoritarian state.

Chapter Three

The Authoritarian State

The emergence of Basque nationalism stems from the specific historical sequence of the Spanish state, more specifically its transition from confederal to centralizing and the agency this change triggered from Bizkaia's conservative elites. Prior to the Second Republic and the Franco dictatorship, nationalism had not really penetrated Basque society. This is hardly surprising since mass politics was still in its infancy in the early twentieth century, which means that any type of popular adherence to a nationalist creed was unlikely. There was also the matter that Basque nationalism was an offshoot of Carlism and that not all Carlists had followed Arana's "conversion" to nationalism. The Carlist origins of Basque nationalism are also central for explaining why Sabino Arana's ideas did not find wide acceptance among the elites of Araba and Navarre. In these two territories, Carlism remained strong and nationalism proved less popular than in Bizkaia or Gipuzkoa.

Despite the fact that provincial differences in the popularity of nationalism remain to this day, there is no denying that Basque nationalism is a mass movement of considerable strength and mobilization capacity. The broadening of social support for Basque nationalism was the product of a major institutional transformation: the end of the Second Republic, through a bloody civil war, and its replacement by a dictatorship.[1] The switch to authoritarianism represents a critical juncture for Basque nationalism insofar as it legitimized Basque nationalism as a political force and gave it broader appeal. The Franco dictatorship represented a strand of Spanish nationalism founded on the sacred unity of Catholic Spain. The authoritarian state sought to project a vision of Spain as united and homogeneous, but its great unintended consequence is that it produced just the opposite. There was no room, in the Franco vision of Spain, for cultural distinctiveness or political autonomy. On the contrary, state structures were centralized and the expression of cultural differences was driven underground by repression. Therefore, the Basque struggle against the Spanish state became closely associated, if not conflated, with a struggle for democracy.

The effect of the authoritarian state on Basque nationalism needs to be understood in relation to prior state forms. The Franco dictatorship is part of a historical process of state transformation that framed the development of Basque nationalism. The territorial structuring of the early Spanish state gave the Basque provinces a legacy of autonomy and exceptionalism. This legacy was then politicized in nationalist terms during the late nineteenth century through the politics of opposition of Arana and like-minded Traditionalists against the centralizing state in the context of a Spanish nation-building failure. From an instrument to articulate a particular group's opposition against liberal-secular centralism, Basque nationalism became, in the Franco era, a symbol of democratic resistance and gained wide acceptance in the Basque provinces.

The authoritarian state was central to the diffusion and legitimization of Basque nationalism, but it also represents a critical juncture for Basque nationalism insofar as it generated a new cleavage within the movement that still marks its politics. Before the Franco dictatorship, there was little division within the Basque nationalist movement: the PNV was the movement's hegemonic party and it was dominated by the Aranist program and ideology. The authoritarian state triggered two different patterns of nationalist action and opposition: the PNV formed a government-in-exile that steadily denounced the dictatorship's treatment of the Basques. ETA, created out of a sense that this type of resistance was ineffective against the Franco dictatorship, opted for guerilla warfare. These different patterns of opposition eventually evolved into distinct ideological frameworks and slightly different programmatic positions: the Basque nationalist movement came to feature "moderates" and "radicals."

Primo de Rivera and the Second Spanish Republic

The participation of the PNV in electoral politics was cut short in 1923 by the takeover of General Miguel Primo de Rivera. Class struggles, social violence, and anarchist movements, combined with international tensions and upheaval resulting from World War I and the Russian revolution, had severely shaken the foundations of Spain's liberal monarchy.[2] This growing instability led several actors to seek political change, namely the powerful Catalan bourgeoisie, the Crown, and the army. The military coup, which was presented by the army as a short-term solution to a political crisis, was not completely unwelcome by a large segment of the population who hoped for the return of law and order.[3] The army was at that time "the only major institution that could be said to support Spanish nationalism directly."[4] As a result, the coup represented the coming to power of a more concrete form of Spanish nationalism than ever before, which sought political modernization and social order while at the same time stressing unity through Catholicism and hispanidad.[5] Primo de Rivera looked to replace the liberal state and its conception of the nation.[6] He showed great enthusiasm for fascism,[7] which he saw as a political doctrine holding much promise for solving the "Spanish problem," that is, the lack of a coherent and convincing definition of the Spanish nation.

Still, for Basque nationalists, there was some hope to the new regime. Primo de Rivera had served in Barcelona and had good relations with several prominent members of Cataluña's regionalist party Lliga Regionalista. He seemed to be open to territorial autonomy: soon after his takeover, the general received political leaders from all three Basque provinces and encouraged them to develop concrete projects.[8] Politicians from Gipuzkoa presented a scheme featuring autonomy for the individual provinces and for a "Basque region." Navarre was left out of the project since its leaders were satisfied with the existing foral arrangement. Even with the exclusion of Navarre, the proposal did not enjoy unanimous support. Bizkaia, then dominated by conservative politicians, refused to endorse the initiative on the grounds that the Basque provinces had never formed a single region.[9] This view demonstrates the relatively limited influence of nationalism in the Basque provinces in the 1920s.

Primo de Rivera soon lost his taste for regional autonomy and forbade nationalist and regionalist political activity. The PNV and its splinter organization Comunión Nacionalista Vasca (CNV) were forced underground. This dictatorship never embarked on mass cultural repression; in fact, Basque cultural expression flourished during this period. From this perspective, the Primo de Rivera regime was different from Franco's. Nevertheless, it generated, albeit it on a smaller scale, a political dynamic similar to the one witnessed during the Franco years: repression of nationalist claims bolstered nationalist sentiments. From a doctrine viewed with suspicion, even considered desperately romantic and frivolous, nationalism was transformed into a legitimate political option. In the first election of the Second Republic held in June 1931, the PNV, running a slate with the Carlist party, won more than half of the seats allocated for Araba, Bizkaia, Gipuzkoa, and Navarre. The Primo de Rivera years were a first sign that the transition of the Spanish state from liberalism to authoritarianism would have a considerable impact on the popularity of Basque nationalism.

The dictatorship also served to strengthen Basque nationalism from an organizational point of view, as it prompted the merger of the CNV and the PNV into a single party. This was less a union than the simple absorption of the CNV by the PNV. The name of the enlarged party, for example, remained PNV. In addition, the terms of the agreements were dictated by the PNV as reflected by the core doctrinal elements agreed upon at the Bergara reunification assembly of November 16, 1930. They read as follows:

First: Basque nationalism proclaims the Catholic religion as the only true religion. . . .

Second: Euzkadi . . . will be Roman Catholic in all the manifestations of its internal life and in its relations with other nations, peoples and states.

Third: Euzkadi is the nation and *patria* of the Basques.

Fourth: Euzkadi, the Basque nation, is in virtue of natural and historical rights . . . master of its destiny.

Fifth: Basque nationalism . . . seeks to:

(a) Preserve and strengthen the Basque race, the fundamental basis of nationality.

(b) Preserve, spread, and purify the Basque language, clearest marker of our nationality.

(c) Reestablish traditional customs, and fight exotic ones that contaminate our character and personality.

Sixth: Reconstitute the historical Basque states, Araba, Bizcaya, Gipuzkoa, Nabarra, Laburdi, and Zuberoa, and their confederation in Euzkadi.[10]

In sum, not only did the dictatorship leave Basque nationalism more popular than ever, it also united it organizationally and focused the movement squarely around the principles laid out by Sabino Arana thirty years earlier.

Nationalist sentiments strengthened under the Primo de Rivera dictatorship found an outlet during the Second Spanish Republic. Primo de Rivera did not make his rule the short-term transitional dictatorship it was initially supposed to be and failed to craft a successor regime. Opposition forces, primarily left-wing segments of society, profited from the fact that the king had closely aligned himself with the dictator to effectively push their favored state model, republicanism. In August of 1930, Republicans met with left-leaning Catalan nationalist/regionalist organizations (Estat Català, Acció Catalana, and Acció Republicana de Catalunya) to seek their support for finishing off the military dictatorship and establishing a new regime. Basque nationalists, whose conservatism clashed with the politics of the Republicans, were not invited and did not seek involvement. In what became known as the Pact of San Sebastián, Catalan nationalists agreed to support the republican movement, and Republicans committed to present to the parliament a project for Catalan autonomy.[11]

The Second Republic, proclaimed in April 1931, was driven by a different variant of Spanish nationalism from the preceding dictatorship and the constitutional monarchy since it came not only with promises of democracy and progressive politics, but also with assurances of regional autonomy for Cataluña. While these values were at the center of a national project for Spain, culture and history remained part of the nation-building strategy. For example, the Republic's minister of public instruction, Fernando de los Ríos, stated in 1937: "We were trying to revive in the mind of the peasant the cultural values of which his ancestors had been the creators. We were attempting to make him conscious of his history, awakening in him a feeling for true "Spanishness.""[12] In concrete terms, the Republican regime organized "pedagogical missions" to spread "Castilian" urban culture to areas considered "isolated" for the purpose of cultural unification.[13] Interestingly, there was relatively little activity on that front in the Basque provinces, perhaps because industrialization was perceived as already doing that work there.[14]

At the same time, Republicans showed tolerance for schemes of regional autonomy. From this perspective, the Second Republic represents an important moment in the development of Basque nationalism because it gave nationalist forces, strengthened by the Primo de Rivera dictatorship, the opportunity to develop projects of autonomy and to put forward their now more widely accepted ideas in electoral politics. Indeed, notions of political autonomy may have been written into the Republican agenda only to satisfy Catalan nationalists, but they quickly caught the eye of Basque nationalists. The PNV was suspicious of the Republic's left-wing orientation and strong anticlericalism, but it did not oppose the new regime. In fact, the party was hopeful that the Republic's openness towards Cataluña's claims for autonomy could translate into the implementation of a statute of political autonomy for the Basque provinces, and perhaps even for all Basque territories as a whole.

Nationalist forces moved quickly to spearhead the drafting of a Basque Statute of Autonomy in the summer of 1931. This statute, which was adopted by nationalist forces at the Lizarra assembly in June, declared the "Basque state" to be autonomous within Spain and specified that individual provinces would also be allowed to administer much of their own affairs.[15] It specified powers reserved for the Spanish government (foreign affairs, armed forces, currency, criminal and commercial law) while leaving most everything else to the Basque government.[16] The statute was revised in the summer of 1932 to adapt it to the new Spanish constitution where Spain was called an integral state (*estado integral*) but said to be compatible with autonomy; references to a "Basque state," were replaced by "Euskadi," and the list of regional powers was shrunk. The document was approved by municipal representatives from all provinces except Navarre, where Carlists had grown suspicious of the centrist character of the project. The dream of uniting all the Basque territories of Spain was dashed by the reality of Navarre's own sense of distinctiveness. In 1933, the statute was modified to include only Araba, Bizkaia, and Gipuzkoa and endorsed in referendum (table 3.1). Majorities were clear in every province, although the level of abstention in Araba was very high. This was a tremendous triumph for the PNV, which followed it by a very good performance in the 1933 elections, where it won, on its own, half of the seats allocated for the four provinces (all of them in Bizkaia and Gipuzkoa). However, politics in both the Basque provinces and the Republic as a whole delayed the implementation of the statute. In terms of Basque politics, there were hesitations on the part of Araba. In the larger context of Spanish politics, the elections of 1933 produced center-right majorities that were less sympathetic to regional autonomy than the Republican left. By 1936, the Left was back in power, but Spanish politics was badly polarized and the Republic was on the verge of disintegration (tables 3.2, 3.3, 3.4). The nation-building program of the Republicans would come crashing down, primarily because "the Spanish state had a weak hold on society."[17] The modernization process in Spain had been uneven territorially, which meant that "the new Republican state had to mediate between a wide range of contradictory social and political forces, none of which held the balance of power in the Cortes."[18] In the end, the Basque Statute of Autonomy was granted on October 1, 1936, in the context of a civil war.[19] A PNV Basque government led by José Antonio Aguirre was formed, but it effectively controlled only Bizkaia and parts of Gipuzkoa. When Franco's forces took control of these last territories, the Basque government was forced into exile.

The Second Republic was a crucial institutional moment for the development of Basque nationalism. After being articulated by Sabino Arana in the context of a centralizing liberal state and paradoxically gaining strength when chased underground by the Primo de Rivera dictatorship, nationalism was allowed to display and increase its strength in a period of electoral politics. The Republic also gave the PNV the chance to create a first, albeit short-lived, Basque government that would serve as a pole of opposition to the Franco dictatorship and a key reference for the institutional structuring of the democratic period.

TABLE 3.1 *Results from referendum on the Basque Statute of Autonomy, November 5, 1933*

Results	Vizcaya (%)	Guipúzcoa (%)	Alava (%)	Total (%)
Electoral census	267.456 (100.0)	166.635 (100.0)	56.056 (100.0)	490.147 (100.0)
Votes	241.629 (90.3)	151.861 (91.1)	32.819 (58.5)	426.309 (87.0)
Votes in favor	236.564 (88.4)	149.177 (89.5)	26.015 (46.4)	411.756 (84.0)
Votes against	5.065 (1.9)	2.436 (1.5)	6.695 (11.9)	14.196 (2.9)
Void	—	248 (0.1)	109 (0.2)	357 (0.1)
Abstention	25.827 (9.7)	14.774 (8.9)	23.237 (41.5)	63.838 (13.0)

SOURCE: Santiago de Pablo, José Luis de la Granja Sainz, and Ludger Mees, eds., *Documentos para la historia del nacionalismo vasco: De los fueros a nuestros días* (Barcelona: Editorial Ariel, SA, 1998), 111.

TABLE 3.2 *Electoral results in the Basque Country, June 28, 1931*

Parties	Vizcaya (%)	Guipúzcoa (%)	Alava (%)	Navarra (%)	Total (%)
Right:					
CT	15,982 (26.0)	35,819 (14.4)	8,016 (37.9)	92,042 (25.3)	151,859 (16.1)
Católicos	—	71,879 (29.0)	—	93,624 (25.7)	165,503 (17.5)
PNV	31,209 (50.8)	35,901 (14.5)	4,615 (21.8)	46,419 (12.7)	211,456 (22.4)
Left:					
ANV	1,458 (2.4)	25,407 (10.2)	—	—	36,316 (3.8)
Republicanos	6,441 (10.4)	52,123 (21.0)	8,513 (40.3)	80,875 (22.2)	211,620 (22.4)
PSOE	6,381 (10.4)	25,612 (10.3)	—	51,393 (14.1)	148,684 (15.8)
PCE	—	1,301 (0.5)	—	—	18,405 (2.0)

SOURCE: José Luis de la Granja Sainz, *Nacionalismo y II República en el País Vasco* (Madrid: Siglo XXI, 1986), 215.

TABLE 3.3 *Electoral results in the Basque Country, September 19, 1933*

Parties	Vizcaya (%)	Guipúzcoa (%)	Alava (%)	Navarra (%)	Total (%)
Right					
CT	20,259 (14.7)	95,381 (18.6)	20,718 (52.2)	322,233 (43.0)	498,649 (25.0)
Monárq., alfonsinos (RE)	19,100 (13.8)	32,320 (6.3)	—	—	91,698 (4.6)
Católicos Independientes	—	—	—	136,923 (18.3)	136,923 (6.8)
Unión Navarra (CEDA)	—	—	—	77,690 (10.4)	77,690 (3.9)
Nationalist					
PNV	79,528 (57.4)	236,177 (46.1)	11,525 (29.0)	69,325 (9.2)	625,263 (31.3)
ANV	—	2,116 (0.4)	—	—	2,116 (0.1)
Republicans					
P. Radical	—	15,698 (3.1)	2,382 (6.0)	25,841 (3.4)	(3,9212.2)
P. Federal	—	12,395 (2.4)	—	—	12,395 (0.6)
Republics., de Guipúzcoa	—	11,901 (2.3)	—	—	11,901 (0.6)
PRRS	169 (0.1)	—	98 (0.2)	5,552 (0.7)	7,897 (0.4)
PRRS Independiente	—	—	4,856 (12.2)	—	54,839 (2.7)
Acción Republicana	9,662 (7.0)	15,333 (3.0)	—	—	75,974 (3.8)
Left					
PSOE	9,337 (6.8)	81,560 (15.9)	—	105,918 (14.1)	297,753 (14.9)
PCE	(338) (0.2)	9,365 (1.8)	109 (0.3)	6,120 (0.8)	59,927 (3.0)

SOURCE: José Luis de la Granja Sainz, *Nacionalismo y II República en el País Vasco* (Madrid: Siglo XXI , 1986), 427.

TABLE 3.4 *Electoral results in the Basque Country, February 16, 1936*

Parties	Vizcaya (%)	Guipúzcoa (%)	Alava (%)	Navarra (%)	Total (%)
Right					
CT	24,726 (17.7)	87,345 (16.5)	16,020 (37.1)	318,014 (43.0)	476,132 (23.5)
Renovación Española	22,089 (15.9)	43,495 (8.2)	—	95,530 (4.7)	
Independientes	—	—	—	76,080 (10.3)	106,356 (5.3)
CEDA	—	43,936 (8.3)	8,681 (20.1)	163,112 (22.0)	245,857 (12.1)
Nationalist					
PNV	72,026 (51.6)	195,647 (36.8)	8,958 (20.8)	14,799 (2.0)	465,205 (23.0)
Popular Front					
ANV	—	—	—	34,987 (4.7)	34,987 (1.7)
Unión Republicana	10,221 (7.3)	—	—	10,221 (0.5)	
Izquierda Republicana		80,724 (15.2)	9,521 (22.0)	67,023 (9.0)	226,952 (11.2)
PSOE	10,424 (7.5)	40,195 (7.6)	—	33,912 (4.6)	223,122 (11.0)
PC de Euskadi	—	39,213 (7.4)	—	32,874 (4.4)	141,265 (7.0)

SOURCE: José Luis de la Granja Sainz, *Nacionalismo II República en el País Vasco* (Madrid: Siglo XXI , 1986), 553.

Spanish Nationalism and the Franco Dictatorship

The vision of Spain promoted by the Second Republic profoundly divided Spanish society. The political structures and culture of the Republic proved unacceptable to most of the Spanish Right. Opposition to the Republic corresponded roughly to the electoral support of right-wing parties[20] such as the Traditionalists, Monarchists, and Agrarians.[21] However, the decisive opposition force was the military, which began rising against the Republican regime in the summer of 1936 and triggered the Civil War. All these elements represented the Catholic-conservative view of Spain that had fought liberal-secularism in the nineteenth century and which was now struggling against the Republicans. For the Spanish army in particular, there were two fundamental flaws to the Republic. First, it was seen as a nest of proletarian politics. In Spain as elsewhere in Europe after the Russian revolution, left-wing politics was feared by many for its destabilizing effects and revolutionary potential. The distaste of the Spanish Right for socialist ideologies was therefore nothing unusual. In the Spanish context where Catholicism had always been central to the state and the articulation of the nation, the stance of the Left on the religious question rendered the politics of the Second Republic even more troublesome for the Right. The burgeoning of socialism in Spain was also interpreted by some in the army as the work of foreign agents. In turn, this perception fed the idea that the Second Republic was weakening Spain and leaving it exposed to the manipulations of foreign powers.

This idea that Spain was weak derived in large part from the second flaw of the Republic as perceived by the military and other right-wing elements: the statutes of autonomy. For right-wing forces, political autonomy was seen as a "slippery slope" to secession rather than a positive strategy of accommodation. The statutes would undo Spain rather than keep it together, or, at least, it would make it weak and uncoordinated rather than strong and united. From this perspective, they constituted unacceptable concessions to nationalist movements in Cataluña, Galicia, and the Basque provinces. The Second Republic therefore represented the abandonment of the right-wing idea of Spain as united by political centralization and cultural homogeneity.

Spanish nationalism as articulated by the Right was about seeking the "regeneration" of Spain,[22] which entailed the destruction of the Second Republic and its replacement by an authoritarian regime. From the Left's perspective, preserving the Republic meant securing democracy, progressive politics, and possibly regional autonomy. The perceptions that the life or death of the Republic was such a high stakes issue explain in large part the particularly ferocious fighting of the Spanish Civil War (1936–1939) between Nationalists and Republicans. After its victory, the Right created an authoritarian regime led by General Francisco Franco, which branded as twin evils the two features of the Second Republic that prompted the military to seek its end: left-wing politics and regional nationalist claims. The two were even considered to be one and the same and were neatly packaged in the idea of *rojos separatistas* (red separatists).

The politics of the Civil War was quite complex in the Basque provinces. Early on, the PNV's support for the Republican side was less than enthusiastic: it was never enamored of the Republic because of its left-wing slant, but viewed it more likely than a Nationalist regime to grant autonomy to the Basque Country. Franco's forces helped the PNV make up its mind as they started victimizing party members shortly after having triumphed in Araba and Navarre.[23] Nevertheless, not all the Basque provinces supported the Republicans: Bizkaia and Gipuzkoa did, but most of Araba as well as Navarre backed Franco. The centralism and Spanishness of Franco's Nationalists would have struck a chord in Araba, the least nationalist of the three provinces, and Navarre, the least Basque of the four territories. The discourse of Franco's Nationalists, with its heavy emphasis on religion, was also close to the Carlist ideology that was still strong there, especially in Navarre. As a reward for their support, Araba and Navarre were then allowed to keep their *conciertos económicos*. Bizkaia and Gipuzkoa were not; they were in fact branded as traitors.

The Civil War might have been a divisive affair in the Basque provinces, but the story is told quite differently by Basque nationalists. From this perspective, the war did not pit Spaniards against other Spaniards, but rather Spain against the Basques. Or, in other words, the war was a matter of resistance against an invader. This discourse is not unlike the one surrounding the Second Carlist War, although there is one major difference between the Basque nationalist interpretation of the Carlist war and of the Civil War. In the case of the Carlist war, the specific ideological nature of the new regime (liberal, constitutional, and secular) was paramount to the Basque opposition. In the case of the Civil War, the fascist nature of Franco's Nationalists was presented almost as an element of secondary importance: the key point was that, after having finally united their three provinces, the Basques now had to endure a foreign occupation.[24] With the Civil War and the ensuing dictatorship, the Basque struggle became more than ever before a struggle against the Spanish state.

Collective memory of the war in the Basque Country was also fed by some very real events. Of foremost importance was the bombing of the city of Gernika (Guernica). The details of this event are fuzzy, but what is certain is that on April 26, 1937, Gernika, a small Bizkaian town of approximately seven thousand people, was the victim of aerial bombardments that caused, depending on the estimates, anywhere from a few hundred to over one thousand deaths.[25] Many have persuasively argued that these bombings were carried out by German planes with the blessings of General Franco. In a statement pleading for the protection of women

and children who had taken refuge in Bilbao, Basque president José Antonio Aguirre said that "for three and a half hours, German planes bombed with a ferocity
never experienced before the defenseless civil population of Gernika."[26]

Franco always denied any role in the attack, stating: "We have respected Gernika
as we respect everything that is Spanish."[27] Despite these denials, it is most probable that these bombings somehow originated from Franco's Nationalists and that
Gernika was chosen for political rather than strategic reasons.[28] Gernika is home
to the famous oak tree that served as a meeting place for foral councils; it is closely
associated with the Basque fueros and is therefore a space of great symbolic significance. The contemporary Basque nationalist standpoint on the bombings is that
they represented a deliberate and nearly genocidal act that showed a profound
hatred for the Basques and announced the intent to exterminate them as a culturally distinct group. If there is one event that symbolizes the Basque view of the
Civil War as a conflict between Spain and the Basques, it is the attack on Gernika.
For example, Pablo Picasso's *Guernica* painting conveys for most Spaniards as well
as the international audience the horrors of war. In the Basque Country, where
Picasso's representation can be widely seen, it symbolizes the oppression of the
Basque people at the hands of the Spanish state. The controversy over the location
of the painting (currently in Madrid but sought for the Guggenheim Museum
in Bilbao) exemplifies the Basque determination to make Gernika, the historical
event, Basque.

While the Franco dictatorship demonized all left-wing political forces, its obses-
sion was national unity: Spain was "better red than broken."[29] Interestingly, the
fascist articulation of the Spanish nation had much in common with the way the
Basque nation was conceived by Sabino Arana. At the center of the fascist discourse
was the idea that Spain was a historic nation of Catholic tradition: Spain was built
through a religious struggle between Christians and Muslims that was not unlike
the struggle between Franco's Nationalists and the Republicans. This religious element of the fascist doctrine gave mystical qualities to the Spanish nation, which
was presented as eternal, immortal, and sacred. There were also strong cultural,
if not racial, underpinnings to this doctrine as Spain was said to be united by a
common character, hispanidad.[30] From the Fascist perspective, Spain was culturally
homogenous; or, at least, it had to be because its unity depended on it. Basque and
Catalan nationalism were therefore the worst enemies of Spain. The very existence
of "Basques" and "Catalans" was a problem because they represented cultural distinctiveness.[31]

For the Franco regime, keeping Spain together entailed cultural repression and
assimilation. From this perspective, democratic practices were problematic since
they allowed "peripheral" movements to undermine the unity of Spain; authoritarianism was justified, at least in part, by the imperative to prevent the disintegration of the country. The exercise of political power under Franco conditioned the

politics of opposition. Authoritarianism discredited state centralization. Democracy became synonymous with decentralized political structures. In the Basque provinces, the consequences of authoritarianism, political repression, and attempted cultural assimilation acquired a particular meaning: the Spanish state, as opposed to only the Franco dictatorship, was seen as an oppressive force bent on destroying the Basques as a culturally distinct community. The presence of the authoritarian state in the Basque provinces, and its determination to forcefully obtain the loyalty of all Basques to Spain, had in many cases the opposite effect. The dictatorship gave new legitimacy to the idea of the Basque nation, above and beyond provincial borders, and made it a symbol of democratic resistance. It transformed nationalism into an instrument of political and democratic opposition. The authoritarian state also shaped the patterns of Basque nationalist politics by giving new meaning to the ideas of moderate and radical nationalism.

From Hegemony to Decline: The Struggles of the PNV Under Franco

Franco's forces took control of the Basque provinces with the firm intent of destroying nationalist sentiments. By all accounts, those who had fought against Franco, resisted the military regime, or expressed support for the Basque Country were imprisoned, tortured, and often executed.[32] This included the many Basque priests who had "strayed" from the Church by siding with the Republicans. A crucial aspect of the early Francoist repression in the Basque provinces was the effort to eradicate all signs of the Basque language. Euskara was banned from schools, mass, and broadcasting. Its use in public was also forbidden. Basque names in civil registries, and in some areas on tombstones, were erased and replaced by Spanish ones.[33] Over one hundred thousand Basques went into exile before the end of the Civil War. They went to France, often the first stop, to other European countries such as Belgium and Britain, and to Latin and North America.[34] This Basque diaspora became an important source of support, financial and otherwise, for the Basque government-in-exile.

In the meantime, the Basque government-in-exile had to manage with the events of World War II. President José Antonio Aguirre left France for the United States after stops in several other countries, including Belgium and Germany; this rendered the Basque government largely incapable of political representation.[35] In response to this vacuum, nationalist forces in Britain formed the Basque National Council (Consejo Nacional Vasco) in 1940. The Council developed a radical agenda that featured the creation of a Republic of Euskadi, whose territory was larger than in any previous plan, together with an Iberian confederation.[36] Of course, the Council had no chance to follow through on this project. It did sign a military agreement with General de Gaulle's French forces that saw the creation of a Basque unit in the French navy, but pressures from Spain through the British government led to the unit's dismantling.[37] The existence of the Council created some tensions within the Basque opposition forces,[38] but it ceased its activities in 1942, shortly after Aguirre arrived in the United States and reestablished the Basque government-in-exile.

With the war, the "Basque question" was internationalized. The political strategy of the Basque government-in-exile consisted essentially in supporting the Allies, primarily the United States, in the hope that a defeat of the Axis forces would lead to the fall of the Franco regime. Of course, the assistance of the Basque government could only be very modest, but the PNV did cooperate with American and other Allied secret services in the gathering of intelligence.[39] During the war, the PNV's program was radicalized. Throughout the Spanish Civil War, the PNV had supported Republican forces. However, Aguirre thought that an Allied victory in World War II had such upside for the Basques that he spoke of the creation of an independent Basque state between Spain and France. A return to the statute of 1936 within a Spanish republic was now a minimalist or pessimistic solution.[40]

The end of the war was therefore a time of great optimism for the Basque government-in-exile as it began its reorganization. This government featured members from many different political parties but was clearly dominated by the PNV.[41] José Antonio Aguirre, who was its unquestioned leader, was present at the 1945 San Francisco conference that saw the birth of the United Nations. There, he took a pragmatic stance and defended the Republican regime.[42] This might not have been a complete return to his self-stated pessimistic solution since any change in the political status of the Basque Country necessarily involved the end of the dictatorship in Spain and its replacement by a different type of regime. In the context of the Spanish authoritarian state, the PNV's emphasis was on the ideas of "freedom" and "liberation," which may or may not have eventually involved the creation of an independent state. At its first postwar meeting held in Europe (Bayonne, France) in August 1946, the Basque government-in-exile stated the following: "The government of Euskadi, interpreting the will of its people, declares as a general principal its determination to increase the resistance against Franco's tyranny until Euskadi is completely free."[43]

It appears, however, that after the grandiose projects of the Basque National Council during the darkest days of World War II, the prospect of a return to the republican regime had the PNV focusing its effort on reestablishing the Statute of Autonomy for an Euskadi composed of Araba, Bizkaia, and Gipuzkoa. Many Basque nationalists in France felt that the Basque government-in–exile was letting them down. One young Basque nationalist chided Aguirre for presenting his government as a regional government of the Spanish Republic and, therefore, discouraging the French government from adopting a positive attitude on the Basque question: "What does the French government and public opinion see in you? A

Spaniard, a Spanish Republican, a Basque political leader who is at the same time a civil servant of the Spanish state. How can the sympathy for the Basque cause of a French minister of foreign affairs, which is at best moderate, weigh on this people's destiny when you have yourself willingly inserted this cause within the destiny of the Spanish people?"[44]

The hopes of the PNV for any type of autonomy for the Basque Country were dashed by the realities of cold war power politics. Starting in 1947 with the Truman doctrine, the foreign policy of the United States would be focused on the containment of the Soviet Union and communism. In this new environment, the Franco dictatorship, with its staunch anticommunism, became a dependable ally. The United States was ready to overlook Spain's support for the Axis during the war and its violations of human rights. In 1953, Spain signed a bilateral treaty with the United States. It entered the United Nations in 1955.[45] The partial end of Spain's isolation, and the normalization of the relationship between the United States and the Franco regime, meant that the PNV's gamble to count on foreign powers to create conditions favorable to Basque autonomy had failed.

Since the PNV's leadership was in exile in France, its options for continuing the struggle against Franco were limited. The PNV's overall strategy was to accelerate the fall of the dictatorship any way it could.[46] At the center of this strategy was the idea that Basque autonomy, or independence, could come only as a result of regime change in Madrid. Only democracy in Spain could liberate the Basques. This led the PNV to pursue three different strategies. First, it established links with other anti-Franco forces as well as with other Christian Democratic parties in Europe.[47] Second, it sought to promote the Basque culture and language, and with them nationalist sentiments. After all, it was crucial that those sentiments still be alive and well when democracy came to Spain for Basque autonomy to be achievable. For example, the PNV was a key actor in the organization of the World Basque Congress in Paris. Such events were also aimed at showing both Basques and Franco that the nationalists were still there. Third, although starting in the late 1940s the PNV could no longer count on very much international support, it still made its presence felt internationally by voicing condemnations of the Franco regime. For example, Aguirre wrote to UNESCO in November 1952 to object to Spain's membership. After having described political and cultural repression in the Basque Country, Aguirre argued that: "If, according to the UNESCO charter, this organization has for objective 'to contribute to the maintenance of peace and security for the purpose of securing the universal respect of justice, law, human rights and fundamental freedoms for all without distinction of race, gender, language, or religion,' then we do not believe that the regime of general Franco is qualified for membership in this organization."[48] Despite Aguirre's letter, Spain gained admission to UNESCO. Indeed, denunciations of the Franco regime by the Basque government-in-exile were not effective; Franco's fascist tactics were trumped by the imperatives of the cold war.

The PNV's strategy of nurturing relationships with other anti-Franco actors and of promoting the Basque culture and language (always abroad of course) brought no immediate results to the condition of Basques living under Franco's regime. In a decade, the 1950s, when the Basque economy was booming, many lost interest in nationalism in the Basque Country.[49] The PNV appeared passive, ineffective, and, after José Antonio Aguirre died in 1960, without firm leadership. These conditions explain the rise of ETA.

ETA and Political Violence

ETA (Euskadi ta Askatasuna, Basque Country and Freedom) is a creature of the Spanish authoritarian state. During the dictatorship, the themes of ETA's struggle were national and democratic liberation. Its existence derived from policies of political and culture repression conducted in the Basque Country by the Franco regime in the name of Spanish unity. More specifically, the creation of ETA should be understood as a consequence of a restlessness toward the seemingly ineffective strategies of the PNV and a disillusionment vis-à-vis the chance of the United States toppling the dictatorship. From a more substantive point of view, the founders of ETA disagreed with the PNV on both the process that could lead to the liberation of the Basque Country and its end result. The founding members of ETA were young. They had not been closely associated with the politics of the Republic and had little confidence that any solution to the Basque question could come through the Spanish state. They therefore favored the creation of an independent Basque state rather than a return to the Statute of Autonomy.[50] These young nationalists had started meeting, first in 1952, as a group called Ekin (To Do). Ekin then merged for a couple of years with the PNV's youth wing, Eusko Gaztedi (Basque Youth), but tensions within the latter organization with respect to both strategies and political objectives produced a split: one group chose to remain within the PNV fold, while the other stayed with Ekin and contributed to the founding of ETA in July 1959.

For Basque nationalism, the creation of ETA meant a return, albeit partial, to the doctrine of Sabino Arana.[51] From Arana, ETA took a belligerent attitude toward the Spanish state. Spain was viewed as an occupying foreign power whose presence in the Basque Country was the source of all problems afflicting the Basques. Consequently, the only way out was to struggle for the complete independence of the Basque Country, which was conceptualized in a maximalist fashion, that is, as incorporating the Basque territories of France as well as those of Spain (including Navarre). ETA did not present its political action as aiming at the betterment of individual Basques; rather, its cause was the liberation of Euskadi, understood as an organic whole.[52] This central objective was specified at ETA's first assembly held in 1962. To generate support for the Basque Country's liberation, ETA

rearticulated Arana's historical narratives that portrayed the Basques as a democratic and egalitarian people whose progress was impaired by a conquest at the
hands of a backward state.[53] ETA was also influenced by Arana when it came to
immigrants from elsewhere in Spain, although the overall position of the organization on this issue was always ambiguous. Since ETA, like Arana, harbored a deep-
seated hatred for everything Spanish, it was instinctively suspicious toward people
it considered a source of "Spanishness" (*españolismo*) and therefore a potential
threat to the cultural integrity of the Basque nation.[54] However, ETA understood
that a large segment of the Basque Country's population was of Spanish descent.[55]
This sociological reality made unthinkable the exercise of excluding from the
nation everybody whose lineage could be traced to "Spain."

ETA also made fundamental changes to Arana's doctrine. Four are particularly
noticeable. First, the emphasis on race was replaced by a stress on the Basque language and culture. This deviation from Arana's articulation of Basque nationalism
was partly the consequence of the important wave of immigration to the Basque
Country from other parts of Spain from the late 1950s to the mid-1970s.[56] In a
period of such a diversification, the politics of liberation would have been greatly
complicated by a racial definition of the nation. Of course, the Basque language
was not exactly a marker around which Basques could rally around easily since a
majority did not speak it fluently. ETA therefore insisted on the need to strengthen
the use of Euskara. In other words, its treatment of language involved a call for language recuperation. For ETA, the marginalization of the Basque language was something serious; it threatened the very existence of the Basque nation.[57] The focus
on language at the expense of race also had another dimension. ETA was formed
as a reaction against the repressive policies of an authoritarian state, and therefore
defined itself as a progressive movement fighting for freedom and democracy. From
this perspective, it is hardly surprising that it avoided references to racial categories
that would have smacked of conservatism. In fact, ETA founders often criticized the
PNV for endorsing Arana's ethnic definition of the nation and accused its followers
of being racist.[58]

The second change made by ETA to Arana's brand of Basque nationalism was
the evacuation of religion from the formal articulation of Basque nationhood.
Here again, the profile of the authoritarian state conditioned the form taken by
the emergent radical nationalism. Since the Franco regime relied on the Roman
Catholic religion as an instrument of political legitimization and used it to project the idea of a homogeneous Spain, ETA could not adopt a similar religious discourse. Also important to ETA's self-professed secularism was the perception that
the clergy had done little to challenge the Franco dictatorship.[59] The radical nationalist critique of the Church was substantially developed in a text that served as
the central inspiration to ETA: Frederico Krutwig's *Vasconia*, published in 1963.
Krutwig, who was not himself a member of ETA, argued that the Church had served

to undermine the Basque national identity. He then proceeded to reinterpret the historical relationship between the Basques and religion. From a religious people, the Basques become atheist: "The Basque people . . . never welcomed with open heart the foreign creed embodied by Roman Catholicism. Even if today the Basques seem to adhere to the Roman Catholic Church, any serious observer can see that the Basque is closer to paganism.[60] All of this being said, it is important to qualify the relationship between ETA and the Catholic church. Despite a discourse that often appears strongly anticlerical, ETA's action never targeted the church; no priest has ever been killed by ETA members. Moreover, Basque priests generally refrained from criticizing ETA during the dictatorship period.

Vasconia was also central in shaping ETA's nationalist rhetoric along the lines of the discourse of anticolonial and revolutionary movements in Latin America and elsewhere in the developing world. This ideological bent is, of course, very different from the conservatism articulated by Arana. As indicated before, ETA founders considered the Basque Country to be under Spanish occupation. From this perspective, the plight of the Basques did not appear much different from that of, for example, the Algerians. ETA identified very strongly not only with wars of independence such as Vietnam's and Algeria's, but also with the revolutions in Cuba and China.[61] In these situations, they saw oppressed and exploited peoples successfully topple repressive regimes through armed struggles. ETA was also inspired by the ideologies of these various independence, anti-imperialist, and revolutionary movements. ETA members and followers were, partly as a result of the United States decision to support the Franco regime once the cold war had begun, staunchly anti-American. They were attracted to, and indeed sought to frame their political action in terms of, anticapitalist revolutionary ideologies such as Marxism-Leninism and Maoism. ETA formally adopted the anticapitalist stance at its third assembly in 1964, and the connection between the class and national questions was endorsed at its fourth assembly in 1965.[62] ETA's focus was therefore on radical change through action. Or, in the words of Frederico Krutwig, "A national liberation movement can never be conservative. . . . A conservative regime, a conservative ideology prolongs the status quo. A struggle for national liberation is by definition a revolutionary ideal. From this fact, we must draw the necessary consequences."[63]

Despite the existence of a broad agreement on a radical left-wing slant, ETA was never a coherent organization ideologically or politically. From its beginnings, it experienced debates over ideology that translated into internal divisions. During the 1960s, there were three different tendencies within ETA: the cultural nationalists, the revolutionary nationalists, and the Marxists.[64] The first tendency was represented by members of the original Ekin group, who believed the organization's central focus should be the "national question," that is, the independence of the Basque Country. The second tendency, guided by Krutwig's thinking, conceptualized the Basque Country as a colonial possession of Spain. This perspective was not too far from the Ekin group's culturalist view in that it put the idea of nation-hood at the forefront of politics. The third tendency framed the Basque question squarely in terms of class struggle. From this Marxist angle, Basque national-ism was really an epiphenomenon of a larger movement for the emancipation of workers. This position brought to the Marxists criticisms of Spanishness from the rest of the organization. In the early 1960s, the Ekin group controlled ETA; however, starting in 1964, the organization slipped into the hands of the Marxist faction, which fought off a loose coalition between the cultural and revolution-ary nationalists.[65] This conflict produced ETA's first split: the Marxist faction was ousted in 1966 and created ETA-Berri (new ETA), which eventually mutated into a Spanish communist organization.[66] Despite this splinter, the relative importance of the national and class questions within ETA remained, as advocates of a workers' revolution were accused of españolismo. In 1971, ETA split again over ideology, with ETA-VI representing the class struggle approach and ETA-V supporting the cultural nationalist vision. In the end, ETA-V prevailed and was able to simply return to the name ETA.

ETA's espousal of radical left-wing ideologies involved the advocating of violence as a political strategy. This is another departure from Arana, who never hinted at such an approach for creating an independent Basque state. In the presence of the authoritarian state, ETA conceived of violence as having an instrumental use. In other words, killings were not simply meant to remind Franco that the Basques were still there and that there was still a political conflict in the Basque Country. Rather, they were viewed as a way to chase the Franco regime from Basque territory. Here again, ETA's source of inspiration was Krutwig's *Vasconia*. Krutwig refers to Clausewitz as he sketches a framework for reaching this objective. "For him," Krutwig says, "any action from the enemy must always be met by a stronger response so that he accepts our will; in our case, the end of the military occupation."[67] Krutwig devel-oped a theory of how the "occupation" of the Basque Country would end, which in turn informed a political strategy. Krutwig's theory revolved around the idea of a cycle triggered by action and perpetuated by repression; the corresponding political strategy was a guerilla war. Krutwig explained that if the state's repression were met by equally punishing acts of violence (killings, torture, etc.), the use of violence would become more indiscriminate (since the *guerilleros* would be difficult to find) and its level would heighten. As a consequence, the Basque population would be increasingly mobilized through this "upward spiral of resistance."[68] In the end, the Franco regime would effectively be chased from the Basque Country, and a Basque government would gradually assume the administration of the territory.[69] For Krutwig, it was therefore not necessary to topple the dictatorship, but only to drive it out of the Basque Country. His perspective was purely a Basque one. It did not involve a change in the nature of the Spanish state, but simply its rollback to Spanish territory.

Krutwig was not an ETA member, but the organization latched onto *Vasconia* as its central manifesto and strategic guide. In 1963, a young member of ETA, José Luis Zalbide, wrote, under the pseudonym K. de Zumbeltz, *Insurrección en Euskadi*, which advocated guerilla resistance within the framework of the action-repression-action theory. The Krutwig-Zalbide approach was formally endorsed by ETA at its second assembly in 1963.[70] The use of violence as a political strategy had its critics within ETA, most notably among the cultural nationalist group, but violence has been ETA's trademark for most of its existence.[71]

At its creation, ETA was a very small organization whose expertise in its chosen means of action, guerilla warfare, was limited. For this reason, it did not become an important factor in the resistance to Franco for several years. In its first two years of existence, ETA primarily held meetings, circulated its literature, and painted its names on buildings.[72] In 1961, five prominent ETA members were imprisoned and then went into exile in France, thereby depriving the organization of much of its leadership. That year, ETA also attempted a bolder action, a train derailment, which failed and led to more imprisonments and exile. By 1967–68, ETA had pushed its action to robberies, shootings, and bombings. In 1968 came the first casualties of ETA violence: an ETA member, Txabi Etxebarrieta, killed a Guardia Civil officer before being shot dead himself.[73] The two killings marked the beginning of the action-repression-action spiral. Etxebarrieta's death sparked much grief and anger among the Basques; he became ETA's first martyr.[74]

That same year, ETA assassinated police commissioner Melitón Manzanas. The assassination of Manzanas, who was known for physically abusing Basque nationalists and other opponents of the regime, was a watershed moment for ETA because it proved both the organization's willingness to take risks and its capacity to reach powerful agents of the state.[75] In other words, ETA was living up to its action-repression-action blueprint; after having had its every move countered with arrests and repression, ETA had upped the ante with Manzanas's killing. That killing had the expected consequence of triggering a swift and indiscriminate reaction by the Franco regime, which declared a state emergency and detained people almost at random.[76] In this sense, Krutwig's approach was working, although ETA's violence had not yet triggered the mass rebellion needed to "liberate" the Basque Country. However, ETA could count on substantial popular support.[77] After all, it struggled, for many heroically, against a brutal dictatorship and therefore embodied ideas of democracy, liberation, and justice. This being said, there was also opposition to the means used by ETA to fight the Franco regime; the PNV, for example, rejected the use of violence, which it presented as contrary the traditional pacific character of the Basques.[78] The immediate absence of a large-scale popular rebellion that would drive the Franco dictatorship out of the Basque Country did not lead to a reexamination of the cycle theory; it was, after all, too early to tell if the strategy could bring about the desired outcomes. However, the repression part of the cycle theory was costing ETA much of its leadership, and it was unclear, in the late 1960s, if the organization would have the structure necessary to pursue its spiraling violence approach to fighting off the dictatorship.[79]

In 1970, the Franco dictatorship inadvertently attracted national and international attention to the Basque question by charging sixteen ETA members with the murder of Melitón Manzanas. The Burgos trial, as this episode was called, triggered multiple protests not only in the Basque Country but also in Madrid and elsewhere in western Europe.[80] The trial also led the international media to narrate ETA's struggle against the dictatorship; various intellectuals (for example, Jean-Paul Sartre) jumped into the debate, while many European states recalled the ambassadors.[81] ETA's spiraling cycle of violence had produced an outcome that shook the Franco regime to its core. Through the Burgos trial, the dictatorship was exposed abroad like never before; in turn, this attention only added to the growing pressures the regime faced at home. In 1973, ETA managed to up the ante once again by assassinating Franco's presumed successor, Carrero Blanco. Once again, the killing brought international attention to the Basques of Spain in addition to depriving the dictatorship of the appearance of political continuity. The action-repression-action strategy was bringing a struggling dictatorship to its knees, albeit it in a slightly different way from the path drawn by Krutwig. Despite these victories, ETA experienced another major schism in 1974 when it broke up into an ETA *politico-militar* (ETA-PM) and *militar* (ETA-M). This split was not the result of an ideological conflict, but rather a strategic one: ETA became divided over the usefulness of engaging in politics rather than being strictly a military organization.

Despite these divisions, ETA survived the dictatorship. ETA was a creature of the Spanish authoritarian state, and it fed on the state's repression against the Basques. Repression was, under Franco, the only management strategy for Basque nationalism, and ETA attacks were consistently met by policing efforts that often involved the indiscriminate use of violence. ETA killed over forty people during the Franco years and managed to attract the sympathy of a considerable portion of the Basque population.[82] This sympathy, even legitimacy, made the question of the future of ETA in the democratic period a less open-ended question that appeared at first sight; ETA was not going to disappear.[83] This connection between ETA and many Basques fostered during the dictatorship provided the organization with the social support necessary to pursue its violent activities after Franco's death. ETA would take seriously Krutwig's ominous warning about violence: "Since guerilla war is not an end in itself, the population of Vasconia will wish its termination. . . . In such a situation, the worst error that the guerrilleros could make is to accept a solution other than one that recognizes the full independence of the nation."[84]

The Authoritarian State: Radicalizing Basque Nationalism

The turn of the Spanish state toward authoritarianism in the middle of the twentieth century represents a third critical juncture in the development of Basque nationalism. The authoritarian state narrowed the development pathway of the Basque Country by broadening the appeal of nationalism. While Sabino Arana was the founding father of Basque nationalism, the Franco dictatorship was responsible for making Basque nationalism a truly mainstream political position by discrediting Spanish nationalism among the Basques. The dictatorship gave substance to many of Arana's ideas. First and foremost, it gave credence to the notion of the Spanish state as a foreign oppressor and to the argument that the Basque political culture, imbued with egalitarianism and democracy, clashed with Spain's. In a classic case of unintended consequence, the authoritarian state created by Franco, to a large degree for maintaining the unity of Spain through the eradication of nationalist sentiments, stimulated Basque nationalism by making this form of politics synonymous with democratic opposition and struggles for freedom. In this political and institutional context, to not be a nationalist was de facto to be a supporter of Franco.

A central argument of this book is the importance of the sequence and timing of institutional transformations for explaining sociopolitical outcomes. The reaction of Basque traditional elites to political centralization in the late nineteenth century, in the form of the formal articulation of Basque nationalism, needs to be understood in the context of an early state that nurtured territorial autonomy and privileges. Similarly, the short-lived Republic that preceded the Franco dictatorship compounded the effect of the authoritarian state on Basque society. The second Spanish Republic was a progressive and democratic regime that, ultimately, offered political autonomy to the Basque Country. It presented a picture of the Spanish state and nation as flexible and tolerant of diversity. The switch to Franco's regime was therefore seen by Basque nationalists, and in time by most Basques, as a clear step back. In other words, the transition from a democratic republic to an authoritarian state galvanized Basque nationalism in a way that a continuous succession of non-democratic or weakly democratic regimes might not have.

Basque nationalism during the Second Republic was shaped by the historical fueros. Taking advantage of the opportunity presented by the new regime, José Antonio Aguirre, leader of the PNV, met with Basque mayors to claim "their right to autonomy within a Spanish federal republic, by the legendary Oak of Gernika."[85] This idea of "right" to autonomy is a legacy of the fueros. Another such legacy is the tradition of *provincial* distinctiveness and autonomy. This last aspect of foralism is crucial for understanding some of the difficulty in implementing a Basque

Statute of Autonomy during the Second Republic; the province of Araba and the Kingdom of Navarre were reluctant to merge into one single Basque political unit. In the end, the Basque Statute of Autonomy represented an amended form of the historical fueros in the sense that the three provinces were subsumed in a single, or at least overarching, political entity.

The authoritarian state served to radicalize Basque nationalism. In comparison to the doctrine of Sabino Arana, the Basque nationalist movement softened its position toward the Spanish state during the Republic. The PNV agreed to work within the Spanish framework and defended the Republican state when it was under attack from the forces of the Right. In fact, the PNV kept its faith in the Republican government well after it was ousted from Madrid. It was this attitude, viewed as weakness and passivity, which eventually became intolerable for some Basque nationalist youths who created ETA. The authoritarian state created a new stream within Basque nationalism since ETA and its brand of radical nationalism developed in reaction to the repressive policies of the Franco dictatorship. Faced with a fascist regime, radical nationalism in the Basque Country adopted a neo-Marxist revolutionary discourse; this was a clear departure from the nationalism articulated by Sabino Arana.

So was ETA's guerilla war strategy. Political violence in the Basque Country is also a direct product of the authoritarian state. During the dictatorship, ETA's killings were widely seen as acts of democratic resistance. As a consequence, the organization gained a level of respect that was carried into the democratic period. Political violence in the democratic period, especially the first decade or so, was to a large extent the product of the social support ETA enjoyed in virtue of its opposition to Franco. Violence therefore outlived the political and institutional circumstances that led to its birth. However, its rationale, that it constituted a means to drive the Franco regime out of the Basque Country, was challenged by the reemergence in Spain of a democratic state.

Chapter Four

The Democratic State

By the time Spain began its transition toward democracy, Basque nationalism was a potent political force. The sequential chain represented by the institutional mutations of the Spanish state had taken it from a marginal movement spearheaded by conservative politicians to a vigorous, popular, and also multidimensional one. By the last quarter of the twentieth century, it was not only that the Basque nationalist movement was fundamentally different from fifty or one hundred years before, but also that the institutional context was changing one more time in a most fundamental way. Basque nationalism was central in shaping this new institutional environment, and the historical trajectory of the Basque provinces' political and institutional development factored heavily in the determination of their own status. As much as Basque nationalism contributed to shaping the specific configuration of the new state, the future and nature of nationalist politics in the Basque Country were very much open-ended in the late 1970s. Basque nationalism was entering near-uncharted territory: it would now operate within a democratic decentralized state, something that had not occurred since the Second Republic.

The main argument of this chapter is that the Spanish Estado de las Autonomías not only allowed for the expression of Basque nationalism, but also stimulated its development by providing an institutional setting that generated political dynamics and patterns of relationships conducive to nationalist politics. Much like in the late nineteenth century or during the dictatorship, the democratic period features a causal mechanism between the Spanish state and the development of Basque nationalism. This causality, however, is not as straightforward as the ones involving the centralizing and authoritarian state, respectively. Rather, it needs some disentanglement.

There are four patterns of relationships stemming from the Spanish system of autonomous communities that have stimulated and configured nationalist politics in the Basque Country. The first pattern involves the political opposition between Basque nationalist and non-Basque nationalist forces within the Basque Country. Nationalism is a powerful force in Basque politics, but it is certainly not without its opponents. The existence of such a dialectical relationship is full of implications for Basque nationalists who, for example, are never in a position to say that their claims are supported by all Basques. The second pattern is also endogenous to the Basque Country and features moderate and radical nationalists. The relationship between these two groups is ambiguous, and its subtle nuances have strongly marked the direction of Basque nationalism, including the use of violence. The third pattern is between the Basque and Spanish governments. This relationship, which is more fluid than sometimes assumed because it is conditioned by the contingencies of electoral politics, is central in shaping discourses and practices about the political position and status of the Basque Country within Spain. Finally, Spain's decentralized framework triggered mainly competitive relations between many of Spain's autonomous communities, including the Basque Country, which spurred claims for autonomy and distinctiveness. This was a rather new element for nationalist politics in Spain since regions such as the Basque Country and Cataluña had typically articulated their claims purely in reference to the Spanish state rather than other territories.

After having discussed the immediate impact of the creation of the new Spanish institutions in the late 1970s, this chapter traces the evolution of Basque nationalism over the last twenty-five years in reference to the four patterns of political relationships mentioned above. Once again, the core argument is that these patterns are the consequence, at least partially unintended, of the new institutional environment designed during the transition.

Basque Nationalism and Spain's Democratic Transition

The death of General Franco in November 1975 signaled the beginning of Spain's transition toward democracy. The dictatorship had considerably weakened during the 1960s and early 1970s, but it is with the passing of Franco that genuine political change became possible and indeed inevitable in Spain. The Spanish democratic transition is generally hailed as a complete success,[1] and, as a consequence, it has contributed to rehabilitating Spanish nationalism. The transition clearly involved a redefinition of this nationalism. The idea of a Spanish nation characterized by cultural homogeneity and mystical unity underpinned by strong centralism was not tenable for a large segment of Spanish society. At the same time, notions of Spanish nationhood anchored in the belief in a common past and future could not be sacrificed. As a result, the political dynamic characterizing the transition involved a delicate balance between an organic and centralist vision of Spain, defended most forcefully by political and military actors close to the Franco regime, and a conception of Spain as plural and decentralized, supported by much of the democratic forces that had opposed the dictatorship. Rather than seeking a complete and immediate rupture with the previous political order, key political actors, most importantly newly crowned King Juan Carlos, opted for a gradual process. This approach is exemplified by the king's designation of Adolfo Suárez, a former civil servant of the Franco era, as head of the transition government. This was endorsed by a significant percentage of the population, as Suárez's Unión del Centro Democrático (UCD) won the first post-dictatorship democratic elections by garnering 34 percent of the vote compared to 29 percent for the newly legalized Partido Socialista Obrero Español (PSOE) and a little under 10 percent for the Partido Comunista de España (PCE).

Nowhere was the balancing act of enacting democratic change without alienating political forces close to the Franco regime, most importantly the army, more apparent than on the question of decentralization. The centralist legacy of the Franco dictatorship strongly shaped the transition period. On the one hand, Francoist elements were extremely wary of any regional autonomy, which they understood as threatening the unity, if not the survival of Spain. On the other hand, forces that had opposed Franco saw autonomy as an essential part of, and safeguard for, any democratic system. This last view was strongest in the two regions where nationalist politics has been at the forefront of the struggle against Franco, Cataluña and the Basque Country. Mobilization in Cataluña and the Basque Country, spearheaded by both left-wing and nationalist forces, triggered similar events in other Spanish cities to protest against the hesitation of the Suárez government toward the issue of regional autonomy.[2]

Of particular significance here were the violent actions of ETA, which had found new life following Franco's death as it sensed an opportunity to shape the political dynamic of the transition. Until 1974, ETA had never killed more than 20 people per year, but between 1977 and 1980 there were 240 deaths attributed to ETA violence.[3] From a theoretical perspective, the high number of ETA killings is not surprising since periods of institutional transformations carry very high stakes, which increase the likelihood of violent conflict. The flurry of killings served to strengthen the PNV, which could argue that its "moderate" demands needed to be satisfied to avoid chaos and a failure of the democratic transition. For the PNV, it was crucial to shape the agenda of the transition, because negotiations would produce the framework for the relationship between the Basque Country and Spain for years to come.

ETA was never a coherent monolithic organization, and when the transition came, it was effectively divided between the político-militar (PM) and militar (M) groups. ETA-PM sought to negotiate a cease-fire with the Spanish state as early as 1977 but without success. The Spanish government was still on shaky grounds at this point and had to be wary of overtures that would be considered treacherous by many.[4] ETA-PM eventually disbanded (starting in 1981) as a result of negotiations on a partial amnesty for Basque political prisoners,[5] and most of its members joined Euskadiko Ezkerra (EE). ETA-M was wholly committed to armed struggle, which it hoped to use for the purpose of dictating, or at least shaping, the terms of any new political arrangement.[6] It put forth, in early 1978, conditions for a cease-fire known as the KAS alternative that featured, among other things, amnesty for "political" prisoners and a Statute of Autonomy recognizing the sovereignty of the Basque

Country. Although the KAS alternative was dismissed by most Spanish politicians, many of its elements would later be found in the Basque Statute of Autonomy.

The politics of the transition therefore made it such that a Jacobin-type centralized unitary state could not present a realistic option as a model of territorial organization for democratic Spain since Catalan and Basque nationalists along with the PSOE and the Partido Comunista de España (PCE) favored decentralization. At the same time, making Spain a formal federation ran the serious risk of alienating the most conservative elements of Spanish society, such as the newly constituted Alianza Popular (AP)—later transformed into the Partido Popular (PP)—and the army, who feared for the integrity of the country.

The result was a political compromise, the Estado de las Autonomías, which created a system of autonomous communities. Nowhere does the Spanish constitution refer to this model as federal. In fact, the central reference is to the state, whose power is said to emanate directly from the Spanish people (article 1.2). In principle, there is no explicit division of sovereignty in the constitution, but article 148 specifies the powers that can be assumed by an autonomous community after its statute of autonomy has been approved by the Spanish parliament (Cortes), while article 149 identifies the exclusive power of the state. Powers that can be assumed by the autonomous communities include social assistance; transportation; the diffusion of the community's culture and the teaching of its language; tourism; and public works in the community's territory undertaken for its interests. Areas where the state has exclusive jurisdiction include international relations; justice; defense; labor law; civil law; social security; immigration; and the defense of Spanish culture. These functions are important enough to trigger attachment to the Spanish political community.[7] The Spanish constitution might not have given birth to a federation, but it is certainly permeated by federal principles. In addition to the formal division of power, the Spanish constitution, much like constitutions of most federations, empowers a constitutional court (tribunal constitucional) to arbitrate conflicts of jurisdiction between autonomous communities and the state (article 161 c). Similar to other federal systems (with the exception of the United States), Spain also has a mechanism to redistribute wealth territorially: the constitution establishes a Fondo de Compensación Interterritorial to enforce the principle of territorial solidarity (articles 2 and 138). Spain departs from the ideal-type federal model in two ways: the amending formula for the constitution does not prominently feature the autonomous communities as constituent units (this is also the case in Belgium), and these communities are weakly represented in the upper house of the Senate.[8]

The change in the nature and configuration of the state stemming from the new constitution also involved a rearticulation of Spanish nationalism, which was in a period of flux. In this context, the compromise of the Estado de las Autonomías featured a creative formula for defining the quality of Spain's nationhood. From the Catalan and Basque nationalist perspective, Spain was to be conceptualized as a multinational state, that is, as a political and legal entity encompassing several different nations. The Spanish Right was uncomfortable with any recognition of cultural and historical diversity framed in the language of nationhood, while the PSOE and UCD held roughly similar positions by favoring a formula whereby the Spanish nation was the "organic whole" that held all others together.[9] In the end, the fundamental nature of Spain was expressed in exactly this type of language, as the constitution (article 2) proclaims the unity and indivisibility of the Spanish nation composed of regions and nationalities that have a right to autonomy. Through this formula, different, even rival, visions of Spain that had unfolded throughout the last century found a temporary form of accommodation, albeit uneasy and unsatisfying for many.

The use of the concept of nationalities, designed with Cataluña, the Basque Country, and Galicia in mind, served a dual purpose. Firstly, it altered the vision of Spain, articulated by Franco but also by the nineteenth-century liberal reformers, as a culturally homogeneous and undifferentiated nation. In fact, article 3.2 and 3.3 recognize the presence in Spain of other languages than Castilian, which form part of the country's cultural heritage and therefore deserve to be respected and protected in the autonomous communities. Secondly, the distinction between nationalities and regions was meant to underline fundamental historical differences relating to culture, identity, and, perhaps most importantly, political organization. Catalan and Basque nationalists pressed hard for some form of recognition of their distinctiveness; they rejected the idea that their autonomous communities should be constitutionally similar to all the others. Their key argument, which in the end proved convincing or, at least, acceptable to most, was that Cataluña, the Basque provinces, and also Galicia had already enjoyed a Statute of Autonomy during the Second Republic. The historical-institutional legacy of these three territories was therefore instrumental in shaping their position within the new Spanish arrangement. Most on the Right who tolerated regional autonomy were much less comfortable with the concept of nationality, which they saw as legitimizing secessionist claims.[10]

The constitutional distinction between nationalities and regions was a powerful symbolic marker of the historical, cultural, and political differentiation of Spanish society the state had attempted to deny, and even obliterate, during most of the twentieth century. This distinction was also meant to have a substantive effect on the process through which autonomous communities could acquire powers, and perhaps also on the relative extent of these powers. The constitution specifies a fast and a slow track toward autonomy (articles 151 and 143.1, respectively). The fast track was clearly designed to quickly meet the Catalan, Basque, and, to a lesser extent, Galician claims of autonomy, while the slow track could be used by other territories that would eventually wish to become autonomous. The language of

the articles is vague, but many observers have argued that the crafters of the constitution envisioned an institutional order where only the "nationalities," using
the fast track, would develop substantial autonomous powers, whereas most other
autonomous communities, if they came to be formed at all, would acquire only
minor powers mostly of an administrative nature.[11]

The constitution was not only contested by Spanish unitarists. In the Basque
Country, the referendum on the constitution was a volatile and divisive affair
that highlighted a pattern of renewed importance in Basque politics: the tension
between moderate and radical nationalism. In the broadest sense, this pattern was
the product of the Franco dictatorship, which superimposed a radical left-wing revolutionary stream to the moderate center-right nationalism of the PNV. It was the
democratic state, however, that allowed the full expression of these two streams,
thereby exposing the tension. Overshadowed by ETA as a vehicle of nationalist
resistance during the Franco dictatorship, the PNV was well positioned to be the
premier voice for Basque nationalism in the democratic context. It could find legitimacy in its history as the party of Sabino Arana and boasted an organization and
leadership, including the presence of recognizable figures such as Manuel Irujo and
Juan Ajuriaguerra, which enabled it to participate in electoral politics. In the first
post-Franco general elections, the PNV won 30 percent of the vote in the Basque
provinces compared to 27 percent for its nearest rival, the Socialist party. The PNV
reentered the political arena with only vague visions of independence, which meant
that it was ready to operate within the new democratic structures. The PNV was
nevertheless dissatisfied with the constitution proposal because it did not recognize
a right to self-determination for the Basques. The PNV therefore called for abstention in the referendum vote.

For ETA, the democratic state was a more puzzling political and institutional context. ETA was not created for, and never had experience in, contesting elections. Its
program and method were ill-suited for the democratic process since violence had
always been at the center of the organization's politics. Nevertheless, in the context
of the transition, ETA could still envision violence as having an instrumental use
insofar as it could hope that fear of an escalation would force Spanish politicians
to accommodate some demands of the Basque nationalist movement as contained,
for example, in the KAS alternative. ETA's radical nationalism and revolutionary left-
wing position became institutionalized as they found expression through Herri
Batasuna (HB). HB was created in 1978, which means it did not contest the elections of 1977, but it was quite vocal in the debate over the constitution, where it
took a harder line than the PNV by advocating a "no" vote in the referendum.[12]
The rationale of HB leaders in calling for a rejection of the document was similar
to the PNV's argument for abstention: the constitution did not acknowledge the
"original sovereignty" of the Basques. In fact, the third Basque nationalist party,
Euskadiko Ezkerra (EE), specifically pushed for a constitutional article recogniz-

ing a right to self-determination.[13] Such an article would have involved, according to the Basque nationalist discourse, a collective right of the Basque population to determine the political status of the Basque Country independently of the preferences of the Spanish state. EE, created in 1977, represented leftist views but was not associated with ETA's violence in the same way as HB. It called for a "no" vote in the referendum on the constitution.

As a result of these positions of nationalist parties toward the constitution, there was a very high abstention rate in the Basque Country for the 1978 referendum.[14] Moreover, support for the constitution was lower in the Basque Country, where it ranged from 63.9 percent to 71.4 percent depending on the province, than in Spain as a whole where it was 87.8 percent.[15] Of course, since the referendum was Spain-wide, the Basque vote did not have a determinant influence on the overall result. However, the consequence of the important abstention rate in the Basque Country was that the constitution lacked legitimacy there,[16] whereas it tended to be viewed almost as a sacrosanct document by politicians in most other parts of Spain. This legitimacy gap further contributed to the negative attitudes held by a substantial number of Basques toward the Spanish state. Therefore, the particular nature of the state might have changed from authoritarian to democratic in the 1970s, but its alien status vis-à-vis an important segment of Basque society remained.

In addition to perpetuating the legitimacy gap of the Spanish state in the Basque Country, the process leading to the approval of the 1978 constitution also generated tensions between various political forces. As we have already mentioned, the slightly different positions toward the constitutional document (most importantly the PNV's abstention call versus HB's "no" vote urging) exposed a tension between moderate and radical nationalists that has marked Basque politics ever since the transition. This tension was confirmed in the 1979 Spanish election, where the Basque nationalist vote was split between the PNV (27.6 percent), HB (15.0 percent), and EE (8.0 percent). Another fundamental cleavage exposed and fed by the constitutional debate was between Basque nationalist and non-Basque nationalist forces. Spanish-wide parties, such as the PSOE, UCD, AP, and PCE, all supported the constitution, which was also endorsed by a majority of Basques, albeit with a high rate of abstention votes. This cleavage was also visible in the first two Spanish elections, as the Basque vote split 50 percent–50 percent between Basque nationalist and non-Basque nationalist parties in the 1979 election, a substantial gain for Basque nationalist parties, which had gathered roughly 35 percent of the vote in 1977.[17]

The new constitution led the way to another major institutional development in the Basque Country: the creation of the Basque Statute of Autonomy. This statute, often called Statute of Guernica, involved the creation of the Autonomous Community of the Basque Country for the provinces of Araba, Gipuzkoa, and Bizkaia. Its provisions are multidimensional. At the most practical level, the statute defines the jurisdictions of the Basque Government (Eusko Jaurlaritza) and its relation with the state with respect to policy making (title 1). It also specifies the workings of the legislative, executive, and judiciary branches. Moreover, the statute makes some statements of greater symbolic importance, such as proclaiming Euskara the language of the Basque people (and one of the official languages of the Basque Country, along with Castilian), and specifying the colors and outlook of the Basque flag.

The Basque Statute of Autonomy also stipulates that fiscal relations between the Autonomous Community of the Basque Country and the Spanish state are to be governed by the conciertos económicos. These conciertos (agreements) allow the Basque Country or, more specifically, its three constituent provinces, to levy almost all taxes on its territory. A portion of these revenues (the cupo) is then transferred to the state for the financing of services it ensures in the Basque Country. The presence of these financial agreements in the statute is entirely the product of the historical legacy of the fueros, which involved financial autonomy. Basque politicians may not have been able to enshrine a right to self-determination in the constitution, but they successfully managed to have recognized the "historical rights" of "foral territories" (article 169, first supplementary clause). It is in this context that the conciertos económicos, viewed as a historical right of fiscal autonomy, were specified in the statute despite the fact that the constitution states that differences in statutes of autonomy cannot involve economic or social privileges (article 139.23). The conciertos económicos make for another asymmetrical feature of the Estado de las Autonomías since they apply only to the Basque Country and Navarre.[18] Other autonomous communities are party to the so-called common system whereby they obtain financing principally from state transfers.[19]

The Statute of Autonomy proved much less controversial in the Basque Country than the constitution. Both the PNV and EE supported the statute, along with the Spanish-wide parties; HB, for its part, advocated abstention despite the fact that the statute included many elements from ETA's 1978 KAS alternative, such as making Euskara an official language of the Basque Country and creating a Basque police force. It would be a stretch to say that the Basque Statute of Autonomy owed many of its dispositions to ETA, but there is no doubt that its actions served as an implicit bargaining chip for Basque nationalist politicians, who could raise the specter of greater political violence if demands deemed as minimalist could not be accommodated. Violence therefore had an instrumental use, although the framework was no longer one of action-repression-action since concessions, rather than the use of force, were now expected from the Spanish state.

A strong positive vote in the 1979 referendum, along with a decent voter turnout, left the statute with greater legitimacy than the constitution (see table 4.1). This being said, radical Basque nationalism has had lingering issues with this document as well. Like the constitution, it does not feature any reference to a right to self-determination. Moreover, the statute does not represent the contours of the Basque community as conceptualized by radical nationalists, since neither Navarre nor the Basque territories of France are included within the Autonomous Community of the Basque Country. Of course, there was no chance that parts of French territory would be incorporated to the Spanish Basque Country, but in the case of Navarre there was no such obstacle as an international border. The main problem was a lack of clear political will for inclusion in the Autonomous Community of the Basque Country, as Navarre was divided between Basque nationalists, who favored such inclusion, and foralists, who supported the erection of Navarre as an autonomous community in its own right.[20] Despite the fact that Navarre went on to adopt its own statute of autonomy, the Basque statute left the door open for a future incorporation (article 2), a possibility also allowed by the constitution (fourth transitory provision).[21] However, the procedure for such a change is long and tortuous, involving, most notably, referendums in Navarre and the three Basque provinces.[22]

The Statute of Autonomy represents a watershed moment in the development of the Basque nationalist movement in several respects. Perhaps most important is the fact that the three Basque provinces of Araba, Bizkaia, and Gipuzkoa become politically united for the first time in their modern history.[23] In other words, the statute involved the creation of a "Basque Country" as a political community. As a result of this political unification, Basque nationalism also acquired a formal anchoring in the sense that it became underpinned by a set of institutions rather than simply by political parties and voluntary associations. Here again, this was a novelty since only during a few months at the end of the Second Spanish Republic was there a Basque government operating in Spain.

The Basque Statute of Autonomy represents the institutional canvass for the expression and struggles of two sets of forces, which already made their presence felt during transition negotiations and campaigning. The first is a very polar and antagonistic relationship that pits Basque nationalists against non-Basque nationalists. At the most basic level, this relationship shows that not all Basques identify with Basque nationalism. Spanish nationalism did have supporters in the Basque Country even during the dictatorship, and the country's successful democratic transition rehabilitated the idea of the Spanish nation for many Basques. The second set, featuring moderate and radical Basque nationalism, involves a more fluid and ambiguous relationship. Analytically, these two sets of forces help shape a perspective through which Basque nationalism in the democratic era can be understood. This being said, focusing on patterns of relationships strictly endogenous to the Autonomous Community of the Basque Country does not give the whole picture about contemporary Basque nationalism. Indeed, the 1978 constitution and the subsequent construction of the Estado de las Autonomías presented an institutional context that generated a third and a fourth pattern of relationship. The third pattern features the Basque and the Spanish governments. The Spain of the autonomies may not be a formal federation, but it certainly is a federal political

TABLE 4.1 *Results from referendum on the Basque Statute of Autonomy,*
October 25, 1979

Results	Vizcaya (%)	Guipúzcoa (%)	Alava (%)	Total (%)
Electoral census	859,843 (100.0)	507,002 (100.0)	174,930 (100.0)	1,541,775 (100.0)
Votes	507,487 (59.0)	303,469 (59.9)	110,604 (63.2)	921,560 (59.8)
Votes in favor	460,554 (90.8)	279,015 (91.9)	92,536 (83.7)	832,105 (90.2)
Votes against	25,072 (4.9)	12,289 (4.1)	10,017 (9.1)	47,378 (5.2)
Void	21,861 (4.3)	12,165 (4.0)	8,051 (7.2)	42,077 (4.6)
Abstentions	352,356 (41.0)	203,533 (40.1)	64,326 (36.8)	620,215 (40.2)

SOURCE: Santiago de Pablo, José Luis de la Granja Sainz, and Ludger Mees, eds., *Documentos para la historia del nacionalismo vasco: De los Fueros a nuestros días* (Barcelona: Editorial Ariel, SA, 1998), 159.

system. Basque nationalism therefore became strongly conditioned by the politics and policies of the central government and, most of all, by its interaction with the Basque government. Finally, the fourth pattern revolves around the existence of multiple autonomous communities. As a result of this territorial structuring, the Basque government operates in a broader decentralized system, which means that Basque nationalism can be structured by the political dynamic surrounding inter-autonomous community relations. It is with this fourfold scheme in mind that we now examine Basque nationalism during the first decade of post-transition politics in Spain.

Between Movement and Stalemate: Basque Nationalism and the Structures of the Democratic State

The constitution of 1978 was a political compromise that set up a system whose exact degree of decentralization and asymmetry was an open-ended issue. The spirit of the document was to provide some measure of autonomy to every autonomous community while treating the "historical nationalities" as special cases. In practical terms, this was expected to translate into a territorial model where only these nationalities (Cataluña, the Basque Country, and Galicia) would claim extensive autonomous powers. The political dynamic triggered by the new institutional arrangement proved more complicated and exemplifies the pitfalls of asymmetrical government. Several autonomous communities took up the slogan "coffee for everyone" (*café para todos*), or "we all want coffee" (*todos queremos café*), as a way to argue that substantial autonomy should be readily available for any regional government ready to assume it. The crucial case was Andalucía, which mobilized in support for a "fast-track" route to autonomy via a referendum held in 1980.[24] After the Spanish government agreed to a compromise on Andalucía's accession to autonomy, several other autonomous communities (most notably, the Canary

Islands, the Balearic Islands, Valencia, and Aragón) expressed discontent with their own perceived second-class status. The immediate consequence was a demonstration, or mimesis effect, which spurred the glorification of distinctive cultural markers and histories as a way of legitimizing political claims. The overall result was greater centrifugal tendency and decentralization than originally anticipated.[25]

This demonstration effect of autonomy claims toward the "regions" had an impact on Basque nationalism in at least two ways. First, the three historical nationalities became concerned with preserving their distinct status (*hecho diferencial*) in the face of other autonomous communities seeking to "catch up." The Basque Country, with its fiscal autonomy, even became a target for Cataluña. This momentum toward what appeared to be the leveling of political statuses between autonomous communities did not help the legitimacy of the new constitutional and institutional framework. In fact, it gave more credence to Basque nationalists who argued that only the recognition of a right of self-determination could allow the Basques to acquire, if they so chose, meaningful political expression of their distinctiveness. Second, the two main Spanish political parties, the center-right UCD and the left-wing PSOE, reacted to a situation they thought was spinning out of control by attempting to slow down and level the process of decentralization through the Ley Orgánica de Armonización del Proceso Autonómico (LOAPA) of 1981. Formally, the LOAPA was about harmonizing decentralization, as the Spanish government was looking for the opportunity to set national norms and standards in areas of jurisdiction otherwise reserved for the autonomous communities. In effect, it represented an effort to limit the extent to which the autonomous communities could design and implement policy autonomously. For most Spanish politicians, the new institutional framework was proving too conducive to decentralist claims and the expression of centrifugal forces. This political dynamic was difficult to accept for a political class not accustomed to operating within a decentralized system but rather used to the hegemony of the state. It was also considered dangerous since Spain was still a fledgling democracy featuring a handful of reactionary elements (for example, in the army) that had little patience for a process of decentralization they associated with the weakening of Spain. The attempted coup of 1981 represented a trigger for a "harmonization" legislation.

The LOAPA was short-lived since it was struck down by the constitutional court in 1983. Nevertheless, this legislation is revealing of the attitude of the main Spanish political parties toward the flurry of decentralist claims in the early 1980s.[26] As a matter of political practice, Spanish governments have been slow at effectively transferring powers specified in the statutes of autonomy of those autonomous communities where substate nationalism is a powerful electoral force. This lack of enthusiasm for fulfilling all the stipulations of the statutes has given greater legitimacy to the Basque nationalist characterization of the Spanish state as rigid and fundamentally antagonistic toward the Basques. Moreover, Basque nationalists have come to view the Statute of Autonomy as a dead-end road for moving the political situation of the Basque Country toward more autonomy because they think that successive Spanish governments are being purposively obstructive. As a consequence, moderate nationalists have discussed alternative frameworks and strategies such as the free association proposal of Basque lehendakari Juan José Ibarretxe.

Basque nationalism in democratic Spain has also been driven by a more endogenous dynamic. The Basque Statute of Autonomy generated a Basque political system featuring three political forces that entertained highly ambiguous relationships: moderate Basque nationalism, embodied by the PNV; radical Basque nationalism, represented by HB and its successors; and Spanish nationalism.

Spanish nationalism is a differentiated phenomenon. At the most basic level, there are two broad visions of Spain promoted by politicians operating in central institutions.[27] The first vision, which was the PP's under José María Aznar, defines Spain first and foremost by organic unity. From this perspective, the coherence of the Spanish nation involves a stress on its (supposed) common origins located in the Catholic struggle against the Moors as well as a common prosperous and democratic future as underpinned by the 1978 constitution. From an institutional perspective, this vision of Spain involves political centralization and constitutional and institutional status quo. The second vision, which corresponds with the PSOE's, incorporates more substantively Spain's cultural and linguistic diversity. This vision is more comfortable with the political recognition of these types of differences through, for example, asymmetry in the autonomous community framework, and more accepting of decentralization as a principle of governance. This brand of Spanish nationalism is less rigid than the first version when it comes to discussing institutional and/or constitutional change with the Basque and Catalan governments insofar as it is more willing to accept a dynamic view of the existing frameworks. This being said, the two main Spanish parties vigorously promote Spain as a political project and defend the basic elements of the 1978 constitution and the system of autonomous communities. In the case of the Socialists, the discourse of Spanish nationalism is "softer" in Cataluña to the point where the emphasis is on the multinational character of Spain.[28] The Basque Socialists stay much closer to the position of the PSOE.

The PNV has long been in an advantageous position in Basque electoral politics for at least two reasons. First, it holds great legitimacy from being the original party of Basque nationalism and having led the Basque government-in-exile during the Franco dictatorship. Second, the PNV is vague enough on the question of the political future of the Basque Country to make it an attractive option for a large segment of the Basque population. The PNV has never come out in favor of pure independence since Spain's system of autonomous communities was put in place, preferring instead the more open-ended notion of self-determination. In this context, it avoids the pitfalls of españolismo, that is, of a firm commitment to Spain, as well as those linked to the near-utopian objectives and violent methods of radical nationalism. Of course, the PNV's political position was also delicate throughout the 1980s. An unequivocal condemnation of ETA violence could then have been interpreted as an act of treason toward the nationalist family. For this reason, the PNV typically "explained" ETA murders by locating them within a wider "political conflict" and insisting on the "violence" and "repression" of the Spanish state. At the same time, it needed to be careful, as a party endorsing democratic principles, not to take this defense of ETA violence too far.

The PNV has been the premier political actor in Basque politics since the transition. In the first few years of democratic politics in the Basque Country (1980 to 1986), the PNV was in a particularly dominant position. In the 1980 and 1984 Basque elections, it gathered approximately 40 percent of the vote, but was left short of an overall majority as a result of the proportionality element in the electoral system. From 1980 to 1984, this shortfall was not a problem since representatives from HB did not participate in parliamentary activities as a way to indicate they considered the new autonomy framework insufficient and illegitimate.[29] This left the PNV (twenty-five seats in a chamber of sixty) with a de facto majority. The PNV's situation became more precarious after the 1984 elections largely as a result of internal divisions. While the PNV had signed a government agreement with the Socialists, the fate of the executive came undone when eleven of the PNV's members (including then lehendakari Garaikoetxea) left after a disagreement over legislation about the (internal) institutional reorganization of the Basque Country and formed the party Eusko Alkartasuna (EA). This split left the PNV with little choice but to govern with the Socialists. As the 1980s came to a close, exercising political power was a more complicated operation for the PNV than it had been at the beginning of the decade. Most significantly, EA was commanding a good chunk of the PNV's past support; for example, in the 1986 elections, the PNV garnered 24 percent of the vote compared with 16 percent for EA. This left the PNV only slightly ahead of the Socialists, who finished with 22 percent of the vote (table 4.2).

From the first Basque elections where they gathered 14 percent of the vote to those of 1984 and 1986 where they received 23 percent and 22 percent, respectively, the Socialists proved the strongest Spanish party. The political importance of the Socialists stemmed not only from their electoral strength, but also from two more structural aspects: the legitimacy held by left-wing movements in virtue of their opposition to Franco and the party's relatively flexible attitude toward decentralist claims. This meant that the Socialists were, in the context of Basque government formation, a potential coalition partner for the PNV, whereas Spanish parties on the right of the spectrum, the UCD and Alianza Popular (AP), were not. These parties were clearly handicapped by their Francoist heritage and never received more than 10 percent of the vote in Basque elections during the 1980s.

TABLE 4.2 *Basque election results in the contemporary democratic period, % of votes (# of seats)*

Parties	1980	1984	1986	1990	1994	1998	2001	2005
PNV	38.10 (25)	42.01 (32)	23.71 (17)	28.49 (22)	29.84 (22)	28.01 (21)	42.72[†](33)	38.60[†](29)
PSE-PSOE	14.21 (9)	23.07 (19)	22.05 (19)	19.94 (16)	17.13*(12)	17.60 (14)	17.90 (13)	22.67 (18)
HB/EH/BAT	16.55 (11)	14.65 (11)	17.47 (13)	18.33 (13)	16.29 (11)	17.91 (14)	10.12 (7)	12.50 (9)[‡]
EE	9.82 (6)	7.98 (6)	10.88 (9)	7.78 (6)	—	—	—	—
PCE/IU	4.0 (1)	1.4 (0)	0.50 (0)	1.42 (0)	9.15 (6)	5.68 (2)	5.58 (3)	5.40 (3)
AP/PP	4.77 (2)	9.36 (7)	4.86 (2)	8.23 (6)	14.41 (11)	20.13 (16)	23.12 (19)	17.38 (15)
UCD/CDS	8.52 (6)	—	3.54 (2)	0.66 (0)	—	—	—	—
EA	—	—	15.84 (13)	11.38 (9)	10.31 (8)	8.69 (6)	—	—
Others	4.03 (0)	1.53 (0)	1.15 (0)	3.77 (3)	2.87 (5)	1.98 (2)	0.66 (0)	3.45 (1)

SOURCE: Basque government, Department of the Interior.

* Starting with these elections, the Socialists and EE were merged.

† In these elections, there was a PNV-EA electoral coalition.

‡ For these elections, Batasuna was outlawed, but the party's leadership urged its voters to support the Partido Comunista de las Tierras (PCTV), a recently constituted party that had never participated in elections before.

The PNV was not the only Basque nationalist party to gain support during the first decade of electoral competition. On the left, EE's support hovered around 10 percent, while HB, the political face of radical nationalism, garnered 16.5 percent in 1980, 15 percent in 1984, and 17.5 percent in 1986. As the voice of ETA, HB was treated mostly as a pariah party throughout the 1980s, with the Spanish parties blaming it for the violence and the PNV never seeking it as a coalition partner. This situation was expressed, if not instrumentalized, by the 1988 Pact of Ajuria-Enea on the normalization and pacification of the Basque Country. The Pact of Ajuria-Enea consisted of a condemnation of political violence, which was viewed as illegitimate and contrary to the Basque popular will, and of an appeal for ETA to abandon the armed struggle.[30] It put the onus on the Basque government to takes steps toward ending the violence. The Pact of Ajuria-Enea was signed by all political parties operating within the Basque political system, except for HB. It formalized two political blocs: the first featured all "democratic parties," that is, parties ready to condemn political violence; and the second was made up of the political party representing radical nationalism and articulating the ideas of ETA, Herri Batasuna.

Of course, HB's isolation was also partly self-imposed since it viewed Spanish parties as representing the enemy (the state) and profoundly distrusted the PNV, which it considered too soft and ambiguous on the issue of the political future of the Basque Country. The electoral strength of HB during the 1980s pointed toward a significant segment of Basque society dissatisfied with the new constitutional and institutional arrangement to the point that it was ready to at least tolerate political violence.

Basque nationalist parties also participated in Spanish general elections starting in 1977. In this context, there existed a connection between Basque political forces and Spanish institutions through the legislative arena. Overall, the results for Basque parties during these elections closely mirrored those of the Basque elections. However, the presence of Basque nationalist parties in the Spanish parliament was not overly significant during the 1980s as a result of the Socialist majorities beginning in 1982. In other words, the PNV, EA, and EE never had the opportunity, during the 1980s, to offer their support for a Spanish party in exchange for the Spanish government meeting some of their claims on autonomy issues the way they did in the 1990s.

The patterns of relationships between Basque nationalist and non-Basque nationalist parties as well as between moderate and radical Basque nationalist parties were heavily conditioned by ETA. Violence forced the PNV to walk on a tightrope. On the one hand, an unambiguous condemnation of ETA had the potential to prove costly politically and electorally. The radical organization still evoked positive feelings for many Basques during the 1980s as its role in fighting the Franco dictatorship was still remembered fondly. A common view of ETA members was that they were the lost sons of the Basque nationalist family whose methods might be questionable but who held commendable objectives. For example, in 1989 23 percent of Basques characterized ETA activists as either "patriots" (5 percent) or "idealists" (18 percent).[31] On the other hand, it would have been difficult for the PNV as a party committed to democracy to push its defense of ETA actions too far, since violence was tolerated by only a minority of Basques.

The PNV's calculated defense of ETA violence strained its relationship with the Spanish parties. This was just the type of outcome sought by ETA. From 1975 to 1980, the logic of ETA violence was primarily to destabilize and delegitimize the institutional architecture under construction. Subsequently, it could be argued that the focus became primarily the dichotomization of Basque politics and society. Most Basques hold a dual identity as both Spaniards and Basques, albeit to different and varying degrees.[32] ETA violence has presented a challenge to this social structure insofar as it has pushed the Basques toward adopting a monist identity, that is, having to choose between being solely Basque and solely Spanish. The gamble, of course, has been that if forced to choose, the Basques would prefer to abandon the Spanish reference rather than the Basque one. ETA killed between twenty and fifty people every year from 1982 to 1989,[33] but made careful use of this violence insofar as it avoided, at least for the most part, any move that could create a serious backlash against it and perhaps tilt the identity scale of the Basques toward the Spanish end. During the 1980s, however, two ETA actions triggered extremely negative reactions: the murder of a former member (María Dolores Gonzáles Catarain, "Yoyes") who had spent time in Latin America, and the bombing of a shopping center in Barcelona.[34] The killing of Yoyes was a message to ETA members who might have been considering "reinsertion" into society, that is, leaving the organization and obtaining a formal pardon from the Spanish government. Here, ETA had miscalculated the public reaction to murdering a woman walking her baby in a public plaza. As for the Barcelona bombing that killed many innocent bystanders and prompted huge public marches against violence, ETA claimed that it had called the authorities to signal the presence of bomb before the explosion. These events showed that, while there existed some tolerance for political violence in the Basque Country during the 1980s, there were certain parameters that could not be ignored by ETA without the organization suffering widespread and stinging public condemnations among the Basques. If the events that set off such a reaction are any indication, it appears that these parameters were more about the nature of the victims (one woman and innocent bystanders) than their actual number.

Violence also needs to be situated in relation to the Spanish government, whose approach to ETA relied heavily on policing and intelligence work. The coercive approach for dealing with ETA also had a not-so-public face, as the Spanish government, through the ministry of the interior, propped up a paramilitary organization known as GAL (Grupos Antiterroristas de Liberación) that hunted down ETA members in the French Basque Country between 1983 and 1987.[35] For the Spanish government, this was a way to put pressure on its French counterpart, which it considered quite passive toward the movement of ETA commandos across the border.[36] Of course, the use of such paramilitaries in a liberal-democratic context was hard to justify and played into the hands of Basque radical nationalists who insisted that nothing had changed and that Spain remained fascist.[37] In this context, ETA violence retained an instrumental value, as it managed to trigger, still in the democratic period, the type of violent and somewhat indiscriminate repression seen to bear the potential to unite the Basques against Spain.

Coercion and policing did not represent the only forms of interaction between ETA and the democratic Spanish state. The official line of Spanish governments that there would be no negotiations with terrorists was never true. Between 1986 and 1989, ETA and Spain's Socialist government were involved in a series of talks held in Algeria and brokered by the Algerian government that featured discussions over the amnesty of political prisoners as well a political framework for the Basque Country.[38] These talks reportedly led to eight tentative agreements, including one calling for the creation of a PSOE-HB forum that would prove extremely controversial among other Basque nationalist parties.[39] The failure of the talks seemed to have been one of political will.[40] On the one hand, ETA might not have been completely decided on abandoning political violence. On the other hand, the Spanish government, bolstered by successful strikes at ETA and increased support by French authorities, might not have sensed the urgency to carry out whatever agreement was negotiated. It might also have feared the political consequences of implementing new policies and frameworks resulting from direct talks with ETA. This was rather at odds with the claims of illegitimacy showered upon ETA by the Basque parties that were signatories of the 1988 Pact of Ajuria-Enea. This last issue demonstrated the limits of direct negotiations between representatives of the

Spanish government and ETA members, because they bypassed a whole range of political actors (most notably the PNV and the opposition party in Madrid) whose support was crucial for major change to have democratic legitimacy and to be actually implemented. Indeed, as the 1980s drew to a close, so did the possibility for ETA to engage in exclusive bilateral talks with Spanish governments.

The Realignment of Political Forces

In the 1990s, the political dynamics emanating from the system of autonomous communities evolved, as did the Basque nationalist movement. More than ever, the path of Basque nationalism was shaped by the complex interplay between Basque nationalists (moderate and radical), Spanish governments, and other autonomous communities. The framework of the democratic Spanish state triggered new political dynamics as social change (for example, the decrease in tolerance for political violence) combined with new party politics configurations to provide a different picture of nationalism in the Basque Country.

The last section explained that the presence of Basque nationalist parties within the Spanish parliament had presented virtually no political consequence for the territorial structuring of the Spanish state during the 1980s. This changed as a consequence of the 1993 and 1996 general elections where the winning party was in a clear minority position (table 4.3).

In 1993, the PSOE won 159 of the 350 seats in the Cortes, which left it in need of coalition partners or, at least, of parliamentary support. Considering that developing a working relationship with either the PP and the left-wing Izquierda Unida (IU, the post-Communists) was nearly impossible (the former because of political rivalry and ideological differences and the latter as a result of its critical stance toward European integration), the only option available was to approach nationalist and regionalist parties. There certainly was some common ground between, on the one hand, the PSOE and, on the other hand, the two nationalist parties with the most significant representation in the Cortes, the PNV (five seats) and Cataluña's CiU (seventeen seats). For example, the PSOE's program featured a commitment to speed up the transfer to the autonomous communities of the remaining powers specified by the various statutes of autonomy. This concern also appeared in the PNV's program.[41] The PSOE sought a formal coalition with the PNV and CiU but without success. The strongest opposition came from the CiU, whereas the PNV was divided, although its leadership was more strongly in favor of a coalition with the PSOE.[42] The PNV shared with the CiU a concern that the Socialists would seek to meet claims for decentralization through a café para todos-type of recipe where any new transfers of power would be extended to all autonomous communities.[43] This approach had long been considered unacceptable by the "historical nationalities,"

TABLE 4.3 *Spanish elections in the Basque Country in the contemporary democratic period, % (# of seats)*

Parties	1977	1979	1982	1986	1989	1993	1996	2000	2004
PNV	29.34 (8)	27.63 (7)	31.88 (8)	27.97 (6)	22.93 (5)	24.44 (5)	25.43 (5)	31.32 (7)	34.19 (7)
PSE-PSOE	26.54 (7)	19.09 (5)	29.30 (8)	26.43 (7)	21.25 (6)	24.91[†](7)	24.04 (5)	24.03 (4)	27.59 (7)
HB/EH/BAT	—	15.02 (3)	14.78 (2)	17.78 (4)	16.98 (4)	14.83 (2)	12.47 (2)	—	—
EE	6.08 (1)	8.04 (1)	7.73 (1)	9.12 (2)	8.85 (2)	—	—	—	—
PCE/IU	4.55 (0)	4.61 (0)	1.76 (0)	1.26 (0)	3.03 (0)	6.42 (0)	9.35 (1)	5.62 (0)	8.31 (0)
AP/PP	4.44 (1)	—	11.70*(2)	10.55 (2)	9.43 (2)	14.92 (4)	18.63 (5)	29.14 (7)	19.15 (4)
UCD/CDS	12.84 (4)	16.92 (5)	—	5.02 (0)	3.48 (0)	0.78 (0)	—	0.06 (0)	—
EA	—	—	—	—	11.24 (2)	10.01 (1)	8.35 (1)	7.80 (1)	6.57 (1)
Others	14.21 (0)	8.69 (0)	2.85 (0)	1.87 (0)	2.81 (0)	3.69 (0)	1.73 (0)	3.03 (0)	4.19 (0)

SOURCE: Basque government, Department of the Interior.
  * In these elections there was an AP/CDS coalition.
  † Starting with these elections, the Socialists and EE were merged.

which sought to preserve their distinct political status. Overall, the PNV leadership (then lehendakari Ardanza and party president Arzalluz) was not as concerned as the CIU's with establishing formal links because its political position within the nationalist landscape at home was looking good. It was recuperating EA votes, HB's support seemed to have reached a peak, and EE no longer existed since it had merged with the Socialists.[44] Of course, this made little difference for party militants, many of whom could not tolerate any type of alliance with a Spanish party. In the end, the Socialists had to count on the parliamentary support of the CIU to survive in government.

The 1996 elections produced an even more complicated situation. This time, it was the PP, which had decried the Socialists' reliance on substate nationalist parties, who came up short of an overall majority (with 156 seats) and was forced to turn toward these same parties for help. This time, formal agreements were struck with the CIU, the PNV, and also Coalición Canaria (CC), which provided for power transfers and additional financial resources.[45] The immediate consequence of the political weight of nationalist parties resulting from minority victories in the 1993 and 1996 elections was a momentum toward decentralization or, from the perspective of the historical nationalities, a more accommodating attitude from the Spanish government. There is a profoundly structural mechanism at work here, since the identity of the party winning a minority does not seem to impact on the likelihood of agreeing to further decentralization by seeking parliamentary support from the nationalist parties. The contemporary party of centralist Spanish nationalism, the PP, behaved in 1996 exactly as the more flexible PSOE did in 1993. Furthermore, under the same leadership of José María Aznar, the PP took a very rigid attitude toward decentralist claims after the 2000 elections when it won an overall majority.

In the Autonomous Community of the Basque Country, the 1990s were a period of major political upheavals and realignment. This movement was not readily perceptible in the overall voting pattern at Basque elections (in 1990, 1994, and 1998). The PNV held its support steady around 29 percent, up slightly from its first post-schism result (in 1986). HB garnered around 18 percent of the vote in each of the 1990s elections, a score similar to previous results. The Socialists, which absorbed EE in 1993, were slightly down from the 1980s, with an average ranging from 17 percent to 20 percent. The only noticeable sign that something different was happening in the Basque Country was the slow but steady rise of the PP, whose precursor AP was only able the muster single-digit support in the 1980s. The PP, which under the leadership of José María Aznar promoted Spanish nationalism through a stress on centralism, unity, and a hard line toward ETA, gathered 14 percent in 1994 and 20 percent[46] in 1998. This signaled the gradual hardening of the dichotomization of Basque politics between Basque and Spanish nationalists.

The PNV was no stranger to this dichotomization. Until 1998, the moderate nationalist party continued its strategy of including the Socialists in the governing coalition and, in adherence with the Ajuria-Enea pact, of isolating HB. In 1990, a PNV/PSE-PSOE coalition would barely have had a majority, while in 1994 it would have had fallen short. Coalition agreements were signed with EA on both occasions. Although the initial split within the PNV that led to the creation of EA was over matters internal to the structuring the Basque Country, the splinter group evolved into a more strongly nationalist party less favorable to collaboration with the Spanish government.[47] This complicated the multiparty coalition of the early and mid-1990s. For example, in 1991, EA's statement in favor of independence led to its expulsion from the government.[48]

This party alignment, consisting of a large bloc of democratic parties on the one hand and HB on the other, was broken by the PNV in 1998 when it accepted the support of representatives from the renamed Herri Batasuna, Euskal Herritarok (EH). Tellingly, the 1994 coalition was terminated when both the PNV and EA voted against a Socialist motion that parliamentarians should swear to respect the constitution and the Statute of Gernika before assuming their responsibilities. These moves were part of a larger reorientation of the PNV that has been dubbed the "sovereignist" or "separatist" turn.[49] In essence, this turn meant that the PNV would look beyond the existing institutional framework to consider other ways to pursue self-determination by engaging with different partners and creating new political opportunities. This change of direction certainly was not a first for a party that had always gone back and forth between nationalist convictions and pragmatism.[50]

In 1998, the PNV moved to showcase this new determination toward the pursuit of self-determination by signing the Barcelona Declaration with Cataluña's CIU and Galicia's Bloque Nacionalista Galego (BNG). This declaration announced the signatories' intent to promote, throughout Spain and beyond, a multinational rather than mononational understanding of the country.[51] It argued that democratic Spain had failed to recognize the national distinctiveness of Cataluña, the Basque Country, and Galicia. The declaration did not put forward any specific institutional solutions, but considering the various ideas that have come out of Cataluña and the Basque Country subsequently, one can read into the notion of multinationalism such principles as asymmetrical government, shared sovereignty, and confederalism. This pact highlights the different dynamics that have emerged from an institutional framework featuring several autonomous communities: there certainly exists competition between these communities but there are also opportunities for cooperation that can present strong challenges to the ways of the Spanish state.

The major PNV initiative exemplifying its sovereignist turn was the Pact of Lizarra signed on September 12, 1998, with EA, the Basque branch of IU, and, most significantly, HB and a myriad of radical nationalist civil society organizations, part of a loose ensemble sometimes referred to as the National Liberation Movement. Neither the PSOE nor PP signed the document, which they criticized as being a sell-out to ETA. For the PNV, greatly inspired by the Good Friday Agreement in Northern Ireland, the ultimate objective of this initiative was political change. The PNV had come to consider the Pact of Ajuria-Enea, as well as the political relationships built around it, as a stalemate: political violence was condemned, but the status quo prevailed. This being said, the PNV considered that change could only occur in the absence of violence. The Pact of Lizarra represented a way for the PNV to set up an ETA cease-fire with the intent of driving a process of political and institutional change.

There was an inherent paradox to the Pact of Lizarra.[52] The pact needed to contain the necessary elements to be sold to ETA and radical nationalism for a cease-fire to occur. For example, the declaration framed the conflict in the Basque Country as political in nature and involving the Spanish and French states (a radical nationalist line); it specified that a resolution process should be open to all parties (therefore ETA could be an actor in this process); it also stated that every and all issues pertaining to the conflict should be dealt with (theoretically including the agenda of radical nationalism). In sum, the Pact of Lizarra was a document written by Basque nationalists for a Basque nationalist audience.[53] As a result, its potential to engage the Spanish parties and, by extension the Spanish government, in a meaningful discussion over the political future of the Basque Country was limited. Even if the Pact of Lizarra was built in a way that fleshed out the keys to the peace process in Northern Ireland and their potential translation in the case of the Basque Country, the political structure surrounding the attempt at peace and conflict resolution was markedly different in the Basque case since the Spanish parties were left out.

As we have just explained, the PNV needed an end to ETA violence to hope to bring about political and institutional change for the Basque Country. But, what about ETA? Why did ETA decide to declare a cease-fire in the fall of 1998? Radical Basque nationalists as well as politicians from the Spanish parties (particularly the

PP) have a straightforward explanation: for the former, ETA was giving peace and a political solution to the Basque conflict a genuine chance, while the latter argued that ETA had been forced to regroup by the relentless antiterrorist campaign of the Spanish state. In all likelihood, both of these factors played a role in ETA's decision to announce a cease-fire, although the first requires a less naïve interpretation. In its September 1998 communiqué published in *Euskadi Información*, ETA spoke not merely of solving this conflict but more specifically of a unique opportunity to move forward toward sovereignty.[54] Overall, there were four main reasons for the cease-fire.[55]

The first reason, and the most important from a structural point of view, was a decline in the social acceptance of political violence. This decline had not been perceptible at the ballot box, although the prospects of HB for the 1998 elections did not appear so good before the cease-fire. There were, however, clear signs that Basque society had lost much of its sympathy or even tolerance for violence. By 1996, over 75 percent of Basques said either that they rejected or were afraid of ETA, up from 57 percent in 1987 and 36 percent in 1981.[56] More evident signs were the increasing number of marches and demonstrations that followed ETA killings. Of particular importance was the murder in 1997 of Miguel Ángel Blanco, a PP councillor from the town of Ermua, which became a focal point for antiterrorism rallies. ETA had taken to target PP politicians, since the right-of-center party had adopted a particularly hard line toward Basque nationalists of any kind by, for example, shutting down the Basque-language newspaper *Egin* for presumed links with ETA. In a way, this is exactly the type of action (or, repression, from the Basque nationalist perspective) that ETA was expecting. Only, ETA upping the ante no longer seemed to work. The action-repression-action spiral approach was backfiring. The associations formed by families of ETA victims were also becoming increasingly powerful political, symbolic, and emotional references in the struggle against terrorism. As a result of this increasing frustration of a great majority of Basques with political violence, the formal political voice of radical nationalism, Herri Batasuna, along with the various unions and organizations making up the universe of radical nationalism, began turning toward a more squarely political approach to the conflict. Since ETA counts on social support, this was a development to which it could not remain insensitive. For the first time, the strict military-political (ETA-HB) hierarchy was, if not inverted, at least shaken.[57]

The second factor that serves to explain ETA's decision to announce a cease-fire is the demonstration effect of the Good Friday Agreement in Northern Ireland. At the most basic level, the fact that a conflict similar to the one in the Basque Country seemed to have found a peaceful solution was something to think about for ETA and radical Basque nationalists. The demonstration effect was particularly strong because there existed links between ETA and the IRA as well as between Herri Batasuna and Sinn Féin. Both ETA and HB could see that, in the case of Northern

Ireland, a cease-fire did not mean a defeat of the Republican side, especially consid-ering the political weight that Sinn Féin managed to acquire.[58]

The impetus for ETA to abandon violence as a political strategy (or at least to put it on hold) was spurred by a third factor, the major setbacks suffered by the organization in the early 1990s. The central logistical problem for ETA was that it had lost its "sanctuary" in the French Basque Country through increased coopera-tion between Spanish and French police forces. As a result, many key ETA members were jailed, and the capacity of ETA to commit acts of terrorist violence dwindled. Therefore, ETA had to find other means to be politically effective.

The decisive factor that pushed ETA toward the cease-fire is the conclusion that it could drive a process of change through political rather than military means. ETA saw that the PNV was switching its focus from an alignment with democratic parties to a pan-nationalist front. In secret negotiations among ETA, the PNV, and EA before the cease-fire, the three parties stipulated three political goals: the cooperation of all parties favorable to the construction of Euskal Herria; noncooperation with Span-ish parties; and, most importantly, the creation of new institutions featuring repre-sentatives from the seven provinces (the three provinces of the Autonomous Com-munity of the Basque Country, Navarre, and three provinces of the French Basque Country) as a way toward terminating the existing institutional framework and proceeding toward the political unification of the Basques.[59] This agreement was really the historical program of ETA. ETA therefore made no concession to its tradi-tional objectives. It only agreed to stop using political violence, which was a good strategic choice at that time considering the lowered social tolerance for violence and aggressive policing strategy. ETA did not relinquish the role of spearheading the Basque struggle through this secret agreement and the subsequent Declaration of Lizarra but simply changed methods. To ensure that it would keep control of the process, ETA made sure to warn the PNV and EA that its cease-fire was conditional upon progress in the realization of these objectives.[60]

In hindsight, there was never a real chance that the cease-fire could yield a long-term solution to the conflict in the Basque Country. The main problem was that it hinged on the full realization of the maximalist program of radical national-ism. Tellingly, ETA revoked its cease-fire after the PNV and EA rejected a new pro-posal for the election of a Basque "national" parliament representing inhabitants of the seven provinces as a way to effectively break out of the existing institutional order.[61] In its communiqué published on November 28 by the Basque newspaper *Gara*, ETA squarely placed the blame on the shoulders of the moderate nationalists, accusing the PNV and EA of portraying the politics of the cease-fire as a "peace-process" rather than a "process of nation-building."[62] More specifically, it charged the moderate nationalist parties with having taken no concrete steps toward build-ing an independent Basque Country, a position interpreted by ETA as akin to a commitment to the Basque Statute of Autonomy.[63]

In short, the cease-fire was artificial insofar as it was the result of a political deal between Basque nationalist parties that offered nothing to Spanish parties and the Spanish government. This being said, Spain's PP government made no substantial effort to take advantage of the cease-fire to explore potential opportunities to resolve the conflict. When ETA declared its truce, Prime Minister José María Aznar stated that: "After thirty years of terrorist activity, we cannot give ETA the benefit of the doubt."[64] Of course, he was right since what ETA really intended was nothing short of the full realization of its program. Nevertheless, it could be argued that there existed a serious opportunity for meaningful discussion. Instead, the Spanish government met only once with ETA (in Zurich) and then proceeded to jail one of the organization's member-negotiators.

As illusory as they were, ETA's truce triggered many promises for the Basque Country. Basque politics and nationalism felt the aftershock of the collapsed cease-fire to the point of being permanently changed by these fourteen months of apparent normalization.

Post–Cease-Fire Nationalist Politics in the Basque Country

The end of ETA's cease-fire represented a crucial moment for nationalist politics in the Basque Country because it reshaped the patterns of interactions involving moderate Basque nationalists, radical Basque nationalists, as well as Spanish parties and the Spanish state. The political context resulting from ETA resuming its armed struggle put the PNV in a particularly difficult position. On the one hand, the PNV was continually attacked by radical nationalists for having failed to seize an opportunity to move the Basque cause forward. From the radical nationalist perspective, the PNV's behavior demonstrated an implicit commitment to Spain and was therefore akin to treason. The rapid deterioration of the PNV-EH relationship was reflected in the rupture of the parliamentary agreement following new ETA killings. Similar partnerships at the municipal level began falling apart at the same time. In 2000, EH left the chamber, which meant that the moderate nationalist parties (PNV-EA) were in a minority position toward the non-Basque nationalists (PSOE-PP). On the other hand, Spanish parties accused the PNV of having surrendered to ETA and its program or, at least, of having been duped by the terrorist organization. Both the PP and the PSOE put tremendous pressure on the PNV to formally announce the death of the Pact of Lizarra and, at the same time, admit the failure of its initiative.

This being said, the support for moderate nationalism (PNV and EA) not only held steady but went up slightly in the 2001 elections. From an electoral perspective, it was the radical nationalist party EH that suffered most from the end of the cease-fire, dropping from a high of 18 percent in the 1998 Basque elections (where radical nationalism was rewarded for ETA's cease-fire) to only 10 percent. The four-teen months of cease-fire elevated the Basques' hope for peace and provided a taste for "normal," violence-free politics. The return to political assassinations meant that ETA's actions were, for most Basques, even more insufferable than before. The cease-fire served to lower Basque society's tolerance for violence, and EH, as the political voice of radical nationalism, saw many of its voters support other politi-cal parties. Feeling this blow, radical nationalists attempted to regain some form of control over politics by suggesting a new nationalist common front late in 2003,[65] but these efforts were ultimately unsuccessful.

In contrast, the PP, whose tough stance toward ETA had translated into a skepti-cal, and indeed a cynical, attitude toward the truce was rewarded in the 2001 elec-tions, garnering 23 percent of the votes. This result, an all-time high for the PP in a Basque election, made it the second party in the Basque Country behind the PNV.

The end of ETA's truce combined with this strong electoral result in the Basque elections emboldened the PP government in power in Madrid to follow hard-line policies toward all forms of Basque nationalism. This approach was already appar-ent before the cease-fire. For example, in 1997 the PP government jailed twenty-three HB leaders for having collaborated with ETA.[66] Several factors account for the PP's tough approach toward Basque nationalism.

First, the PP is a party whose historical and ideological legacy involves strong stands in support of the unity and indivisibility of the Spanish nation. As a conse-quence, it has a philosophical predisposition toward centralization and symmetry of status between regional governments. As a right-of-center party that finds some roots in Francoism, it is also unflinching on issues of law and order.

Second, the PP was personally targeted by ETA beginning in 1997, which led to the murder of several of its municipal representatives. This is not at the heart of the PP's policies toward Basque nationalism, but may have reinforced its determination not to compromise.

Third, starting in 2000, the PP could count on a majority of seats in the Spanish parliament. Consequently, it was able to form a majority government and no lon-ger needed to show flexibility in accommodating the claims of substate national-ism. Of course, the hard-line attitude started before 2000, but it certainly was made easier by the fact that no support from other parties was needed thereafter.

Finally, and most importantly, the PP developed an understanding of ETA as being so closely intertwined with radical nationalist circles and even the larger Basque nationalist movement that it did not distinguish these political forces. From a sociological perspective, the idea of a network of connections between ETA and the various civil society organizations making up the National Liberation Movement was fairly uncontroversial insofar as ETA could count, to varying degrees, on their active social and political support.[67] The PP's political use of this reality, however, was very controversial in the Basque Country since it consisted of shutting down, through requests to Spanish courts, Basque political and cultural organizations for supposed collaboration with ETA. The prime examples of this strategy were the closing of the Basque-language newspaper *Egunkaria* in 2003[68] and the outlawing of Batasuna (the renamed Euskal Herritarok) for a three-year period in 2002 and then permanently in 2003. Both moves triggered sharp criticism from all sectors of Basque nationalism (the Socialists supported the decisions). This brought together, albeit temporarily, moderates and radicals and worked to further break down the relationship between moderate Basque nationalists and the Spanish government. In the case of Batasuna, the PP government was arguing, for example, that financial resources were diverted to ETA.[69] The outlawing of Batasuna proved particularly controversial, as it was argued that this move effectively disenfranchised a segment of Basque society, radical nationalism. It triggered a major political conflict, since the speaker of the Basque parliament, Juan María Atutxa, refused to eject Batasuna representatives as he was required to do.[70] Predictably, these PP policies fed the radical nationalist discourse, which perceived no major changes in Spain since Franco's death and accused the Spanish government of being fascist. It also led to gains for the PNV in municipal elections where radical nationalist candidates could no longer run.

As a result of the PP's conflation of terrorism and nationalism, the Spanish government's relations with the PNV-led Basque government were very poor. In fact, they were really nonexistent since Spanish Prime Minister José María Aznar simply refused to speak to his Basque counterpart, lehendakari Ibarretxe. For example, asked about the possibility of establishing dialogue with the Basque leader, Aznar said: "Dialogue to achieve what? I have nothing to say on the question of self-determination."[71] In this context, the political climate in the Basque Country from the end of the cease-fire to 2004 was one of intense confrontation and polarization.

Caught between radical nationalists and the PP, the PNV looked for a way out or, rather, for a way to regain the political initiative. It was in this context that in 2002–3 lehendakari Ibarretxe put forward his "plan" or "proposal" for a pact of "free association" with Spain. The idea behind the proposal was to move beyond the existing institutional framework, which the PNV saw as deadlocked by successive Spanish governments refusing to transfer the whole range of powers specified in the Statute of Autonomy.[72] This so-called Ibarretxe proposal suggests a new political framework for managing the relationship between Spain and the Basque Country based on the idea of shared or co-sovereignty. The exact political and institutional configuration that would result from the full implementation of this proposal is difficult to pinpoint. At a minimum, it would rearticulate Spain as a multinational composite state with asymmetrical government. At a maximum, the Ibarratxe proposal would create a loose confederation between Spain and the Basque Country.

Predictably, the Ibarrexte proposal came under heavy criticism. For radical Basque nationalists, it fell short of independence and excluded Navarre as well as the French Basque Country from the project. For the PP, it went against the constitution and was therefore unacceptable. The PNV leadership had anticipated this type of reaction and appeared relatively unruffled. One way to see the Ibarretxe proposal is as a long-term plan through which the PNV can guide a process of recomposition of the various Basque forces. On the one hand, the PNV sought to draw support away from radical nationalism by proposing an institutional framework that represents a break from the Statute of Autonomy. Or, in the words of lehendakari Ibarretxe himself, it involved "getting ETA out of our lives."[73] On the other hand, it looked to engage in some form of dialogue with the Spanish government about the political status of the Basque Country.

The March 2004 bombings in the Atocha train station in Madrid and the result of the subsequent general elections brought a substantial change in Spanish politics that seemed to give the Ibarretxe proposal some type of future. Immediately following the bombings, the PP blamed ETA, a position it maintained even as information began suggesting that the attack was instead the work of Islamic fundamentalists. The political dilemma of the PP was clear. Announcing that an Islamist organization had perpetrated a terrorist attack in Spain was going to make the party's (unpopular) decision to support the American military intervention in Iraq a damaging issue in an election it was fully expecting to win. At the same time, hinting at ETA would somehow validate its hard line toward Basque nationalism. As a consequence of the bombings, and especially of the ensuing effort of the Spanish government to blame ETA and withhold information, the momentum switched and the PSOE won the election. For the moderate nationalists of the PNV, this was a welcome change since it could hope to have some type of conversation with the Spanish government. Indeed, one of the first political moves made by the new Spanish prime minister Zapatero was to meet with lenhendakari Ibarretxe. Substantively, there seems to be little in the way of agreement on the Ibarretxe proposal, which the PSOE does not support. For example, public administration minister Jordi Sevilla stated that the Spanish government was "certainly willing to participate in a project together [with the Basque government], but that project is called Spain."[74] In any case, the resumption of a dialogue was rightfully hailed as a significant development.[75]

The results of the 2005 Basque elections, fought in large part around Ibarretxe's proposal, cast serious doubts on the first of the two political objectives behind it. The electoral results for radical Basque nationalism went up two percentage points,[76] while the PNV-EA coalition went down four. This data clearly indicates that there was no move of support from radical to moderate Basque nationalism. Moreover, the hit taken by the parties supporting lehendakari Ibarretxe's initiative, the PNV and EA, could hardly by interpreted as an endorsement of the plan. In fact, non-Basque nationalists suggested that the election outcome meant its death.

This being said, these elections were similar to previous ones insofar as substantial support for Basque nationalist parties of all stripes indicated that there was still a "Basque issue" to be solved, or at least further managed.

ETA's Announcement of a Permanent Cease-Fire

On March 22, 2006, ETA declared, for the first time in its history, a permanent cease-fire. In a videotaped statement, three hooded ETA members announced that this move had as its objective "the launching in the Basque Country of a democratic process for building a framework where our rights as a people can be recognized and where all political options can be explored."[77] How can we explain the timing of this cease-fire?

The foremost reason is a declining tolerance for political violence in the Basque Country and increasingly negative perceptions of ETA itself, to the point where by late 2005 only a small minority of Basques accepted and did not condemn the organization outright (fig. 4.1). By the time ETA resumed its violent activities following the end of the 1998 cease-fire, there existed a powerful antiviolence social movement featuring various elements of Basque society, most notably families of ETA victims, Socialists, and PP politicians as well as columnists and intellectuals.[78] A watershed moment for political violence in the Basque Country was the 2004 Atocha train station attacks. These attacks demonstrated the extent to which political violence had become intolerable for the Basques. As the PP was blaming ETA for the killings, massive marches and vigils were organized in the Basque Country, and the PNV was categorically condemning the (supposed) ETA attacks. Basque leader Ibarretxe stated that "those who commit these atrocities are not Basque" and that "ETA writes its own ending with terrible actions." (Only Batasuna leader Arnaldo Otegi, who would have been in the know about ETA plans, never accepted that ETA was responsible). Overall, there was tremendous repulsion to the killings of hundreds of innocent people. Although these attacks were of a totally different scale from what ETA usually does, they nevertheless provided an example of the type of negative reaction the terrorist organization could expect if it were to kill again.

Significantly, the critical stance of the Basques toward violence and ETA was accompanied, especially in the aftermath of the Atocha bombings, by an expectation for "normalization." In late 2005, for example, a survey found that 75 percent of Basques thought that the situation had improved in the last year with respect to the problem of violence (fig. 4.2). This was the product of episodic rumors that the terrorist organization was considering a cease-fire. ETA even had well-publicized contacts with the Catalan nationalist (and secessionist) party Esquerra Republicana de Catalunya (ERC) for the purpose of discussing a separate "truce" in Cataluña. It was also the consequence of the organization's greatly diminished activity after

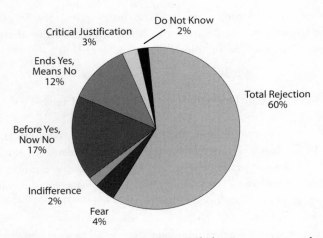

Fig. 4.1. Attitudes of the Basques Toward ETA. *(Euskobarómetro November 2005)*

2002. Following a wave of post-cease-fire violence that resulted in fifty or so victims in three years (including, for the first time, two in the same day when Ibarretxe was sworn in as lehendakari in July 2001), ETA killed three people in 2003 and none afterward.

In addition to these attitudes of the Basques, the change in Spanish government in 2004 is also crucial for understanding the permanent cease-fire announcement. With the PP in power in Madrid, ETA could hardly expect anything to come out of a cease-fire. After all, the PP was not amenable to changes to the constitution or to statutes of autonomy, nor was it open to any negotiation with ETA. The PSOE, on the contrary, had not closed the door on reforming the statutes of autonomy. Moreover, in May 2005, it passed a resolution in parliament supported by all parties except the PP stipulating that the Spanish government was ready to negotiate with ETA if the organization formally renounced violence. The call for negotiations represented an invitation to surrender since these negotiations would focus on ETA's disbanding and the status of their prisoners rather than on the political status of the Basque Country.

For ETA, the most striking display of potential for change with a PSOE government in Madrid most likely came from the negotiations, in late 2005 and early 2006, between the Spanish government and the Catalan Generalitat for a reform of the Catalan Statute of Autonomy. As a result of these reforms, Cataluña will have increased fiscal autonomy and is recognized as a nation.

Finally, ETA might also have been keen to consider a permanent cease-fire because a formal proposal for substantially restructuring the relationship between the Spanish state and the Basque Country, the Ibarretxe plan, had already been put forward by the Basque government and supported by the Basque parliament. In addition, Basque lehendakari Ibarrexte had declared there would need to be an absence of violence to move the proposal forward through the organization of a referendum in the Basque Country. In this context, ETA probably considered that opportunities for meaningful change were greater if it formally ceased its violence.

Will the cease-fire hold? The chances are good if only because tolerance for violence will only diminish as the "normalization" of politics becomes a reality. Still, ETA has not disbanded, nor has it condemned violence, and while the political context in the summer of 2006 looks promising, at least two types of development could produce tensions that might frustrate ETA.

The first relates to the process of negotiations over the hundreds of ETA prisoners currently in Spanish jails. As soon as the cease-fire was announced, the PSOE government declared itself ready for "peace" negotiations. The PP initially opposed this position but eventually came on board. Is the Spanish government ready to accept some form of amnesty for ETA prisoners? If it is not, would ETA stick to its cease-fire?

A second potentially tricky situation would be if institutional change toward the greater autonomy and national recognition of the Basque Country would fail to materialize. Basque politics remains more polarized than Catalan politics, which means that the likelihood of change is not quite as great. How would ETA react in such a situation, especially if it is able to place the responsibility of whatever failure occurs on the shoulders of the PNV or the "Spanish" parties? A reactivation of ETA, or of a splinter group, although unlikely, is therefore not completely out of the question.

Conclusion

The establishment of a democratic Estado de las Autonomías in Spain represented a critical juncture in the historical development of Basque nationalism in many respects. At the most basic level, it transformed Basque nationalism from an underground movement with no institutional anchoring or formal means of representation to not only a legitimate and strongly institutionalized political force, but at times a dominant one. From this perspective, the processes of identity-building and mobilization generated by the interactions between the various historical forms of the Spanish state and Basque elites and society culminated in nationalism being established as the normal form of politics in the Basque Country. At the same time, the successful democratic transition and "normalization" of Spain rehabilitated Spanish nationalism for a significant segment of Basque society. As such, the Basque identity and Basque nationalism are not uncontroversial or endorsed by every Basque. If this were the case, we could speak of a "banal" nationalism of the

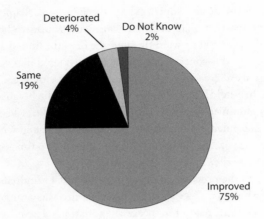

Fig. 4.2. View of the Problem of Violence in 2005. (Euskobarómetro November 2005)

type most often associated with established democratic states such as France and the United States.[79] On the contrary, Basque society is immensely polarized between those feeling completely or primarily Basque and seeking complete independence from, or increased autonomy within, Spain, and others feeling more Spanish and basically defending the status quo. It is these types of conflict that characterize Basque nationalism as they do most instances of substate nationalism.

We saw how the institutional architecture of the democratic state triggered various patterns of relationships that define nationalist politics in the Basque Country. The creation of an Autonomous Community of the Basque Country involved the establishment of a Basque political system where all societal tendencies relating to the issue of the political future of the Basque Country and its relationship with Spain would be played out, reproduced, and/or transformed. At the most general level, these tendencies featured a pair of bipolar options: Basque nationalism versus non-Basque nationalism and moderate versus radical Basque nationalism. Put differently, Basque politics became clearly defined by a triangle of political and social forces: moderate Basque nationalism, radical Basque nationalism, and Spanish nationalism in its various forms. This being said, nationalist politics in the Basque Country was often in flux as forces in this triangular relationship underwent periods of tension and rapprochement shaped by party politics, ETA, and the larger Basque society. Moreover, this chapter has explained how the politics of Basque nationalism is also greatly affected by the actions and policies of the Spanish state as well as by the relationship between the Basque government and other autonomous communities. The choice of a basic approach for managing Basque nationalism has had an impact on the configuration of forces within Basque politics as did responses to ETA and to the claims of the PNV. In this context, the uncompromising attitude of the Aznar government (especially between 2000 and 2004), including the absence of any serious dialogue with Basque nationalist actors, was especially noticeable and most likely explained the serious polarization in the Basque Country during this period.

It appears likely at this point that the democratic Estado de las Autonomías will have a long life (certainly longer than the Franco dictatorship), which means that Basque nationalism could be molded by the types of relationships described in this chapter for some time to come. Of courses, there are sources of possible institutional changes, which could then produce new configurations for Basque nationalism. One of these sources is endogenous to the current framework and could involve a serious disjunction between the Estado de las Autonomías and the preferences of Basque society about the political future of the Basque Country. Currently, Basque societal preferences are divided between various options, but if one option for change were to gather overwhelming support (for example, the Ibarretxe plan) it is likely that a significant transformation would occur with the Spanish state, or at least in the way it relates to the Basques. The other source, which is exogenous, is the European Union (EU). If the EU were ever to evolve into a multilevel governance polity that seriously engaged substate governments, its structure would then have to be considered as a significant transformation of the Spanish state and its relations with Basque institutions, parties, and society. Of course, the EU has already had an impact on Basque nationalism. Perhaps most importantly, involvement of the Basque government in EU decision-making is now a central claim of the PNV. This claim is still unmet, but the Basque government has in the meantime developed all types of European as well as transatlantic links. I consider this "paradiplomacy" in the next chapter.

Chapter Five

Basque Paradiplomacy

The last chapters showed how the historical trajectory of the Basque Country from the late nineteenth century onward involved the development of nationalism as an increasingly powerful political force. The previous chapter explained that the transition to democracy in Spain featured the creation of the Autonomous Community of the Basque Country and that, in the democratic state, Basque politics became centered around the Basque autonomous institutions and their relationship with the state. There is also an international dimension to Basque politics, since nationalism, combined with the political and institutional context generated by Spain's Estado de las Autonomías, has led to the development of a Basque paradiplomacy.

Paradiplomacy refers to regional governments developing international relations. This is by no means a phenomenon unique to the Basque Country. Many regions in Europe (including some of Spain's other autonomous communities), North America, and elsewhere around the world conduct bilateral relations with other regional entities (sometimes even with sovereign states) and participate in multilateral forums.[1] They do this in order to achieve a variety of objectives, most often economic but in some cases also political and cultural. A sine qua non condition for paradiplomacy is, of course, decentralized political structures. But territorial political autonomy alone does not lead to paradiplomacy. The development by regional governments of international relations is spurred by a variety of international processes such as economic globalization and, in the European context, supranational integration that work to decenter the state. In some cases, paradiplomacy is driven by a desire to strengthen, promote, and project an identity distinct from the one associated with the state.

This chapter suggests that Basque paradiplomacy is primarily about identity politics. This is not to say that this paradiplomacy is not concerned with achieving economic gains through, for example, the facilitation of exports, but only that its scope and intensity are a function of nationalism. The idea of a connection between identity and paradiplomacy does not mean that distinctive collective identities necessarily lead to cases of paradiplomacy such as the Basque Country's. In other words, the chapter's argument is not that the Basque Country conducts international relations because many Basques feel more Basque than Spanish; this would be an oversimplification. Rather, the idea put forward here is that the development of foreign affairs by the Autonomous Community of the Basque Country is the consequence of a nationalist movement.

The specific rationale provided by the Basque government for its right to an international presence is strongly rooted in the evolution of the Spanish state. Basque politicians stress the idea of a right to self-determination to argue that the Basque Country should be able to conduct its own international relations. They invoke the precedent of the Basque government-in-exile, which, during the Franco dictatorship, acted autonomously in the international arena. The legacy of the authoritarian state spurs Basque paradiplomacy in other ways. Cultural repression and the ensuing struggle for cultural and identity preservation have become enduring aspects of Basque politics that are now seen to have global dimensions. The diaspora provides the Basque government with natural partners for international activities. Finally, the political violence that emerged as a reaction to the dictatorship prompts the Basque government to undertake various initiatives to present a different, more positive face of the Basque Country internationally.

Paradiplomacy: Regional Governments as International Actors

Regional governments are most often treated as domestic actors. This is hardly surprising since their overwhelming agency occurs within regional or national frameworks. The primary role of regional governments is arguably to design and/or implement public policy applicable only within the boundaries of the federated unit or decentralized territory in question. In regions with directly elected assemblies, responsible executives, and a distinct political class, these governments also serve functions of representation and political legitimization, which are also regionally bounded. This dimension of the action of regional governments has been widely recognized by academics. Indeed, a significant number of scholarly writings analyze the politics of specific regions[2] much as if they were sovereign states.[3]

The agency of regional governments also takes place within a national context. Regional governments necessarily have some relationships with the central state. These relationships can be structured in many different ways: sometimes regional governments and the center are relatively equal partners, and the relationship involves exchanges of information and policy coordination (for example, Belgian federalism). In other cases, central-regional relationships feature the subordination of the latter to the former. This is observable not only in nonfederal regionalized states such as France, but also in many federations (Venezuela, Germany, Austria). Regional governments can also be part of a more complex web of intergovernmental relations that involve other like units. This is the case in Belgium, Canada, and, as we have just seen, in Spain. The agency of regional governments in the national context has also been widely recognized. It is central, for example, to most studies of federalism.[4]

Sometimes forgotten is the fact that regional governments also operate within the broader international context, that they can be international actors. This phenomenon of regional governments developing international relations is most often called "paradiplomacy." The concept first appeared in the English-language literature during the 1980s through the pioneer studies of Duchacek, Latouche, and Stevenson, and Michelmann and Soldatos.[5] It has grown through inputs from both comparative politics and international relations specialists.[6] From the comparative angle, paradiplomacy is closely associated with federalism studies and is meant to address phenomena of bilateral relations between regional governments of different countries, their participation in multilateral forums, as well as transnational/transborder connections. From the international relations perspective, paradiplomacy also tends to be studied in reference to federalism,[7] although the focus, or at least the starting point, is more often the global web of diplomatic relations rather than the domestic grounding of regional governments. In other words, paradiplomacy is studied more from the top down; it corresponds to a "localization" of diplomacy that makes it a multilevel process.[8]

From either perspective, paradiplomacy conveys a sense of both parallelism and subordination. It expresses the idea that the international actions of regional governments run parallel to state foreign policy without contradicting it. In a sense, the concept does not adequately reflect the tensions that can arise from regional governments conducting international relations. Paradiplomacy is rarely welcomed by states, especially since, in many cases, it touches on a very wide range of issues: culture, language, education, environment, trade, technological and scientific cooperation, and so on. These issues used to be considered of secondary importance to defense and security in world politics, but as the "low politics"/"high politics" dichotomy has largely broken down, the core of state foreign policy has grown increasingly more multidimensional. Hence, regional governments attempt to exploit opportunities for international projection without taking on the state headfirst. Of course, their influence on international outcomes or on the behavior of other international actors is not very important, but it cannot be completely discarded. For example, criticism by the Quebec government of France's decision to have air traffic control at Charles De Gaulle airport function in English may have contributed to the policy being abandoned a mere fifteen days later.[9]

The development by regional governments of international relations is more recent than their policy making or involvement in intergovernmental relations. Regional governments need to have policy-making capacities to project themselves internationally. It is also useful for them to have experience in dealing with other governments in a domestic context before establishing relations with entities abroad. This being said, regional governments having international relations is not a completely new phenomenon. The Basque Country had an early experience of contact with foreign governments when it was forced into exile by the Franco dictatorship. Quebec developed international ambitions and links during the Quiet Revolution of the 1960s.[10] States of the American South began seeking out foreign investment in the late 1950s, while northern states did the same in the 1970s.[11]

While there are early cases of paradiplomacy, this phenomenon has acquired new importance over the last fifteen to twenty years. The Basque Country, Cataluña, Flanders, Wallonia, Quebec, as well as many German *länder* are all running quite significant paradiplomacies. Moreover, paradiplomacy is now a global phenomenon; that is, it is no longer strictly associated with the regional governments of Western democracies, but can also be linked to non-Western and/or democratizing states.[12] Many Russian republics have shown international ambitions; in some cases these ambitions are underpinned by religious distinctiveness and/or nationalist aspirations, while in others they result from socioeconomic problems. In Latin America, economic integration has spurred cross-border cooperation. Some instances of paradiplomacy are also visible in southern Africa and China.

Why this growth in paradiplomacy? Several factors contributed to it. First, the federalization or decentralization of several states (Spain, Belgium, South Africa, and even France) over the past twenty years has made paradiplomacy possible. After all, there could be no such phenomenon without regional governments with genuine political autonomy. Second, just as the end of the cold war and its bipolarization allowed nonstate actors such as nongovernmental organizations and social movements to play a more important role in international relations, it also opened up room for regional governments on the international stage. The end of the cold war context also meant a relative decrease in the importance of security (at least, as it has been conventionally defined) in favor of other issues, such as economic development, the environment, and culture, which typically fall within the domestic jurisdiction of regional governments.

Also important was economic globalization, taken as corresponding to the liberalization of trade and the construction of free-trade zones. These processes have had two consequences that favored paradiplomacy. First, they have altered trading patterns: from primarily national to continental and global. Second, they reduced the ability of the state to oversee the economy and its capability to address issues of regional economic development. In this dual context, there was an impetus for regional governments to take it upon themselves to nurture new trade relationships, seek out foreign capital investment, and promote their exports.

Finally, in Western Europe, paradiplomacy was spurred by the political integration of the European Union (EU). At the broadest level, the EU presents shades of multilevel governance[13] that has legitimized the agency of regions. It is probably not coincidental that regional groupings, such as the Four Motors of Europe and the Atlantic Arc, were created and flourished during the relaunching of the

European Union integration project in the mid-1980s.[14] The connection between the European Union and the myriad of transborder associations is even clearer since most of those were formed through the EU's INTERREG program (for example, the Euregio Meuse-Rhin).[15] The EU also fosters direct regional-supranational links through its cohesion policy and the Committee of Regions (COR).

Of course, there is, in Europe, a debate about the exact meaning of all these connections and activities. From a European federalist perspective, these relationships are intrapolity and therefore do not fit very well with the concept of paradiplomacy, which involves an international aspect. However, considering that the state is still the central actor in European politics, an equally good case can be made that inter-regional and cross-border networks in Europe are cases of paradiplomacy. It is the view taken in this chapter.

Nationalism and Paradiplomacy

Not every regional government approaches international relations in a similar way. It is important to make distinctions between three different types of para-diplomacies. The first type of paradiplomacy sees regional governments focus on economic issues; they aim at developing an international presence for the purpose of attracting foreign investment, luring international companies to the region, and targeting new markets for exports. These paradiplomacies typically do not have an explicit political dimension, nor are they concerned with cultural issues. They are primarily a function of global economic competition. Regions with this type of paradiplomacy typically locate an international unit within a commerce and trade department, and their foreign representation consists almost exclusively of trade offices. The prototypical example here is the American states, whose international activity consists essentially in the pursuit of economic interests. Australian states, whose international presence is weaker than their U.S. counterparts, also fit in this category.[16] So do Canadian provinces other than Quebec, namely Ontario and Alberta, that have had some international experiences.

The second type of paradiplomacy juxtaposes the economic dimension with political and, sometimes, cultural ones. Here, paradiplomacy is more extensive and more multidimensional. Institutionally, it tends to be supported by bureaucratic units devoted to international relations rather than simply external trade. Some German *länder* fall into this category, most notably Baden-Württemberg, which has been a leader in the creation of the Four Motors of Europe and the Assembly of European Regions. Baden-Württemberg has also spearheaded many transbor-der initiatives and has been involved in north-south cooperation and development assistance.[17] At least one French region, Rhône-Alpes, also presents a fairly devel-oped and multidimensional paradiplomacy.[18] In addition to membership in the

Four Motors of Europe and several transborder associations (for example, with the Swiss cantons of Geneva, Vaud, and Valais), Rhône-Alpes has developed a series of bilateral relations with subnational entities in various African, Asian, and Central European countries (Mali, Senegal, Tunisia, Vietnam, Poland, etc.). These relations, conceptualized as "decentralized cooperation," take the form of development assistance and cultural and educational exchanges, as well as scientific and technical cooperation.

There is a third type of paradiplomacy that is driven primarily by political and cultural considerations, although the economic dimension is certainly not absent. This paradiplomacy features prominently the international expression of an identity distinct from the one projected by the central state.[19] It tends to be very ambitious; this is not always manifested in the scope of its networks (some are fairly specifically targeted) but in the logic driving the international ventures. Here, regional governments seek to develop a set of international relations that will affirm the cultural distinctiveness, political autonomy, and, indeed, the national character of the community they represent. Paradiplomacy can therefore become a highly conflictual process domestically. There are not that many instances of paradiplomacy that fit this category. As we will argue in the next section, the Basque Country's does.

The Basque Country, as well as other cases of multidimensional and ambitious paradiplomacy such as in Cataluña, Quebec, and Flanders, all share one underlying feature: nationalism. This type of paradiplomacy is a function of nationalism. Nationalism involves at least two processes, linked respectively to identity and political mobilization, that can be logically and theoretically related to paradiplomacy.[20]

The first process is the construction, consolidation, and expression of a collective identity. Nationalism is a form of identity politics. It involves establishing boundaries between groups by providing objective markers such as language with subjective meaning. Identities are constructed and consolidated through a variety of mechanisms whose relative importance varies from one situation to another: cultural change, institutional development, socioeconomic transformations, political context/competition. However, above and beyond these structural variables, the articulation, and therefore construction, of the identities underlying nationalism is ultimately the product of discursive practices. Creating and shaping national identities necessitates speaking the nation, that is, promoting the idea of a national community.

The development of a region's international presence constitutes for nationalist leaders an additional opportunity to build, consolidate, and promote a national identity.[21] Indeed, the discourse of international relations is one of nations and, considering that states and nations are systematically conflated, so is international relations practice. In other words, the very definition of international agents, at least with respect to territorial-institutional units, entails nationhood. From this perspective, the development of international agency on the part of a regional government is full of symbolic meaning. In creating networks of paradiplomacy, regions contribute to their own legitimization as international actors. The relevance for identities of paradiplomacy is not limited to the agreements the regional governments sign or the forums they attend; as important is the fact that paradiplomatic activities, particularly those most visible and prestigious, give nationalist leaders the opportunity to play to their domestic audience. They provide a scene from which nationhood can be proclaimed most forcefully, because foreign, regional, or even international focus offers legitimacy and discursive/communication opportunities. In short, through paradiplomacy, regions can both behave as nations and present themselves as such.

The second process of nationalism is political-territorial mobilization. Nationalism is a form of politics, and therefore is fundamentally about power. The development of nationalist movements is the product of power struggles between and within groups. It involves most importantly competing political elites claiming to speak on behalf of communities, that is, presenting themselves as their legitimate voice. The peculiar feature of nationalism compared to other forms of politics is that mobilization needs to have a territorial basis; indeed, nationalist leaders need to structure mobilization in a way that transcends social cleavages and emphasizes a commonness linked to territory. Political-territorial mobilization, although generally sporadic and fluctuating in intensity, is necessarily a feature of nationalism because it underlies both claims for power and for policy/institutional change. The power of nationalist leaders rests on the prominence, even the hegemony, of nationalism as a form of politics. In turn, this state of affairs is itself conditional on popular support, as is the ability of these leaders to bring about policy and institutional change corresponding to their specific claims, usually formal recognition/distinct status, autonomy, federalization, or independence.

Political-territorial mobilization as a process of nationalism may be logically related to regional governments looking to develop international agency.[22] The peculiarity of paradiplomacy as a form of international expression is its highly conflictual domestic dynamic. Paradiplomacy does not merely feature conflict over the definition of foreign policy objectives, as is the case for traditional (state) diplomacy; it also involves struggles over the very expression of the foreign policy. States rarely welcome the idea of regions going abroad; in fact, they tend to oppose it vigorously if only because paradiplomacy may be seen as undermining the unity of the nation projected by the state. In other words, paradiplomacy often clashes with state nationalism. Some regional political forces subscribing to the nation promoted by the central state may also oppose the ambitious paradiplomacy stemming from substate nationalism. Consequently, paradiplomacy, particularly in its most visible forms (regional-international conferences, bilateral relationships with states, and so on), presents nationalist leaders with opportunities to stimulate mobilization because it pits the region against the center, and sometimes regional nationalist forces against non-nationalist ones. Since foreign policy is one of the last reserved domains of the state, paradiplomacy represents, in domestic politics, a statement about power. It can therefore be understood not only as the emergence of new actors on the international scene, but also as the most recent dimension of historical territorial conflicts whose most prominent and acute manifestation is nationalism.

Paradiplomacy is closely linked to political-territorial mobilization not only because it represents an additional variable in political conflicts and power struggles that tend to provide opportunities for stimulating this process, but more specifically because it can serve as a tool for achieving domestic policy objectives. A region that is very active internationally projects the notions of distinctiveness and autonomy in a way that may lower the degree of contention surrounding certain regional claims and demands. Or, at least, the development of a strong international personality gives regional leaders a prestige that can be used as leverage in negotiations on constitutional and institutional change.

In sum, there is a special type of paradiplomacy that is particularly multidimensional, elaborate, and, most importantly, strongly driven by considerations of identity. This paradiplomacy is a function of nationalism, and its structure and dynamics need to be understood as such. This understanding of paradiplomacy will guide our discussion of the international relations of the Basque Country.

Basque Paradiplomacy

Basque paradiplomacy corresponds to the development by the Autonomous Community of the Basque Country of bilateral relationships and partnerships with actors outside Spain, including the departments covering the French Basque Country and organizations representing Basque communities across the world, as well as its involvement in European Union politics. However, there are historical antecedents to the post-Franco international action of the Basque government. These antecedents are solidly grounded in nationalism.

At the broadest level, the articulation of Basque nationalism by Sabino Arana in the late nineteenth century involved a conceptualization of Euskadi beyond Spanish borders, that is, as involving parts of France. As a consequence, Basque political claims, subsumed for most of the nineteenth century into Spanish conflicts, the Carlist wars, were given an international twist: while these claims primarily targeted the Spanish state, they also touched upon France. In addition to creating Basque nationalism with an inherent international dimension, Arana looked internationally for support for his project of an independent Basque state. Indeed, there is evidence that Arana was counting on some form of international action, possibly involving France and Great Britain, which could lead to the dismantling of Spain.[23] Arana sought to alert foreign powers of the "Basque question." For example, he sent a telegram to American president Theodore Roosevelt congratulating his country's recognition of Cuba's independence; if Europe were to apply a similar logic, Arana intimated, the Basques, as an ancient people, would recover their freedom.[24] In a similar vein, Arana also sent a telegram to British Prime Minister Lord Salisbury, who ended the Boer War in South Africa.[25]

The international outlook of Basque nationalism survived Arana's death. Some ideas about using international links to advance the Basque cause never led to anything tangible: for example, the project of a "League of Oppressed Nations" that would include, among others, the Basque Country, Cataluña, Ireland, Egypt, Morocco, India, and the Philippines.[26] More concrete actions were also undertaken, such as formal visits to the Vatican (1911 and 1936) as well as Uruguay and Argentina (1934); a participation at the Third Congress of the Union des Nationalités (1916) and the Congress of European Nationalities (1929–30); a congratulatory telegram to American president Woodrow Wilson, hailing his doctrine (1918); the presentation of a memorandum to the League of Nations (1929); and the establishment of relations with Sinn Féin (1922).[27] From the Basque nationalist point of view, the idea behind establishing contacts with foreign interlocutors was to present Spain's treatment of the Basques as a form of oppressive colonialism and hope that external pressures would force the Spanish state to grant independence to the Basque Country. Overall, the scope and intensity of the international action of Basque nationalism increased throughout the 1910s and 1920s and declined during the Primo de Rivera dictatorship, only to return with the establishment of the Second Republic in 1931.

The international initiatives undertaken by Basque nationalists between 1900 and 1936 were motivated by the desire to trigger a change in the situation of the Basque Country within Spain. With the beginning of the Civil War in 1936 and the subsequent exile of the Basque government, international networking and lobbying aimed primarily at the status quo ante, that is, at a return to the Basque Statute of Autonomy under a republican regime, although ideas of independence surfaced intermittently. International action therefore became almost a necessity. Having been forced into exile by Franco's forces, the Basque government was almost powerless in influencing events at home. It was in a much better position to exert pressure from the outside by seeking condemnations by various foreign actors of the Francoist side. During the Civil War and the first decade or so of the Franco dictatorship, the Basque government-in-exile enjoyed the legitimacy associated with the Second Republic. The government's external actions,[28] whose ultimate objective was the autonomy or independence of the Basque Country, focused on denouncing the Franco regime and calling for the reestablishment of the Republic. As a return of the republican regime began appearing very unlikely with the onset of the cold war, the international initiatives of the Basque government-in-exile gradually diminished. In the 1960s and 1970s, when ETA emerged as the main resistance force in the Basque Country, the struggle of the Basques against the dictatorship attracted much international interest. The efforts of various actors, from priests to guerilla fighters, to have the international community take a critical look at the Franco dictatorship and its treatment of the Basque population did not represent paradiplomacy in the strictest sense since it was not a regional government leading the charge. From this perspective, there was a first stretch of Basque paradiplomacy from 1936 to the 1950s, while the second and current one began in the 1980s.

For PNV-led Basque governments, there has never been any doubt that the political autonomy recognized by the Statue of Autonomy necessarily involved an international dimension. A document published by the Basque government argues that: "the new Basque self-rule, which has crystallized into extensive authorities over matters such as establishing tax regulations and collecting taxes, Industry, Police, Mass Media, Health and Education, Transport and a long list of other competences, also required a particular foreign action policy in order to correctly perform these functions."[29] This argument has not been easily accepted by the Spanish state. Not surprisingly, the 1978 Spanish constitution confers to the central state exclusive jurisdiction over international affairs (article 149.1.3). The Basque Statute of Autonomy is mostly silent on the jurisdictional issue of foreign affairs. The statute specifies that the state must keep the autonomous community informed of the signing of treaties in matters falling within its range of powers, and empowers the Basque government to implement these treaties (articles 20.5 and 20.3). It also allows the autonomous community to have some input with respect to treaties leading to the establishment of cultural relations (article 6.5). Nowhere is it clearly specified what is meant exactly by international relations and what room there exists for autonomous communities (ACs) to be active internationally.

The Basque government has argued for a limited understanding of the concept of international relations that reduces it to formal diplomatic representation, war and peace issues, and the signing of treaties: it views most everything else as domestic activities that have, in a globalized world, an international extension.[30] On the contrary, the central state has defended a much more comprehensive understanding of international relations as well as a rigid distinction between international and domestic politics. From there, it has argued for its exclusive jurisdiction in the former and situated autonomous communities strictly within the latter. This conflict surfaced clearly in the mid-1980s when the Basque Office for European Affairs was created and then sought to open a Basque delegation in Brussels. In response, the Spanish state contested in the courts the constitutionality of the Basque government having representatives abroad. During a lengthy judicial process, the Basque government conducted European affairs for nearly ten years through a publicly funded nonprofit organization, INTERBASK. Finally, in 1994 Basque paradiplomacy emerged from this gray zone when the constitutional court confirmed the right of the Basque government to be officially represented in Brussels (ruling 165). Despite this legal clarification, Basque paradiplomacy remains fairly conflictual in terms of the relationship between the Basque government and the central state. Spanish nationalism, at least in its harder PP version, views Basque paradiplomacy as a challenge to the unity of the country. Of course, the tensions over paradiplomacy cannot be separated from the larger confrontational climate. In fact, the broader tensions and attitudes of mistrust on both sides are informing the state's suspicion of Basque external action. Paradiplomacy is therefore another terrain of confrontation for Spanish and Basque nationalism.

The foreign affairs ambitions of the Basque Country have inspired many other autonomous communities to develop paradiplomacies, but those have been more easily accommodated by the central state, partly because they tend to be less ambitious. Even in the case of Cataluña, whose paradiplomacy is quite ambitious but does not present issues as starkly and radically as the Basque Country's, relations with Madrid have been mostly "normalized."[31]

Institutionally, Basque paradiplomacy is conducted by the General Secretariat on Foreign Action (Secretaría General de Acción Exterior), which is attached to the presidency. This is a testament to the importance given to foreign affairs by the Basque government. Cataluña is the only other autonomous community to have given such bureaucratic prominence to external relations. The General Secretariat on Foreign Action was created in 1991, taking over from the Office for European Affairs. At the broadest level, its role, as specified by the 1995, 2000, and 2003 decrees stipulating its reorganization, is the definition and coordination of the foreign action of the Basque government.[32] Foreign action is defined in terms of involvement with the European Union, bilateral relations with other substate governments, and participation in interregional forums. The General Secretariat also has as a formal task the application of European law in the autonomous community and coordination of the Basque government's input into the state's position in EU affairs.[33] In reality, however, the state is not receptive to the idea of autonomous communities actively participating in the definition of a Spanish position within the EU. The General Secretariat is organized through a combination of sectoral and geographical dimensions; there are units (*direcciones*) for European affairs, relations with Basque communities abroad, cooperation and development, and the delegation in Brussels. There also exists an Interdepartmental Commission for Foreign Action (Comisión Interdepartamental de Acción Exterior), created in 1993, which is directly accountable to the presidency and includes the head of the General Secretariat, its director for European affairs, as well as representatives from the various departments of the Basque government. The commission is most oriented toward European and EU affairs. Its role is to support the policy making of the secretariat through analysis and evaluation.[34]

The importance of foreign affairs for the Basque government stems from the idea that the Basque identity should be expressed and promoted on the international stage, and that maximizing the power and prestige of the Basque government can also be aided by international action. These concerns clearly come across the four main axes of Basque paradiplomacy: European affairs; extra-European bilateral relations, including aid to development; the Basque communities abroad; and transborder cooperation with the Basque Country of France.

Europe has been the primary focus of Basque paradiplomacy. In the action plan for 2004, the General Secretariat lists as the first objective of Basque external affairs an active participation on the European scene and in the debate over the future of the EU.[35] The Basque government describes Europe as "the natural habitat of the Basques" and argues that Basque history is "closely linked to that of Europe."[36] It also speaks of the Basques' "pro-European vocation."[37] There is a strategic rationale behind this discourse, which is to provide for the Basque Country a context that does not link it to the Spanish or French states. Basque paradiplomacy in Europe clearly follows this logic. The Basque government is an enthusiastic supporter of the European Union, more specifically of a federalist model where regional governments could play a central role and where cultural diversity would be respected. The determination to have a Basque delegation in Brussels can therefore easily be understood; in addition, the delegation provides a channel for the Basque government to nurture its relationship with other European actors, states or regional governments. The Committee of Regions is also seen in this light and therefore prioritized by the Basque government, despite its lack of political power. The Basque government, through the General Secretariat on Foreign Action, has created a Basque Network of European Information (La Red Vasca de Información Europea, REVIE), whose role is to provide Basque citizens, as well as public bodies and private companies, information on European affairs.[38] This serves as a good example of a linkage strategy of the Basque Country to Europe that "loses" the Spanish state.

What the Basque government wants most of all when it comes to European affairs is the opportunity to directly participate in EU institutions, most importantly the Council of Ministers. It would like to have a representative within the Spanish delegation and, in cases of matters exclusive to the ACs, to have their governments flesh out the Spanish position.[39] There is a constitutional opening to do this from the EU side (Belgium and Germany have such an arrangement) in virtue of the ambiguity of article 146 of the Masstricht Treaty that defines representation in the council. However, the Spanish state has so far refused to let the Basque government take part in such a way in EU affairs. Short of this, the Basque government can discuss European affairs with the central government through a Bilateral Cooperation Commission (Comisión Bilateral de Cooperación Administración del Estado-Administración de la Comunidad Autónoma del País Vasco para Asuntos Relacionados con las Comunidades Europeas) created in 1995. This is much in keeping with the Basque preference for bilateral relations with the state rather than for a multilateral approach. There exists a multilateral forum where ACS can discuss the Spanish position at the European Union, the Conference for Matters associated with the European Communities (Conferencia para Asuntos Relacionados con las Comunidades Europeas); however, the Basque government made it a question of principle that it would need to have a bilateral mechanism as well.[40]

Beyond the European Union per se, the Basque government uses a variety of channels to establish links with other regional governments and build up the scope of its political activity. It participates in the Assembly of European Regions (AER), the Conference of Peripheral Maritime Regions (CPMR), Atlantic Southern Europe (ASE), the Working Community of the Pyrenees (Communauté de Travail des Pyrénées, CTP), and the Association of European Border Regions (AEBR). As a region with considerable political autonomy and a willingness to develop and project its political personality continent-wide, the Basque Country has created, jointly with other regions, two of these organizations (ASE, CTP) and assumed leadership in others (CPRM, AER). The Basque government has also sought to develop bilateral relations in the European context. Its preference has been for "strong regions" that share its commitment to a region-friendly European Union and the promotion of cultural diversity.[41] Most notably, it has cooperation agreements with the Jura canton, Bavaria, and Flanders. This choice of partners underlines the political and symbolic importance of paradiplomacy for the Basque government; even for the economic, technological, and scientific aspects of cooperation, the Basque government looks for regions with a strong sense of their own culture and political status. Official visits and meetings with high-profile politicians are a particularly effective way to play up the profile of the Basque Country. For example, Basque presidents have met, in the last twenty years, with such personalities as Jacques Delors, Valery Giscard d'Estaing, Edmund Stoiber, and Juan Antonio Samaranch. From an economic development point of view, the Basque government's Sociedad para la Promoción y la Reconversión Industrial (SPRI) has created a global network of centers to develop the international dimension of Basque business.[42]

For the Basque government, bilateral relations are viewed as an opportunity to improve the international image of the Basque Country. This is particularly, although not exclusively, the case outside Europe where the only image of the Basques is political violence. For example, studies have found that "90 percent of the international coverage of the Basque is 'bad news,'" while in the particular case of the *New York Times* (most likely representative of non-Basque newspapers) the focus has been on ETA, described primarily as "terrorist" and "separatist."[43] Extra-

European bilateral relations that are not strictly development-related have tended to focus on Latin America, where Basque expatriates often serve as an access point for the Basque government and where Spanish as a working language facilitates economic, scientific, and educational exchanges. Since 1988, Basque presidents have visited Mexico, Chile, Uruguay, Venezuela, and Colombia. They have also been to the United States, where a considerable Basque diaspora provides useful contacts. It was during a visit to the United States in 1992 that an agreement was reached to build the Guggenheim Museum in Bilbao. Throughout the 1990s, the Basque government did not rely on permanent foreign delegations to maintain a presence abroad; there existed only one, in Brussels. This has changed since. Between 2003 and 2005, delegations opened in Mexico, Chile, Argentina, Venezuela, and Madrid![44] The General Secretariat on Foreign Action has made the creation and consolidation of delegations a major strategic objective.[45]

Political violence represents an impetus for the further development of Basque paradiplomacy because paradiplomacy is seen as the best way to improve the image of the Basque Country abroad. At the same time, bilateral relations are complicated by the negative connotations carried by the Basques. For example, Quebec enjoys very good and close relations with Cataluña, but does not seek a similar relationship with the Basque Country. For the Quebec government, especially when it is formed by the PQ, any association with a nationalist movement that features a violent radical stream constitutes unnecessary bad publicity that can complicate its position at home and within Canadian politics. The announcement by ETA of a permanent cease-fire in 2006 may trigger a reconsideration of Quebec's relationship with the Basque Country.

The Basque government is also very much involved in aid for development. In fact, the Basque Country is the autonomous community that contributes most to development cooperation.[46] It has developed cooperation programs in Asia (most of them in India and the Philippines), Africa (primarily in Rwanda), and, above all, in Latin America (Peru, Venezuela, Chile, Bolivia, etc.) Of course, there is a purely humanitarian spirit to this dimension of Basque paradiplomacy. However, understanding this spirit requires an appreciation for the historical markers of Basque nationalism, most notably the period of dictatorial rule. A main governmental document on foreign affairs puts it like this: "The Basque Government has wanted to incorporate a clear element of solidarity into its foreign action. The Basques have been given shelter and help on numerous occasions when our people were living in difficult situations. And we are very aware that it is now our turn to help."[47] Moreover, this political choice of emphasizing aid and development cooperation plays into some popular notions of Basque identity. Indeed, Basque political and cultural elites have historically spoken of the Basques as a people imbued with progressive virtues such as egalitarianism. These elites have often characterized the Basques as the most ancient people of Europe, which makes for a connection with the societies of Africa and Asia. Also, during the Franco dictatorship, Basque nationalism developed a strong "Third World revolution" stream that equated the contemporary plight of the Basques with the fate of colonized societies.

Another priority of Basque paradiplomacy is to maintain and foster links with the Basque communities abroad.[48] The Basque diaspora, particularly important in Latin America and, to a lesser degree, in the United States, features prominently in the composition of the Basque identity. Contrary to other cases (for example, Scotland), being Basque is not understood in relation to particular geographical borders. The Basque government therefore provides support to Basque communities abroad in order to keep Basque culture and identity alive and strong. In turn, fostering this attachment to the Basque Country helps the Basque government to maintain links abroad, and works toward the improvement of the Basque image. Legislation was passed in 1994 to provide a framework for the relationship between the Basque government and the Basque diaspora. "Its goals are the institutionalization of social, cultural, and economic relations, as well as the integral protection and promotion of all these groups, while acknowledging a set of individual and collective rights and imposing on the Basque Administration a set of obligations toward them."[49]

The main instrument for the institutionalization of the relations between the Basque government and the Basque communities abroad are the Basque Centers, or Euskal-Etxeak. There are over 130 Basque Centers around the world, more than half of which are in Argentina and the United States. These centers are not, in the strictest sense, run by the Basque government, since they are created by the Basque diaspora and do not represent formal delegations of the Basque government; however, the Basque Centers receive subsidies from the Basque government and take part in the implementation of some programs. In partnership with the centers, the Basque government organizes "Basque weeks," which are celebrations of Basque culture (dancing, music, food, etc.). It also offers bursaries, organizes programs (such as Gaztemundu) that allow youths to go to the Basque Country, and publishes a magazine (also called *Euskal Etxeak*) that informs the Basque diaspora of Basque affairs. Among the Basque Centers, there are some that have the more specific designation of institutes or foundations. They are found in Argentina, Chile, Mexico, Venezuela, and the United States. These entities are closer to the delegation model than the regular Basque Centers. They have the specific mission of serving as intermediaries between the Basque Country and whichever country they are located in. They facilitate not only formal political visits, but also business ventures, academic exchanges, and so on.

A last strategy used by the Basque government to reach out to the Basque diaspora is the world congresses of Basque communities, which are set to be held every four years as specified by the 1994 legislation on relations with the Basque communities abroad. The congresses, the first one of which was organized in Vitoria-

Gasteiz in 1995, provide a forum for members of the various Basque communities abroad to meet with one another and with representatives of Basque institutions.[50] The congresses are not simply meeting places; they serve to define the policy of the Basque government toward the diaspora and, more specifically, lead to strategic action plans. Typically, the emphasis of these plans is on the diffusion of the Basque culture and language through, for example, the Internet and television.

Finally, Basque paradiplomacy puts great emphasis on cooperation with the Basque Country in France. This cross-border cooperation should be seen as a para-diplomacy category in its own right rather than as a subset of European affairs, bilateral relations, or relations with Basque communities abroad. For Basque nationalism, Euskadi is composed of the Basque population of Spain and France. From a political perspective, this is largely a principled position, since the formal "unification" of all Basque territories is not a realistic option. Basque paradiplo-macy cannot and does not treat the Basques of France simply as another European partner or as a community "abroad." There is even some reticence in using the concept of transborder cooperation (often preceded by "so-called"),[51] since from the Basque nationalist perspective there is an Euskadi south and north, rather than a Spanish and a French Basque Country.

Cross-border cooperation presents some important problem for the Basque gov-ernment. First of all, nationalism, as well as simply the Basque identity (at least in its exclusive or preponderant form) is much weaker in France than in Spain. Second, police cooperation between Spain and France with respect to ETA members taking refuge in France has tightened the border.[52] Third, and most importantly, there is no Basque political institution in France. The French Basque Country is included in the department of Pyrénées Atlantique, but at least half of the department's popu-lation is not Basque. The creation of a Basque department is a long-standing claim of French Basques, but this outcome remains unlikely. Even if such a department were to exist, the political weakness of this type of administrative structure would still make institutional cooperation difficult. In the context of France's regional arrangement, the Basque Country is part of Aquitaine, but makes up barely 10 percent of its population. This is a considerable obstacle to a Basque-focused coop-eration. In addition, relations between the Autonomous Community of the Basque Country and the Aquitaine region are hampered by the different political statuses of the two units within their respective states as well as by a significant discrepancy in financial means. Moreover, neither the French nor the Spanish state is keen on cross-border cooperation between the Basque populations. France has no major problems with its Basques, and certainly does not want to encourage the develop-ment of a stronger Basque identity. Spain tightened the border to better fight ETA and has no reason to encourage Basque nationalist sentiments in France since they could lead to an increased support for the project of creating an independent Basque state. In this context, and considering the absence of a Basque institutional partner in France, it is difficult for the Basque government to implement a program that will target the Basque population in France, even if the initiative appears fairly banal (for example, the extension of Basque television to more homes in the French Basque Country). Most often, the Basque government has to communicate its idea to the Spanish government, which then has to relay it to the French government. This process almost never works.[53] Here again, we can see how paradiplomacy involves tensions between state and substate nationalism.

Despite these obstacles, there are activities of cooperation across the border. The framework for these activities is an agreement signed in 1990 between the Autonomous Community of the Basque Country and the Aquitaine region (the Foral Community of Navarre joined the agreement in 1992). The agreement involves an exchange of information in various policy areas: social, economic, communications, and research.[54] It also sets out the objective of promoting the Basque culture and language.[55] The most significant aspect of this cooperation agreement is the creation of a common fund for the financing of Basque projects. As a result of the lack of Basque autonomous institutions on the French side, some initiatives of the Basque government have necessitated the involvement of the French state. For example, the Basque government signed an agreement with the French Ministry of Education to widen the teaching of the Basque language in the French Basque Country. Also as a result of the paradiplomacy of the Basque government, the Basque language academy (Euskaltzaindia) has been officially recognized by the French state, which provides it with funding. We could also mention the Basque Eurocity of Bayonne-Donostia, a forum for cooperation created in 1993 by the Bayonne-Anglet-Biarritz district and the Diputación of Gipuzkoa.

Basque Paradiplomacy in Comparative Perspective

The paradiplomacy of the Basque Country is driven by nationalism. Of course, the Basque government seeks to reap economic benefits from its external action through the promotion of exports, the development of access points to foreign markets, and the attraction of foreign capital. However, the raison d'être of Basque paradiplomacy is not economic, but rather political. It has to do with the strengthening and the expression of the Basque identity as well as the bolstering of the political prestige, status, and autonomy of the Autonomous Community of the Basque Country. In the end, Basque paradiplomacy needs to be understood in the context of the political struggle between the Basque government and the Spanish state; for example, the objective of improving the image of the Basques abroad involves strengthening the self-appreciation of the Basque community and the political legitimacy of its government's claims. This type of ambitious and multifaceted paradiplomacy driven by considerations of identity and nationalist mobilization has three parallels in the West: Cataluña, Quebec, and Flanders.

Cataluña's paradiplomacy resembles the Basque Country's. At the broadest level, foreign affairs have been made a priority in Cataluña. For example, it has its own administrative structure, which has been inserted within the Department of the Interior and Institutional Relations.[56] Moreover, Cataluña's central preoccupation in developing international relations is to make a statement about nationhood through the projection of the Catalan culture and identity. The main objective is therefore recognition:[57] Catalan paradiplomacy seeks to generate, from foreign actors and the Spanish state, discourses and practices that show Cataluña as a nation. Having the objective of recognition in mind, culture becomes an opportunity structure, and Cataluña, much like the Basque Country, uses a network of cultural centers (Catalan Houses) to diffuse Cataluña's unique language. Catalan paradiplomacy is also similar to the Basque Country's insofar as its regional focuses are Europe (although it is involved in different organizations: for example, the Four Motors) and Latin America, and special attention is given to Catalan communities living abroad.

There are two main differences between the paradiplomacy of Cataluña and the Basque Country. First, there was, with Jordi Pujol as leader, a great personalization of Catalan paradiplomacy, which has had no equivalent in the Basque Country during the democratic period.[58] This personalization involved the use by Pujol of paradiplomacy to bolster his own personal prestige and that of his party,[59] Convergència i Unió (CiU). The development of external relations became a weapon in a Catalan political struggle involving the CiU and the Catalan Socialists. This dimension is less present in the Basque Country. The Basque Socialists also represent the main opposition to the nationalists, but they are more squarely viewed as a Spanish party than their Catalan counterparts, and therefore political competition in the Basque Country simply plays into a Basque Country–Spanish state dichotomy. As a result of political violence and more radical claims, relations with the central state are much worse in the Basque than in the Catalan case. Of course, these tensions reverberate on the issue of paradiplomacy.

Perhaps a better point of comparison for paradiplomacy in the Basque Country is Quebec. Quebec paradiplomacy clearly falls within the category of extensive and multifaceted paradiplomacies. In fact, Quebec's international activity and network is more developed than the Basque Country's: the province has international representation in over twenty-five countries; it posts more than 250 people abroad; and it has signed, since 1964, several hundred international agreements.[60] Paradiplomacy in Quebec is clearly driven by nationalism. Much as is the case for the Basque Country, one of the central objectives is the promotion of the international image of the province. For the Parti Québécois (PQ), for example, the federal government presents a negative picture of Quebec nationalism abroad; therefore an international presence is necessary to set the record straight. The PQ also argues that Quebec needs to be active internationally because the federal government is unable or unwilling to defend the province's specific interests. For example, it sees the federal government foreign policy objective of promoting Canadian values and culture as incompatible with Quebec's own culture.[61] When the Parti Libéral du Québec (PLQ) is in power, this discourse is considerably muted, even absent, but the province's stand on the legitimacy and necessity of an international presence stands. For example, the Jean Charest government has made the formalization of such presence through a bilateral agreement with the federal government a political priority.[62]

The link between nationalism and paradiplomacy in Quebec is also exemplified by the fact that the development by the Quebec government of international aspirations coincided with the 1960s Quiet Revolution that saw a rapid modernization of the province's social, political, and economic structure, which triggered, among other things, claims for decentralization of the Canadian federation. Therefore, Quebec governments began arguing, much like Basque governments did starting in the 1980s, that the policy sectors specified as provincial prerogatives in the constitution (or interpreted as such by the courts) should also constitute areas of provincial jurisdiction in the international sphere; this is the so-called Gérin-Lajoie doctrine. As is the case in the Basque Country, the federal government has never supported this interpretation. The Canadian government tends to see the province's paradiplomacy as an instrument for promoting nationalist positions abroad. This is particularly the case when the PQ holds power in Quebec. Quebecois, like Basque nationalism, features a secessionist stream; in this context, when PQ governments take international initiatives, or make claims to an international presence, it is viewed as an attempt to legitimize the secessionist option, or even secure support for an eventual declaration of independence. The relationship is slightly less conflictual when the autonomist PLQ is in power. In 2006, the major development surrounding Quebec's paradiplomacy has come from the election of a Conservative government in Ottawa. Whereas the Liberals clearly viewed the federal government as the sole legitimate voice in the international arena for Canada and were uncomfortable with the most visible aspects of Quebec's paradiplomacy, the Conservatives have shown more openness, even suggesting that Quebec could be given the opportunity to speak at UNESCO.[63]

Although Quebec is the paradiplomacy case that most resembles the Basque Country, the objective of the Basque government is to be able to operate within a framework such as the one enjoyed by the Belgian federated units. In Belgium, the catalyst for paradiplomacy has been Flanders.[64] The ambitions and motivations of Flanders with respect to foreign affairs are similar to the Basque Country's. Flemish leaders seek to develop an international presence to project Flemish culture (it targets partners, such as the Netherlands and South Africa, with whom there are cultural links)[65] and above all its nationhood. Flemish leaders were able, during the federalization of the Belgian state that they instigated, to constitutionalize the idea that fields of domestic jurisdiction should extend to the international sphere. The result is an institutional arrangement whereby Belgian regions and communities have exclusive power over certain elements of foreign affairs. In this context, they can, within formally recognized parameters, develop bilateral relations with states and (collectively) flesh out Belgian positions at the EU Council of Ministers.[66] From a conceptual point of view, the framework for the international relations of the Belgian federated units means that their foreign action may represent something other than paradiplomacy since it is not subordinated to the will of the central state. In other words, regions and communities no longer act as regional governments in international affairs; they are statelike. This development is specific to Belgium and its political dynamic. Flemings are a numerical majority and hold political power; they have been able to drive the federalization process and achieve most of their objectives such as the decentralization of much of foreign affairs. Of course, this structure is not present in Spain (or in Canada), which means that the emergence in these two countries of a similar constitutional-institutional arrangement is very unlikely.

Paradiplomacy, Nationalism, and the State

Paradiplomacy is a differentiated phenomenon. In many cases, it is exclusively about economic gain (American and Australian states). In some other instances, the economic aspect is combined with some elements of cooperation (French regions and German länder). The pressures of globalization and processes of regional integration are instrumental in explaining these types of paradiplomacy. There are also cases of paradiplomacy, such as the Basque Country's, that are much more ambitious and multidimensional; these usually have an economic aspect, but their logic is cultural and, above all, political. They are the product of substate nationalism. Multidimensional paradiplomacy needs to be understood historically, even if it is often a fairly recent occurrence; more specifically, it should be seen as a particular outcome of state development. In other words, types of paradiplomacies that are infused with political, cultural, and identity considerations are driven by nationalism, which is itself a phenomenon inseparable from state development as a historical process. Global economic conditions may provide a favorable context for these paradiplomacies to thrive, but they are not the main forces behind them

In the Basque case, paradiplomacy ties into every historical form of the state. The structure of the early Spanish state gave Basque leaders the sense of a right to self-determination that they argue justifies the Basque government conducting foreign affairs. The centralizing state of the late nineteenth century led to the articulation of Basque nationalism by Sabino Arana and therefore underscores the Basque government's effort to promote the Basque identity and bolster the political status of the Autonomous Community of the Basque Country. The authoritarian state had multiple legacies that provided the impetus for the development of a Basque paradiplomacy: the Basque government-in-exile, which represents an important precedent; ETA, which forced the Basque government to work on the Basque image abroad; the formalization of a conceptualization of a Basque nation (initiated by Arana) artificially separated by an international border, which leads the Basque government to look for transborder cooperation; the development of the Basque diaspora, which also pulls this government abroad because it perceives a responsibility to support Basque culture wherever it is found. Finally, the democratic state not only opened up room for the Basque government to make claims about an international presence but, with its system of autonomous communities, provides a dynamic of political competition over identity and power that made the development of such an international personality as much an end in itself as an instrument to achieve specific objectives.

Regional governments, such as that of the Basque Country, that develop ambitious and multidimensional paradiplomacies are international actors of a unique type. On the one hand, they clearly are not states since they either operate within constitutional frameworks where sovereignty is shared (Quebec within Canada, the Belgian regions and communities, and, although this is a more borderline case, the historical nationalities within the Spanish autonomous communities system), or lack any appropriation of formal sovereignty even if they can exercise a good measure of political power autonomously (Scotland in the United Kingdom). Moreover, these actors are typically not recognized as equals by states, which typically refuse to have formal relations with them. On the other hand, regional governments are not "nonstate" actors in the conventional sense of the term; they do not have the fluidity or transnational character of social movements, nongovernmental organizations, or multinational corporations. Rather, they are territorial-institutional units that tend to interact with international actors in a statelike fashion. The Autonomous Community of the Basque Country, along with a few other cases, suggests, in virtue of its international action, that the conception of global politics as composed of two "worlds" (state and nonstate actors)[67] may need to be revisited.

Chapter Six

The Management of
Basque Nationalism in Spain

The contemporary sociological reality of Spain is characterized by multinationalism, which means that a segment of the country's population identifies, at least to a degree, with a different national community from the one projected by the state. The Spanish state has been unable to forge a common and unchallenged nation such as the one constructed by the French state (largely through cultural assimilation) or the Swiss state (through mechanisms of political integration that excluded cultural homogenization). It is therefore faced with the task of managing nationalist movements, that is, of responding to their claims. This chapter examines what approaches and strategies the democratic Spanish state has favored in responding to Basque nationalism, and it analyzes the consequences of these choices. In this context, the chapter also discusses the most recent proposal put forward by moderate Basque nationalists for restructuring the relationship between the Spanish state and the Basque Country.

The perspective adopted in this chapter for discussing issues of nationalist conflict management involves some ontological and normative positions. First of all, the core of this book has shown how the process of historical transformations of the Spanish state into various forms has produced the development of a Basque nationalist movement that has found in the structures of the Estado de les Autonomías fertile ground for its expression and consolidation. In this context, it would be illusory to speak of "solving" the "national question" in the Basque Country since the political conflict around this issue is strongly institutionalized. What can be "solved" is the problem of political violence; Northern Ireland stands as a striking example of such a solution, and the permanent cease-fire declared by ETA in 2006 opens up the opportunity for a similar "peace process" in the Basque Country. The larger objective of *resolving* nationalist conflicts (assuming they take nonviolent forms) may not be realistic, at least in a liberal democratic context, in the short or even medium term. It is therefore more accurate to speak of conflict "management" or "regulation."

Why, then, would it be necessary for states to respond in some way to the claims of nationalist movements if no violence is involved? In other words, why would states bother devising strategies to manage these movements? At the most basic level, it could be argued that the claims of substate nationalism are no different from the constellation of political demands that are articulated in a liberal democracy and that, therefore, they need to be at least acknowledged and incorporated into the political dialogue. National politicians may fear that a complete nonresponse might trigger violence, or some form of civil disobedience. Their concern may be that if no measure is being taken to accommodate (or eradicate) substate nationalism, the shift in loyalty from the nation projected by the state to the one promoted by nationalist leaders might translate into potentially successful secessionist attempts. There is also the more banal issue that the claims of substate nationalism can remain on the national political agenda for a long time. In this context, there is less time and energy to address other important policy issues.

Finally, this chapter avoids treating substate nationalism as a "problem," or a bothersome force that states need to obliterate. From a normative point of view, it is suspect to view substate nationalism as being always and consistently morally inferior to state nationalism. The question is not one of right versus wrong; rather, it has to do with the peaceful and satisfactory coexistence of populations identifying with different nations.

Nationalist Management Strategies: Theoretical Perspective

There are different approaches for responding to the claims of substate nationalism.[1] These approaches are not mutually exclusive but rather tend to be used in combination.[2] In addition, one particular approach can be implemented through different strategies. For example, a state looking to boost the power of a group in central institutions may use consociational devices, assign to the group's political representatives a disproportionately large number of seats in the legislature, create a special cabinet position for the articulation of the group's preferences, and so on. As a result, the configuration of political practices and institutional arrangements put in place to manage nationalist movements varies from one case to the other.

In liberal democratic states, certain options are not available or, more to the point, acceptable. This is obviously the case for approaches involving the use of violence such as genocide or ethnic cleansing. Similarly, strongly coercive approaches such as population exchanges, segregation, or the subordination of one group to the other[3] are incompatible with liberal and democratic principles. Perhaps more important is the fact that political integration through linguistic and cultural assimilation, an approach favored by many states in contemporary history and used perhaps most successfully in France, has been rendered problematic by the globalization of minority rights.

States operating in the context of multinationalism typically seek to capture, or recapture, the loyalty of citizens who have come to identify with another nation. At a minimum, these states work to maintain the loyalty of citizens that is challenged by substate nationalism. Therefore, states look to deploy their own nationalism.[4] There are different ways to do this. A central force in the process of state nationalism in multinational liberal democracies has been the welfare state.[5] The development of the welfare state meant a "social citizenship"[6] whereby national social programs brought citizens together through common sets of rights, responsibilities, and values. In other words, social policy was integrated into, and fed, national identity.[7] Globalization has complicated the process of states seeking integration through welfare politics since states have been under pressure, resulting from global economic competition as well as the constraints and rules of continental integration, to reduce or eliminate budget deficits. Nevertheless, states in multinational societies understand the value of social policy as a common bond. In Canada, the federal government has shown a willingness to defend and even expand its national social programs in recent years. In a different context, Francophone Belgians, as well as some Flemish parties, are fighting off claims from the most nationalist parties in Flanders to "defederalize" Social Security; they are convinced that social policy is the crucial element holding Belgium together as a political community.[8]

This national politics of social protection is typically part of a larger design for political integration that features a focus on liberal individual rights and on the documents that formally protect them.[9] Canada has used this strategy with the introduction by the government of Pierre Trudeau of a Charter of Rights and Freedoms in 1982. This same Trudeau government also sought to foster the identification of Francophone Quebeckers with Canada by making the Canadian state officially bilingual (in 1969) and branding the Canadian nation as bicultural.[10] States in a situation of multinationalism can also choose to promote and foster a specific, usually dominant, culture. In this context, the state's nationalism involves the projection of historical narratives and symbols[11] that are, most often, drawn from the experience of the dominant cultural group. This strategy for political integration features tendencies of cultural assimilation that fit into a perspective that some authors have described as dominant ethnicity.[12]

Most of the time, the approach consisting of the explicit promotion of the national identity projected by the state is not sufficient to successfully manage multinational societies. Indeed, once the situation of multinationalism is in place, nationalist movements are unlikely to be satisfied unless their claims for political power and recognition have been met. In this context, states in multinational societies typically have to adopt approaches that can yield strategies aimed at meeting, at least partially, these claims. These approaches should not be seen strictly as alternatives to the promotion of the (state) national identity; in fact, most of the time they are superimposed on it.

A first approach that can be employed to meet the claims of nationalist movements consists of bolstering the power of the minority group(s) at the center. The most formal and extensive strategy for doing this is to construct consociational/power-sharing arrangements.[13] The logic of consociational democracy is to accept the presence of distinct national identities and groups within a society rather than seek assimilation or integration in a larger alternative identity. In other words, consociationalism seeks to build on multinational structures rather than to destroy or supersede them. From this perspective, it is fairly at odds with the "state national identity promotion" just discussed. The mechanisms of consociationalism involve the sharing of political/executive power between the groups and the use of collective vetoes on matters deemed to affect vital group interests. This means that consociational arrangements work better in binational societies. It also means that the majority group needs to accept *not* to behave as a majority, or has to be presented with certain incentives not to do so. In Belgium, for example, the demographically dominant Flemings have accepted to share political power with Francophones at the federal level, while Francophones do the same in the region of Brussels-Capital where they are a majority.[14]

The most serious criticism of consociational arrangements is that they build up, consolidate, and politicize identities that are by nature fluid and malleable.[15] This argument is strong because it is based on the widely accepted idea that identities are constructed rather than primordial. However, transforming identities is a long-term process. Furthermore, the degree of fluidity and malleability varies depending on the level of institutionalization of the distinct national identity. All things considered, consociational democracy is a reasonable solution when nationalist conflicts become too serious. For example, the 1998 Good Friday Agreement in Northern Ireland that set up consociational arrangements to manage the conflict between Unionists (Loyalists) and Nationalists (Republicans) was a more adequate response than any attempt to deconstruct or supersede the respective identities.[16]

The empowerment of minority groups at the center can be operationalized through means other than consociationalism. For example, a certain number of seats can be reserved for representatives from minority groups in the central parliament. This is done in New Zealand for the Maori people. A cabinet position may be designated to articulate the preferences of a group as well as to relate and adopt public policy to it. This was the central accommodation practice in the United Kingdom for Scotland and Wales before devolution. Moreover, informal practices can develop within political parties to give, when they are in power, prominent cabinet positions to members of the minority group. Parties can also make sure that their own internal structure is well populated by representatives of the minority group and that the position of leader is at least occasionally occupied by someone from the minority group. An extreme example of this is Canada, where the prime minister has represented a Quebec riding for approximately thirty-four out of the last thirty-eight years and where the politically dominant party, the Liberal Party of Canada, has featured a disproportionate number of Francophone Quebeckers in positions of influence. Canada presents other interesting means of securing power for Quebeckers within federal institutions: there exists an understanding that a certain number of Quebeckers need to be in the cabinet, that three out of nine Supreme Court judges will be from Quebec, and that the position of governor general (the head of state, purely symbolic) will be alternated between Anglophones and Francophones.

An alternative, or complementary, approach to empowerment at the center is territorial autonomy. From a formal perspective, this approach is most often operationalized through one of two models. The first type of model is a federation, where sovereignty is divided between levels of government and the division of power cannot be altered unilaterally because it is written into a constitution. In this context, territorial autonomy becomes a general governing principle and there exist multiple units with specified powers. Canada, Belgium, and Spain (albeit not formally) are the Western multinational states that fit this model. The second type of model is the granting of autonomy to one or selected territories. Here, autonomy is targeted rather than part of a larger framework and may not be the result of a formal division of sovereignty. Devolution in the United Kingdom, for example, provided autonomy to Scotland and Wales without stripping Westminster of its sovereignty. Countries with this form of territorial autonomy might fall short of being federations, but they are shaped by federal principles.[17]

Independently of the formal structures used to implement it, territorial autonomy as an approach for managing situations of multinationalism follows a logic whereby the decentralization of decision making reduces majority-minority conflict. It is therefore no coincidence that decentralized matters are almost always linked to the cultural differences that are central to the discourse of nationalist movements (for example, linguistic policy and education). The theory behind territorial autonomy makes the assumption that policy making in fields that involve a clear cultural dimension presents great potential for conflict in situations of multiethnicity or multinationalism. For example, one group might want to promote a language regime favoring its own tongue or an education curriculum presenting its own vision of the state or national history. Of course, federated units or autonomous territories are not often completely homogenous, and in units/territories where the statewide minority group is dominant, it often needs to coexist with communities from the state-wide majority group.[18] In this context, there is still potential for conflict, but it can be argued that a federal liberal democratic system offers modes of accommodation through minority-rights guarantees. There is also the fact that members of the state-wide majority group who are in a minority position within a federated unit/autonomous territory retain power and representation at the center. With this same logic, we could say that schemes of territorial autonomy are attractive not only because of the specific policy fields they decentralize but also because they provide minority groups with political power. Territorial autonomy also produces a new forum for political representation,[19] through a regional legislature, as well as a distinct political class for the minority group. These are important references for a group in search of cultural and political security.

Territorial autonomy as an approach to managing multinationalism represents a framework for territorial governance that can lead to many different actualizations. For example, the extent of the powers assumed by the regional government is variable and subject to negotiations. If cultural and linguistic issues are often decentralized, disentangling responsibility for social policy, for example, is usually more complex. Financial transfers and arrangements are also something that typically need to be discussed and rediscussed, especially since central states often have the greatest revenues while regions typically administer expensive programs (for example, health care). In this context, center and region most often cannot live in isolation from one another and there needs to be some mechanisms for intergovernmental relations. These relations can be structured in a variety of ways. They can be driven by political parties, particularly if these have a unique organization across territorial levels (as in the case of the United Kingdom). They can take the form of central-regional executive meetings (like in Canada). In this last context, intergovernmental relations involve a particularly important potential for conflict. Federal and autonomy arrangements are unlikely to eliminate conflictual relations in multinational societies. In fact, some would say that they can increase conflict and even pave the way toward secession.[20] A more optimistic view is that these strategies may serve to "banalize" conflict by placing it within a complex system of territorial governance and that, if territorial structuring involves several units, the structure of the conflict can be shifting since potential alliances provide fluidity to the situation.

Finally, states in the context of multinationalism can also utilize "recognition" as a political strategy.[21] Nationalist movements cannot be compared to interest groups. Their leaders are not primarily in pursuit of material benefits for the group members, although this is often part of the equation. The central concerns of nationalist leaders are to secure for members of their group (including themselves) access to political power, and to obtain for their group the recognition that they form a nation. This last quest is mainly of symbolic nature, although it may have political implications. The status of nation is closely related to the right of self-determination. Although international law typically reserves secession as a form of self-determination for colonial and dictatorial contexts, the notion of self-determination is often too close for comfort for states. States may also opt against the recognition option because it goes against the national identity they are trying to project. In Canada, for example, state nationalism is erected on the basis of bilingualism and biculturalism, but not binationalism. The failure of constitutional accommodation with Quebec stems in large part from the difficulty that many leading Canadian politicians had, especially during the 1980s and 1990s, with the idea of constitutionally recognizing Quebec's "distinctiveness." By contrast, British politicians have routinely spoken about the "nations" of the United Kingdom. For example, even Margaret Thatcher stated that she would never hold the Scots in the United Kingdom against their will.[22] In keeping with British traditions, this recognition is not formally specified, but the British state allowing Scotland to keep separate societal institutions such as the church, and the education and legal system, albeit in the absence of political autonomy, is testament to this view of the United Kingdom as a "nation of nations." In Canada, despite the absence of a discourse of multinationalism, the federal government has also implicitly accepted the legitimacy of the secessionist option by participating in the two referendums (1980 and 1995).[23]

The Spanish State and Basque Nationalism

Historically, the Spanish state has used a variety of approaches to manage Basque nationalism and, before it, foralism. In premodern Spain, the fueros of the Basque provinces involved a bilateral relationship with the state, which meant that each of the provinces had a confederal-type link with Spain. In the nineteenth century, the slow and uneven process of integration through centralization begun by the Spanish state two centuries earlier reached the Basque provinces through an attempt on the part of the state to promote the idea of a liberal Jacobin Spanish nation. After this effort failed, the Spanish state experimented with approaches of territorial autonomy and recognition during the Second Republic. During the Franco regime, all of these approaches were abandoned in favor of the imposition, through repression, of a monocultural Spanish nation viewed not only as one and indivisible but also as sacred and eternal.

In the democratic era, the management of Basque nationalism by the Spanish state has involved a combination of various approaches. One option excluded, for at least two reasons, was integration through cultural assimilation. First, the Franco years had created a strong association between this type of practice and fascist regimes. Second, there was in the 1980s and 1990s an extensive diffusion and institutionalization of a human rights culture, of which minority rights were a particularly closely scrutinized component. In this context, the Spanish quest for acceptance as a "normal" liberal democracy and, more specifically, for membership in the then European Community, made cultural assimilation, even in a nonviolent form, an unattractive alternative.

A central element of the Spanish management of Basque nationalism in the democratic era has been the promotion of the Spanish nation and identity. This approach is typically not acknowledged by some Spanish politicians, who refuse to see themselves as nationalists of any kind.[24] This is primarily because of the negative connotations attached to the term "nationalist." Not only was this the term chosen by Franco during the Civil War and thereafter, but it is also, of course, the reference for Basques and Catalans who either articulate a different vision of Spain or want to leave it altogether. In this context, the Spanish project of a strong and united Spain, multicultural but not multinational, is typically viewed as postnational in nature.[25] This is best seen in the discursive practice of branding "constitutionalists" against "nationalists,"[26] which places Spanish politicians at a normative advantage that would be absent if the debate were between "Spanish nationalists" and "Basque (or Catalan) nationalists." Behind this discourse is the theoretical and philosophical foundation of constitutional patriotism. The Habermasian theory,[27] which celebrates the identification with, and loyalty to, constitutional frameworks of liberal rights, found a warm reception in Spain during the late 1990s partly because of a transformation in Spanish self-perception.[28] In the years following the democratic transition, the Spanish national identity and the idea of the Spanish nation were heavily marked by links with authoritarianism, Catholic traditionalism, militarism, and hyper-centralism. Moreover, the weight of Spain's history as a perceived failed state (at least from liberal democratic criteria) and an abnormality in Western Europe was still strong. In the last twenty years, several developments worked to change the image of Spain, most notably the successful democratization, the membership in the European Union (1986), and robust economic growth. In this context, Spain came to be seen as a "normal" Western state: it was liberal and democratic, integrated in the process of European construction, and presented a well-functioning market economy. As a result, Spanish politicians, societal leaders, and intellectuals, both from the Left and the Right, renewed with Spanish nationalism.[29]

As we will now discuss, there is no doubt that Spanish parties, especially the PP starting in the 1990s, have sought to vigorously promote the Spanish national identity. But there are different conceptualizations of this identity. Spanish nationalism is a differentiated phenomenon, which ranges from Jacobin visions of the country, where the emphasis is on unity, cohesion, and centralism, to more multi-composite views highlighting plurality, diversity, and decentralism. One influential vision of Spain, especially popular on the Right, carries the implicit assumption of a nation characterized and united by its Castilian roots and language. For example, PP politicians can still be heard recounting the development of the Spanish nation using references to the Reconquista against the Moors.[30] From this perspective, Spain's history thereafter is about the expansion of Castile and the making of the Spanish state, empire, and nation. Spain's national holiday, El Día de la Hispanidad, commemorates the "discovery" of the Americas. Tellingly, the Aznar governments, together with the Real Academia de la Historia, were very much concerned with the way autonomous communities taught history in school, fearing a "distortion" of the Spanish historical developmental process.[31] From this vision of Spanish nationalism, multilingualism is considered to threaten one of the bonds holding Spain together. This vision is strongly present in Spain's language regime. Different languages are spoken in Spain, but only Castilian is an official language of the Spanish state, which all Spaniards have the duty to know. Catalan, Basque, and Galician are official only within the corresponding autonomous community. Despite the multilingual nature of society, Castilian (which, outside Spain, has come to be referred to simply as "Spanish") seems to assume a status as the only legitimate language when it comes to expressing the Spanish national identity.[32] For example, there is no formal status for minority languages in the Spanish parliament, while in the Senate the use of these languages is allowed only one day per year. The Spanish national identity card is written only in Castilian. The Aznar government, which vigorously promoted the Spanish identity through linguistic references, pushed autonomous communities to emphasize a strong education curriculum in the Castilian language and literature.[33]

For this Spanish nationalism suspicious of diversity and decentralization, nationalist movements such as the Basque movement are reactionary and even totalitarian since, somewhat ironically, they are viewed as imposing a single culture on residents of their communities.[34] From this perspective, there is a "demonization" of substate nationalism that features prominently in the construction process of the "new" Spanish identity. The Basque Country has been a prime reference in this discourse of Spanish nationalism. Moderate Basque nationalism is viewed as endangering the unity of the country with its insistence on self-determination and the demand to modify the constitutional framework and the Basque Statute of Autonomy. The most intense denunciation of substate nationalism, however, came in the form of the discourse about terrorism and ETA. ETA was a central reference point against which Spain was defined for much of the democratic period. Through this reference, the Spanish state could be put in a positive light since it was depicted as a modern, liberal, and democratic entity struggling against violent illiberal terrorists seeking to destroy Spain and all the positive values it stood for. It is no coincidence that the PP's hard-line policy toward ETA was so successful among the Spanish population; it was presented as a basic good-versus-evil struggle featuring Spain and the enemies of Spain.[35]

Spanish nationalism also comes with a focus on the 1978 constitution. As opposed to the more culturalist articulation of the Spanish nation discussed above, the so-called constitutional patriotism provides, theoretically speaking, room for greater recognition of diversity. At the same time, the emphasis on universality and individual rights may also be used to resist such recognition. There is therefore considerable room for conceptualizing the Spanish nation in different ways while making the 1978 constitution its institutional and normative basis.

The terminology chosen is interesting, with patriotism being favored over nationalism. This is to meant to highlight that contemporary Spain is modern, open, democratic, and forward-looking. Therefore, the participants in this political project are "patriots" rather than "nationalists." The concept of constitutional patriotism seeks to project a "civic" nationalism (although, again, this last word is almost never used), where the Spanish nation is united by an allegiance to values (rule of law, liberal rights and freedoms, etc.) described as universal. In the Spanish political context, this constitutional patriotism has taken the form of a staunch defense of the 1978 constitution, which is seen as the foundation for all Spanish successes since the death of Franco. For the PP, this focus on the constitution involves a strong preference for the institutional status quo. Under the prime ministership of José María Aznar, the constitution acquired a near sacrosanct status, and any suggestion by Basque (or Catalan) nationalists that the document should be amended to modify the status of their autonomous community was met with stern refusals. From the PP's perspective, this was an offensive by narrow-minded particularist forces against the universalist bedrock of Spanish democracy. On the Left, the PSOE also considers the 1978 constitution a fundamental reference for the Spanish nation, although it sees the constitutional framework in a more dynamic fashion. The PSOE's view of Spain is more compatible with meaningful diversity than the PP's, as the 2006 reform of the Catalan Statute of Autonomy and its recognition of Cataluña as a nation demonstrates.

The PSOE under Zapatero has brought the "soft" constitutionalist vision of Spain closer than ever before in the democratic period to the conceptualization of Spain as a "nation of nations." This multinational conception of Spain is advocated by Basque, Catalan, and Galician nationalists, but admittedly remains marginal within Spanish nationalism. From the Spanish nationalist perspective, the main argument associated with this view is that being Spanish should be the result of a genuine political choice deriving from the principle of self-determination.[36] This approach to Spain is mostly present on the Left: it represents a (fairly small) segment of the Socialist party and is the formal doctrine of Izquierda Unida (IU).[37] Spain as a multinational polity is a much less popular concept on the Right. The only influential voice there is Miguel Herrero de Miñón, who appeals to Spain's foral tradition as a way to manage contemporary nationalist movements.[38]

Along with promoting attachment to Spain through various and changing national models, the democratic Spanish state adopted political and institutional approaches designed to manage rather than supersede the Basque (and other) national identities. These approaches are permeated by the tensions over the various existing visions of Spain.

The foundation approach was territorial autonomy, expressed through the Estado de las Autonomías and the corresponding system of autonomous communities. The constitution of 1978 establishing this model does not formally call Spain a federation, but its specification of a division of power between the state and the autonomous communities makes it a federal system. The rationale of decentralizing decision making, especially in potentially contentious policy fields involving linguistic and cultural considerations, was at the center of the autonomy statutes for the Basque Country and Cataluña. This being said, the Spanish arrangements fall short of other multinational federal systems such as Canada and Belgium when it comes to the extent of territorial autonomy. Spanish governments have been generally unenthusiastic about transferring the full extent of powers specified in the Basque Statute of Autonomy. Even in some areas where the Basque government is formally autonomous, this autonomy is often challenged in practice by central policies. The Autonomous Community of the Basque Country, however, enjoys a very extensive fiscal autonomy; this is rare in federal systems. We could also note that the amending process for the Spanish constitution gives the last word to the Spanish parliament.

In the case of the Basque Country, a particularly important point is that autonomy pertains to the legislative and executive branch, but not to the judiciary. The Spanish justice system is centralized, and judges working in the different autonomous communities are appointed by the Spanish government. As a consequence, the courts are not perceived by Basque nationalists as neutral; rather, they are viewed as the simple extension of the state.[39] This is a point of contention in the Basque Country because the problem of political violence politicized the judicial system. These centralized structures feed the perception that Basque nationalists may not always be treated fairly. In other words, the judiciary's lack of autonomy translates into a lack of legitimacy that serves to fuel nationalist mobilization. For example, court decisions to close the Basque-language daily *Egunkaria* and outlaw Batasuna were seen as having been dictated by the Aznar government and triggered important demonstrations. So did staunch refusals to relocate ETA prisoners in the Basque Country.

One approach that has not been used by the Spanish state in its attempt to manage substate nationalism is empowerment at the center. The new Spanish democracy was built on majoritarian principles. Consociationalism would have been difficult to practice for several reasons. First of all, it is unclear how many "groups" would have needed to be incorporated into a power-sharing arrangement. The Spanish situation is quite complex and fluid. In this context, constructing a consociational arrangement with the Basques, the Catalans, and the Galicians would have had the predictable consequence of triggering complaints for Andalusians, Valencians, and so on. Second, defining the exact contours of the majority group (probably Castilian) would have been a tricky proposition. In any case, this group (however defined) would in all likelihood have represented a clear majority of the population, which makes consent to power-sharing less likely. Third, compounding this demographic imbalance is the possibility that power-sharing arrangements might have lacked support in some of the regions involved. Certainly, the Basque Country is a very polarized society where Basque and Spanish nationalists coexist, the latter more supportive of majoritarian practices.

Of course, there are other ways to seek to empower minority groups within central institutions, such as having them well represented in statewide parties. This has happened to some degree in Spain with Catalan and Basque politicians having played important roles within both the PSOE and PP (Narcis Serra, Josep Borrell, Javier Rojo, Jaime Mayor Oreja, etc.). Of course, the position of politicians from the Basque Country or Cataluña in Spanish politics does not match that of Quebeckers in Canadian federal politics, but Canada can be considered an exceptional case. There is also the possibility of using institutional mechanisms. Spain currently does not have an upper house representing the voice of the autonomous communities, but proposals for reforming the Senate into a Bundesrat-type chamber have been discussed. Nationalist movements have been able to exert political power in Madrid, but that has been as a result of minority government situations. In this context, empowerment at the center has been a matter of constraint rather than principle, although nationalist leaders by and large like the idea of bilateral relationships with Madrid.

A difficult question in democratic Spain has been recognition. As we have seen, Basque (and Catalan) nationalists insisted at the time of the transition that the new constitution needed to recognize their historical, political, and cultural distinctiveness. This was done through an acknowledgment of the existence of "historical nationalities" in Spain. This was a political compromise since the existence of these nationalities is situated within an indivisible Spanish nation. In the 1980s, the Spanish government's attempt at leveling the status and powers of autonomous communities was an early sign of a discomfort with the symbolic implications of this differentiation. It is in the context of the preference of Spanish governments for symmetry that substate nationalist parties engaged in cooperation efforts, such as the Barcelona declaration, aimed at promoting the restructuring of Spain along multinational lines.

In the case of the Basque Country, claims for recognition have centered on the question of self-determination. Basque nationalists want the Spanish state to recognize such a right for the Basques: this was the major obstacle preventing moderate nationalists from endorsing the 1978 constitution, and it is still an underlying source for the conflict in the Basque Country. For Basque nationalists, the Basque provinces never relinquished their sovereignty to the Spanish state; they only agreed to a foral arrangement with Spanish monarchs. As a result, the contemporary Autonomous Community of the Basque Country is said to hold not only a natural but a historically grounded right to decide its political future independently of Spain. In this context, recognition could have institutional consequences: these might not include secession, although this option is not rejected out of hand.

The potential consequence of formally recognizing a Basque right to self-determination explains in part what deters the Spanish state. Secession would be an unacceptable outcome, at least for the Spanish political class if not for a majority of the population. This is not so much because the secession of the Basque Country would mean losing an economically vibrant part of the Spain or even for the potentially dangerous precedent it would set for Cataluña and other autonomous communities. More important is the fact that there exists a very firm idea of the Spanish nation, and that the amputation of this nation would be intolerable. This view of Spain is also at the heart of the refusal by centralist Spanish politicians to characterize Spain as multinational. This is hardly surprising considering that the democratic Spanish state has sought to vigorously project the Spanish national identity as an approach to tackle substate nationalism.[40]

The Ibarretxe Plan: A New Foralism?

The previous discussion has explained how the democratic Spanish state has managed Basque nationalism. For their part, moderate Basque nationalists have always been vague and ambiguous about their preferred political and institutional arrangements; this ambiguity is reflected in the use of the concept of self-determination, which can lead to a wide range of political and institutional avenues. This being said, Basque nationalists have set aside certain options. They opposed, from the first days of the transition, a centralized unitary model. Moreover, they have come to view the current Statute of Autonomy as the protector of a status quo considered too centralist. Interestingly, Basque nationalists also reject the creation of a formal federation as an adequate framework for securing greater autonomy within Spain. Even a concept such as asymmetrical federalism, which holds considerable currency in Cataluña, is not popular among Basque nationalists. This is primarily because Basque governments prefer to deal directly with the Spanish state rather than get involved in various alliances with other substate nationalists they consider too "soft." From this perspective, there seems to be a strong path-dependency effect stemming from the fueros since bilateralism is always favored over any type of multilateral frameworks. This general approach is consistent with a recent initiative of Basque lehendakari Ibarretxe This so-called Ibarretxe plan suggests parameters for restructuring the relationship with Spain.[41]

The Ibarretxe plan proposes a type of confederal arrangement between the Basque Country and Spain, which is reminiscent of the traditional foral system. The basic ontology for this plan involves two parties, Spain and the Autonomous Community of the Basque Country. From a philosophical perspective, the Basque nation, through its government of the Autonomous Community, is free to make decisions about its own political future. It is supposed that the Spanish government has similar legitimacy to make these type of decisions on behalf of all of Spain. The Ibarretxe plan suggests that the two parties enter into a free association. This idea of a bilateral dialogue between the Basque nation and the Spanish state is really the central message put forward by this plan, which is presented as open to debate and negotiation.[42] Of course, this dialogue needs to be understood, from the Basque nationalist perspective, as a way to create more political autonomy for the Basque Country. At the same time, and still from the moderate Basque nationalist perspective, the Ibarretxe plan seems to exclude outright independence as exemplified by its central concept of "co-sovereignty."[43] Not only has lehendakari Ibarretxe stated several times that his proposal does not represent independence, but he has also sought to differentiate the "statute of free association" (his proposal) from the presumably more radical option of a "free and associated state."[44] The Ibarretxe plan is definitely a nationalist project, and its chances of engaging any Spanish government remains slim despite its stated focus on dialogue and mutual consent as well as on the idea of negotiability. Certainly, ETA's announcement of a permanent cease-fire in 2006 will help muster a dialogue that can include some elements of the plan, although support from radical nationalism is far from assured despite the mention in the document of some forms of association with Navarre and cooperation with the French Basque Country *if* all the populations involved should so choose (articles 6 and 7).

The Ibarretxe plan features specific details concerning the division of power between the Basque government and the Spanish state. The key features of the proposed arrangement are the following: the creation of a Basque judicial system; exclusive powers of the Basque government over virtually all major policy sectors such as culture, education, social policy and social security, transportation, and the environment and natural resources (articles 46 to 54); direct representation in European Union institutions (article 65) and the right to have representation abroad and to sign international agreements in fields that are domestically in the jurisdiction of the Basque government (article 67); the establishment of a Basque Country–Spain Bilateral Commission (Comisión Bilateral Euskadi-Estado), as a forum of coordination and information exchange (article 15), a special tribunal (Tribunal de Conflictos Euskadi-Estado) to arbitrate conflicts (article 16); and mechanisms for amendments preventing unilateral change from Madrid (article 17).

Overall, the content of the Ibarretxe proposal suggests a confederal, or perhaps a foral, framework. The commission and tribunal are common institutions, staffed by an equal number of representatives and judges from both sides, where the Basque government and the Spanish state stand as equals. The amending formula also embodies the confederal nature of the structure. The decentralization of the judicial system (which is of central importance for the Basque government, considering that such decisions as the outlawing of Batasuna have come through the courts) is something commonly found in federations, but the complete decentralization of so many key powers is not. Typically, federations work a lot with shared competencies, which means that the central government typically remains active in policy areas that directly affect the daily life of citizens (for example, social policy). The Ibarretxe proposal would leave the Spanish state with power only over matters such as citizenship, defense, and "high" diplomacy. The formal decentralization of substantial components of international relations is also rare in federations (Belgium being an exception). The presence of the king in the proposed arrangement (he would formally appoint the lehendakari) gives another foral taste to the Ibarretxe plan.

This plan also comes with a blueprint for a process toward ratification (article 17). The first step is to gain approval of the Basque parliament. The second step is to conclude an agreement, within six months, with the Spanish state. The third step consists of a referendum in the Basque Country on that agreement. Interestingly, the PNV government has said that it would be looking for a bigger majority than 50 percent + 1; in fact, it would want this proposal to have greater legitimacy than the 1978 Spanish constitution.[45] It is also seeking a majority in all three provinces. If no agreement can be reached with the Spanish state, the Basque government could, with the support of the parliament, organize a referendum nevertheless with the hope that a clear popular endorsement would force the Spanish government to negotiate.

When lehendakari Ibarretxe initially presented his plan in 2003, this process faced some major obstacles. The first obstacle was ETA. The Basque government said that the process for negotiating on the basis of the Ibarretxe plan, and then seeking ratification for whatever would come out of it, could only unfold in the absence of violence. Without a permanent cease-fire, or better still a permanent renunciation of political violence, any progress on the Ibarretxe proposal was unlikely. The 2006 announcement by ETA of a permanent cease-fire provides at least a theoretical possibility that the Ibarretxe plan, or something derived from or akin to it, can be put to a referendum.

The second obstacle for the Ibarretxe plan to serve as a blueprint for institutional change is the lack of consensus about it among Basque politicians and within Basque society. From the beginning, the plan received the formal support of the PNV (of course) as well as that of EA and the Basque Left, Izquierda Unida (IU). This would have, in almost any Basque parliament, left it short of an overall majority, but in the fall of 2004 some radical nationalist representatives unexpectedly opted to support the plan Ibarretxe, providing it with majority endorsement. Radical nationalists had initially criticized the plan for falling short of independence and not corresponding to their (maximalist) conceptualization of the Basque nation, which includes Navarre and the French Basque Country. They argued for the need of an independent state before forging any type of association with Spain. Why did some radical nationalist representatives support the plan? In all likelihood, bearing the responsibility for the demise of this ambitious proposal in the Basque parliament would have created a serious political handicap. Moreover, in allowing the proposal to be supported by the parliament, radical nationalists placed the burden back on lehendakari Ibarretxe and his plans for a referendum. This being said, the

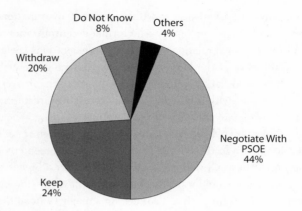

Fig. 6.1. View of Ibarretxe's Proposal in Light of New Circumstances.
(Euskobarómetro November 2005)

overall support of radical nationalism toward the Ibarretxe plan, or anything fall-ing short of independence, is still uncertain. ETA announced a permanent cease-fire because its methods were no longer tolerated and because a successful policing strategy limited its capacity to carry out attacks.[46] However, support for its politi-cal option has not gone away. There still exists a "radical nationalist community,"[47] reproduced through extensive social networks featuring bars and organizations[48] as well as through carefully organized demonstrations against the Spanish state.[49]

The PP and the Socialists also oppose the Ibarretxe proposal. In the PP's case, such opposition is entirely predictable and derives from the strong conviction that the existing constitutional and institutional arrangement has brought prosperity and stability to Spain and therefore should under no circumstance be altered. Also, the PP is the party presenting the strongest and least compromising version of Spanish nationalism. The condemnation of the Ibarretxe proposal by the Basque Socialists is more revealing of the deep polarization between Basque nationalists and non-Basque nationalist Socialist politicians. Intellectuals as well as antiterror-ism civil society organizations such as ¡Basta Ya! have denounced the Ibarretxe as an antidemocratic, anticonstitutional, divisive, and ethnically driven national-ist machination.[50] This being said, a majority of Basques questioned about the Ibarretxe plan in light of the "new circumstances" represented by the election in Madrid of a Socialist government in 2004 thought that it should be either main-tained or negotiated with the PSOE (fig. 6.1).

Surveys show that Basque society is evenly divided on the Ibarretxe plan, with 50 percent of Basques supporting it and a like percentage opposing it.[51] The key element for determining the preferences of respondents is the cleavage between Basque nationalist and non-Basque nationalist: Basques approving the plan are supporters of the PNV, EA, and, interestingly, Batasuna. That same cleavage also determines if respondents think the plan serves "harmonious coexistence" (*convivienca*) or confrontation. As for the provinces, the survey shows that the Ibarretxe proposal would be soundly defeated in Araba, find even support in Bizkaia, and get a slim majority in Gipuzkoa. Another survey conducted at the request of the Basque government, and published by it, shows more interesting answers for the Basque nationalist side, but to different questions.[52] Questions about general principles such as the right to self-determination for the Basques received support from over 80 percent of respondents. Questions on specific policy issues (for example, closer relationship with Navarre and the French Basque Country and more power for the Basque government over selected policy areas) also found strong support (over 60 percent). The most controversial question was the recognition of a double Basque and Spanish nationality, with only 52 percent of respondents supporting this idea.

The idea of holding a referendum on the Ibarretxe proposal raises some questions. First, one can wonder about the context in which such a vote would be held. Even in the absence of violence and with majority support in the Basque parliament, a referendum in the Basque Country (at least if it were held in the short term) would surely be a very tense affair. The Spanish government, along with all the other actors opposing the Ibarretxe plan, would probably not recognize the legality or even legitimacy of the referendum. What type of legitimacy would the final result have, especially if there is a high level of abstention? The biggest problem, however, would be the (un)willingness of losers to accept a loss and, perhaps more to the point, coming to an agreement about the exact percentage at which the proposal is considered sufficiently endorsed. Lehendakari Ibarretxe has said that he would want greater support for his plan than there was for the constitution, which would mean in the 60 percent range. By all accounts, and considering survey data just cited, this result is very unlikely in the short term. What happens if support for the Ibarretxe plan fails to reach this threshold range? Radical nationalists are unlikely to accept this result as definitive, and a frustrated ETA could, especially if it has not disbanded, resume violence. This is especially likely if the result in favor of the Ibarretxe proposal is in the 50 percent range. And where would that leave moderate Basque nationalists? Certainly in a major existential crisis.

What if a referendum organized by the Basque government produced a strong majority in favor of the Ibarretxe plan? The previous PP government reacted swiftly to the plan by pushing legislation specifying that anybody holding a referendum on an anticonstitutional proposal could be jailed and asking the courts to prevent it from being debated in the Basque parliament. The PSOE largely supported these initiatives, although electoral pressures and incentives partly explain this support. Now in government, the Socialists have said they are open to dialogue, but this probably does not involve recognizing as legitimate and legal a referendum on what they view as secession. If this were the case, even an ideal result from the Basque nationalist perspective (strong endorsement of the proposal with high level of voter turnout in a peaceful context) could end in a stalemate. Many Spanish politicians do not accept that Spain can be divided, and considering the centrality of the 1978 constitution to their vision of the country, they are not likely to accept processes and outcomes of change that fall outside the current constitutional framework. Such a situation would be very conflictual: it could trigger more political violence from ETA and possibly strong opposition from Madrid. In short, it is the deep split within Basque society about the Ibarretxe plan that would make a referendum an unpredictable and potentially explosive affair. Few societies can go through this type of exercise in such conditions of polarization and come out the better.[53]

Above and beyond the specific contents of the Ibarretxe plan, as well as the nuts and bolts of the process outlined by the Basque government for its possible implementation, the plan should be understood as a political tool. It is a way for the PNV to take control of "mega" politics in the Basque Country, set the political agenda, and hope to facilitate political and institutional change. So far, this has been quite successful; indeed, the existence of this proposal most likely facilitated ETA's decision to announce a permanent cease-fire. In the end, however, the proposal is more likely to serve as a launching pad for the renegotiation of the Basque Statute of Autonomy, as has happened in Cataluña, than to result in the creation of a Comunidad Libre Asociada de Euskadi. As a Basque nationalist initiative supported almost exclusively by Basque nationalists, it lacks the legitimacy to be an actual template for new political and institutional arrangements, and it is doubtful that a referendum could do anything about that.[54]

The Management of Substate Nationalism: What Is Spain to Do?

It is immensely difficult to make generalizations about the management of nationalist movements, for at least two reasons. First, each case comes with its own political configuration, historical legacy, as well as social, economic, and cultural context. This means that the wholesale transfer of the "Belgian model" to Canada or of the "Canadian framework" to Spain is not a realistic option. In other words, there are no ready-made "solutions," nor are there universal templates for managing substate nationalism. Second, timing is important in devising management approaches, which means that certain avenues that seem adequate at a certain moment in time might not be appropriate at another. This is a point often lost in discussions on nationalist conflict regulation that tend to speak of potential strategies for particular cases independently of time, that is, as if their potential effectiveness remained constant despite the unfolding of sociopolitical processes. These caveats should not, however, preclude attempts at learning from cases.

What should be made of the case of Spain and its management of Basque nationalism? It would be easy to say that it has been a failure, considering not only the presence of political violence until very recently but also the level of political (and social) polarization between Basque nationalists and non-Basque nationalists. This type of judgement would, however, be overly critical. It is unclear how the Spanish state could have put an end to ETA violence before the most recent cease-fire since there seemed to be no willingness on the part of ETA to compromise on its objective of creating an independent Basque state made up of the seven Basque provinces, an unrealistic project supported by only a small minority of Basques. For example, the 1998 cease-fire was conditional upon the realization of ETA's traditional agenda. This being said, the Spanish state may have missed opportunities to provide ETA with alternative scenarios to violence. Despite the many contacts Spanish governments had with the terrorist organization, they seemed not to have seriously considered solving the problem of violence through political negotiations until the election in 2004 of Zapatero's Socialist party.

From the perspective of analyzing the consequences of various management strategies, it is revealing that the level of tension and polarization in the Basque Country was highest between 1999 and 2004. The end of the 1998 cease-fire followed by mutual accusations by moderate and radical Basque nationalists accounts for some of this tension, but so do the policies and the discourse of the Aznar government. The idea of cracking down on all forms of nationalism for their suspected links with violence proved counterproductive because it fed into the discourse of radical nationalists. Whatever benefits were gained from the logistical problems these actions might have created for ETA (for example, diminished access to financial resources), they were overshadowed by political losses, as Basques became more likely to accept the nationalist portrayal of the Spanish state as rigid, intolerant, and even fascist. The tendency of the Aznar government to demonize all forms of substate nationalism and to promote a Castilian-flavored Spanish nation with a continual stress on unity contributed to a hardening of Basque nationalism. The Ibarretxe plan was largely a product of these antagonistic moves.

So what is Spain to do? I would suggest three realistic avenues that could contribute to lessening the conflict with the Basque Country and take advantage of the cease-fire. First, there needs to be a new discourse that recognizes substate nationalism as a legitimate political option. This would involve speaking about Spain in a way that makes room for communities that have different, or at least, split allegiances. Such a change has already happened to a degree with the election of the PSOE in 2004. At this level, a more ambitious project would be to articulate Spain along the lines of multinationalism. This would be a radical departure from past practice, but the reform of the Catalan Statute of Autonomy, with its recognition of nationhood, represents a step in this direction. Second, the Spanish government could finish transferring the competencies in dispute included in the Basque

Statute of Autonomy. The reluctance to do this stems in part from the notion that centralization equals strength and unity, and from the fear that transferring power to Basque nationalists will only served to strengthen them. However, there is an alternate logic that suggests that accommodation of these types of modest demands can foster increased loyalty to the state. This is the logic of federalism, which in Spain has not been fully accepted. Those powers whose transfer is still pending seem for the most part innocuous (for example, scientific research and technological development), yet they are a major irritant in the relationship between the Basque Country and the Spanish state. Finally, turning the Spanish Senate into a true and effective house of territorial representation could create among the Basques a sense that they can have greater say in the policies of Spanish government.

The idea behind these suggestions is to soften the stance of Basque nationalism and possibly undermine its support. Setting out the objective of eradicating a nationalist movement is likely to lead to counterproductive policies. For states such as Spain, the time to think about destroying substate nationalism is long gone.

Contemporary Spanish Nationalism: The Nineteenth-Century Liberal Influence

It is not uncommon for Basque nationalists to make rhetorical links between contemporary Spanish politicians, especially from the PP, and the Francoist era. Radical Basque nationalists have sometimes argued that the Spanish state was fascist, for example when Batasuna was outlawed. This is, of course, false; Spain is a liberal democratic state, which, unlike most of its Western counterparts, had to deal with an illiberal movement. More to the point, a strong argument can be made that the political and philosophical inspiration for the current governance of Spain is not to be found in the military-authoritarian nationalism of General Franco, but rather in variants of nineteenth-century Spanish nationalism. This was not so much the case in the first fifteen years or so of the democratic period, because centralization and explicit references to the Spanish nation smacked of fascism and, therefore, were somewhat discredited ideas in Spanish politics. In more recent years, with democracy firmly entrenched in Spain, the idea of Spanishness has been more easily spoken, although the notion of "Spanish nationalism" is rejected by most Spanish political elites and many intellectuals.[55]

As discussed earlier in the chapter, there are many different versions of Spanish nationalism today, but a common conceptual and discursive reference among Spanish politicians is the notion of "constitutional patriotism" borrowed from Jürgen Habermas. In the Spanish context, constitutional patriotism closely resembles the nineteenth-century liberal project insofar as it seeks to establish the Spanish nation on the basis of universalist principles and individual rights. For its proponents, constitutional patriotism in Spain involves a civic national community, not to be confused with Spanish nationalism deemed to be a phenomenon of the past.[56] As could be expected, this thinking is influential with the PSOE as well as left-wing intellectuals[57] since it seemingly appeals to "neutral," and therefore progressive, parameters of societal cohesion rather than ethnic or cultural ones.

Constitutional patriotism is also in fashion with the PP, whose main discursive reference when it comes to the idea of the Spanish nation is the 1978 constitution. Contrary to the authoritarian state, the democratic Spanish state as conceptualized by the PP should not seek to erase, or even to deny, Spain's cultural diversity, but rather to transcend it by fostering loyalty to the constitution and its liberal principles. From this perspective, the Spanish nation is presented as civic and constitutional, and, from a moral standpoint, is viewed as standing above all other claims of nationhood within Spain.[58] In its program for the 2000 general election, the PP devoted one out of five chapters to "The Constitutional Spain, Guarantor of a Common Project."[59] The PP attributes all the successes of democratic Spain to the stabilizing effects of the constitution: "If Spain was able to make, in recent years, a fantastic jump forward, building an open society, confident in its own strengths, with a significant presence in all areas of the international community and ready to tackle future challenges, those results—made possible by the collective efforts of all Spaniards in the last quarter of a century— under governments and administrations of various political colors were possible because of the 1978 constitution."[60]

For the PP, the constitution is the focal point of the Spanish nation. It underpins all that is good about Spain: democracy, economic success, European vocation, and so on. In this context, it is hardly surprising that any proposal from Basque or Catalan nationalists to alter the constitution, or even hint at political change that could represent a departure from the constitution, was badly received when PP formed the Spanish government. These claims (greater decentralization, federalism, multinationalism, associated statuses) were viewed as threatening the cohesion and "common project" of the Spanish nation. For the PP, the constitution provides the room necessary for the expression of the distinctiveness of the historical nationalities and regions.

The view that a liberal-constitutional model of nationhood best represents Spain's approach to national integration, and its best hope for maintaining the unity of the Spanish nation, has recently been expressed by Basque scholar Edurne Uriarte.[61] Uriarte argues that Spain's "ethnic" or "peripheral" nationalisms conditioned the political agenda for the better part of the early democratic period (something which she deplores), but that increasingly the discourse of the Spanish nation is being spoken. Uriarte borrows explicitly from Habermas in advocating a model of constitutional patriotism, with its focus on the constitution, the rule of law, and the welfare state to foster loyalty to Spain.[62] She nevertheless suggests that such a model risks being an empty shell if it is not explicitly related to Spanishness, or the idea of Spain. She still views Spanish "patriotism" as weakly articulated in the Spanish political discourse: the Left, she argues, has accepted the argument of substate nationalists that any reference to the Spanish nation is a provocation. Only the democratic Right, she suggests, is willing to explicitly frame a model of constitutional patriotism underpinned by liberal principles in terms of a united Spanish political community.

The fear expressed by Uriarte that fostering loyalty to a set of institutions without a substantive "idea" of Spain could produce a weak sense of nationhood is, somewhat paradoxically, shared among enthusiasts of constitutional patriotism. On the Right, the promotion of a civic community often comes with a historical narrative emphasizing the continued existence of a common political project stemming from the Christian struggles against the Muslims.[63] On the Left, there is a more multicultural view of Spain, but even in this view the Spanish nation still precedes the 1978 constitution, which only provides it with a liberal-constitutional framework.[64] In fact, the crucial role of the 1978 constitution for both the Right and the Left is the promotion of the Spanish nation, just as it was hoped the Cádiz constitution of the early nineteenth century would generate nation-building in Spain. As such, the notion that there is no such thing as Spanish nationalism does not hold, and using the concept of patriotism is only a politically motivated choice of terms. Spanish nationalism (or rather nationalisms) does exist, and its manifestations should be foremost in accounting for the development of substate nationalist movements in Spain.

Chapter Seven

Basque Nationalism in Comparative Perspective

There are relatively few studies putting Basque nationalism in a comparative perspective with other nationalist movements in the West such the Quebecois, the Flemish, and the Scottish.[1] The literature on Basque nationalism tends to highlight its exceptionalism.[2] Basque nationalism is, after all, one of the only nationalist movements in the West to have had a violent stream in recent years.[3] It could therefore be assumed that the Basque Country is not a "comparable case" when it comes to studying nationalism in Western societies. This assumption is wrong. Basque nationalism is not fundamentally deviant. Its structure and dynamics are not unlike those of other nationalist movements in Europe and North America. There is, therefore, no methodological or theoretical reason for treating Basque nationalism as an exceptional case. Political violence needs to be considered as an important analytical variable for understanding nationalism in the Basque Country; it does not, however, invalidate comparisons with movements that were always nonviolent. Perhaps there is also a normative issue that explains the relative absence of comparisons with substate nationalism in Canada, Belgium, and the United Kingdom. Scholars in Quebec, Flanders, and Scotland, many of whom are not unsympathetic toward the aspirations of their nationalist movements, might have found it bothersome to compare Quebecois, Flemish, or Scottish nationalism with Basque nationalism. From this normative and political perspective, Cataluña, with its moderate and nonviolent nationalism, is a more attractive case than the Basque Country, which tends to be associated with the violence of ETA.

This chapter places Basque nationalism in a comparative perspective with four other nationalist movements in Western societies that are profoundly shaping politics in their respective countries: Quebecois, Flemish, Scottish, and Catalan.[4] Quebecois nationalism presents a continuous challenge to the structures of the Canadian federation, specifically through the Parti Québécois(PQ) that favors independence. Flemish nationalism has transformed the Belgian unitary state into a decentralized federation, and many Flemish parties envision further constitutional change, perhaps leading to a confederal model. Scottish nationalism, for its part, has forced a renegotiation of the terms of Scotland's involvement in the United

Kingdom. The outcome of this renegotiation was devolution, or home rule, which has provided a new institutional dimension to Scottish nationalism that could eventually complicate Scotland's relationship with Westminster. Catalan nationalism has spearheaded, along with Basque nationalism, the federalization of Spain. Catalan nationalism is a major issue in Spanish politics. Not only is Cataluña's population one-fifth of Spain's, but it is less polarized than the Basque Country and its position toward Spain more moderate.[5]

The primary objective of this chapter is to demystify Basque nationalism by showing that its internal workings and many of its features are very similar to those of other nationalist movements in the West. Of course, this does not mean that Basque nationalism is perfectly similar to Catalan, Scottish, Flemish, or Quebecois nationalism. Most importantly, the impact of political violence on the structure of Basque nationalism since the transition cannot be underestimated. Basque nationalism also features a definition of the nation that involves issues of international borders not typically encountered in other cases.[6] This chapter will bring these differences to light within a comparative framework without exaggerating the supposed exceptionalism of Basque nationalism.

Substate Nationalism as a Modern Phenomenon

The resurgence or emergence of substate nationalism in Western societies during the 1960s and 1970s was a surprising development. Strongly influenced by modernist narratives predicting the homogenization of national societies, both scholars and political practitioners saw Western states as being on a unidirectional track toward the full "integration" of their "peripheries" through the process of state centralization. This view was best embodied by the so-called diffusionist theory, which held that political centers would necessarily project their culture on peripheral territories in order to facilitate the functioning of an advanced industrialized society.[7] These processes of assimilation correspond to what James C. Scott calls "high modernist" projects insofar as they are designed to render societies more intelligible through standardization, or "normalization."[8]

Diffusionist theory represented an ahistorical perspective on the politics of Western states because it did not allow for alternate outcomes to the complete homogenization of their societies. Diffusionists wrongly assumed that integration and cohesion could only come by the way of homogenization and centralization. They ignored, for example, the federalist perspective on integration with its ideas of self-rule and shared-rule, and considered backward and even dangerous forms of political integration other than the centralized nation-state. Diffusionists also made the misleading assumption that political, economic, cultural, and intellectual centers coincided. This was never the case in Spain, where the political center of

Madrid coexisted with the economic centers of Barcelona and, starting in the late nineteenth century, of Bilbao. The idea of cultural and intellectual centers is obviously problematic since the relative value of culture and ideas can hardly be measured. In this context, numerical strength and political power seems to determine what is the dominant culture and intellectual tradition. This clearly happened in Spain, where the state has pushed for the diffusion of the Castilian language and culture throughout the country in several different eras: in the context of the nineteenth-century project of liberal constitutionalism; during the Franco dictatorship; and, to some, extent, in the democratic era as well. Political power at the service of culture promotion was also a feature of Belgian politics from the creation of the country in 1830 to the mid-nineteenth century as Francophone elites sought to assimilate Dutch-speaking Flemings into a Francophone Belgian nation.[9]

Diffusion theory suggested that processes of national integration through centralization, bureaucratization, and homogenization were synonymous with modernity, progress, and enlightenment. Correspondingly, it assumed that substate nationalism, or "peripheral resistance," was backward, parochial, and caught in the past. Diffusion theory per se might have been proven wrong by empirical evidence, but these normative underpinnings still shape the thinking of many scholars. Eric Hobsbawm, for example, has described nationalist movements as "reactions of weakness and fear" and "attempts to erect barricades to keep at bay the forces of the modern world."[10] This type of view has been countered by many scholars who have argued that nationalist movements in the West are fundamentally modern and in tune with current processes of globalization and continental integration.[11]

This argument for the modern character of nationalist movements in Western societies is the most convincing. These movements overwhelmingly espouse liberal democracy and the capitalist market economy. They seek to make use of new technologies to connect their citizens to the outside world and generally encourage cultural exchanges. Nationalist movements in Europe typically look favorably at political integration, while Quebecois nationalism has supported free trade with the United States since the 1980s and is vying for extended integration in the Americas.[12] Moreover, some of these substate nationalisms are on the political left and advocate progressive social policies of redistribution. For example, the Scottish Executive has implemented a publicly funded program of long-term care for the elderly and eliminated up-front university tuition fees, two policy innovations so far not taken up by Westminster.[13] These programs are offered to residents of Scotland independently of cultural background or origins. The Scottish Executive has also adopted innovative approaches to combat social exclusion and homelessness.[14] These progressive measures certainly do not reflect conservative or reactionary positions attributed to substate nationalism by such scholars as Hobsbawm. Similarly, the Quebec government, especially when led by the secessionist PQ, has developed many progressive social policies over the last ten years or so, most notably subsidized ($7 per day) day care and universal drug insurance programs. Quebec governments have also frozen university tuition fees, keeping them the lowest in North America. Flemish nationalism is more on the center-right when it comes to redistribution and fiscal issues, but it has nonetheless enacted a long-term care for the elderly program similar to Scotland's.[15] The PNV-led Basque government is not social democratic like Scottish Labour or the Scottish National Party (SNP), or like the PQ, but it still speaks of extending the depth and reaches of social protection.[16]

The claim that substate nationalism is backward and reactionary is also contradicted by the position of some nationalist parties on social and "moral" issues. For example, the Quebec government makes use of the "civil union" legal category to extend rights to homosexual couples. Homosexual rights have proven a more difficult subject in Scotland, as shown by the controversy over the abolition of section 28, a legal clause prohibiting schools from teaching pupils about homosexuality as if it were a "pretended family relationship."[17] Overall, however, there is little difference between the position of substate nationalists and state policy on these types of issues. The partial exception is Flanders, whose radical nationalist and far right-wing party Vlaams Belang (VB), formerly Vlaams Blok, adopts strongly conservative, intolerant attitudes.[18]

This is not to deny that, in some instances, substate nationalism emerged as a reaction against the economic and political forces of modernization. Basque nationalism was originally grounded in traditionalist and anticapitalist ideologies. This was hardly surprising since the Basque nationalist movement was articulated by Sabino Arana and other like-minded conservatives who were threatened by the centralizing Spanish state. As a result, early Basque nationalism was a reactionary movement grounded in religious fundamentalism. This is by no means exceptional. French-Canadian nationalism was also led by traditionalists until the 1960s. It was strongly shaped by the Catholic church, and its best known voice, abbé Lionel Groulx, was a figure not unlike Sabino Arana.[19] The raison d'être of French Canadian nationalism, much like that of early Basque nationalism, was the defense of a traditional economy, social structure, and way of life. As a result, the interests of French Canadians were conceptualized as involving a struggle to preserve the province's autonomy. During the post–World War II welfare state expansion, this meant opposing the development of new federally run social programs on Quebec's territory. Of course, it is an exaggeration to say that Quebec was a "traditional society" until the 1960s:[20] urbanization and industrialization had been under way since the beginning of the century.[21] However, the Catholic Church's influence was strong, as it, for example, ran key social services such as education and health care. The province's conservative politicians, most importantly Maurice Duplessis and the Union Nationale party, supported this social structure by struggling against "socialist forces" such as trade unions. The Flemish Movement also had a strong conservative slant in the nineteenth and early twentieth centuries. In a story somewhat similar to Basque nationalism, Flemish nationalism was spearheaded by a lower bourgeoisie who saw the construction of a centralized unitary Belgian state functioning almost exclusively in French as a threat to its socioeconomic status.[22] The Flemish Movement was strongly penetrated by religion.[23] Territorially grounded in a largely rural and relatively underdeveloped area, early Flemish nationalism was critical of capitalism and secular ideas. As such, it became closely associated with the Christian Democratic family.

The important point to be made here is that these nationalist movements have changed. Contemporary Basque nationalism has shed the traditionalist overtones of its origins. Basque nationalists are not looking to re-create (or create) a Basque Country modeled on preindustrial times. Religion is still central to Basque nationalism, but it does not define its political program. Of course, references to the early days of Basque nationalism are still present in Basque society—for example, through the use of Sabino Arana's name for public places—but contemporary moderate nationalists distance themselves from the ideology of this period. The same is true in Quebec, where most nationalists are uneasy with many dimensions of the older French-Canadian nationalism despite public references to its main figurehead.[24] The case of Quebec represents a spectacular transformation in the form taken by nationalism, as the new Quebecois nationalist movement was inspired by objectives of economic development and representative democracy.[25] For example, the PQ of the 1970s was driven by the ideal of social democracy in its sovereignty-association project, describing Francophones in terms of a social class in need of emancipation. Overall, the 1960s Quiet Revolution transformed Quebec from religious and conservative to secular and progressive. The development of the Flemish Movement is, in this respect, more similar to Basque nationalism since Flemish nationalism has evolved from its conservative roots while remaining associated with Christian Democracy.

Of course, Basque nationalism uses references and symbols drawn from the past—for example, the fueros and Sabino Arana. It formulates narratives tracing the evolution, or rather the survival, of a people with mysterious origins that has had to deal with a intruding and sometimes belligerent state. In turn, these narratives foster images and self-perceptions of the Basque as a special people. This type of interpretation, reinterpretation, or simply reinvention of history or tradition is not peculiar to the Basque case; it can be found in all nationalist movements. Catalan nationalism is fed by its own references to a glorious past when Cataluña was a Mediterranean power.[26] Scottish nationalism comes with a collective memory about pre-Union Scotland and the struggles against England featuring William Wallace and others.[27] Flemish nationalism recounts ancient and epic battles such as the 1302 Battle of the Golden Spurs against French armies. Quebecois nationalism, at least in its most nostalgic form, is still marked by the Conquest of 1789.[28] This type of storytelling is an inherent part of nationalism, since it serves to produce and reproduce the nation and to stimulate mobilization when needed. The necessary references to the past always introduce a tension within nationalism since they speak primarily to a core ethnic community and recall, or actualize, ancient grievances. It is important to recognize that states also use history to erect symbols and construct narratives to build up their own national identity and rally the support of their citizens. The existence of these processes should not be confused with a yearning for a return to the past. In other words, historical narratives do not invalidate the idea that substate nationalism in the West operates through political movements that are essentially modern.

From a comparative perspective, Basque nationalism stands out insofar as it features a radical stream espousing neo-Marxist revolutionary ideas and, at least until the 2006 announcement by ETA of a permanent cease-fire, rejecting an existing liberal-democratic framework. This made radical Basque nationalism incongruent with most assumptions about how a modern nationalist movement should be, and it remains to be seen to what extent ETA's most recent cease-fire will change that. Moderate Basque nationalism, however, qualifies as a modern movement insofar as it is committed to liberal-democratic principles, supports a free market economy, and generally welcomes globalization. From this angle, it is similar to other nationalist movements that have evolved from traditionalist roots involving not only anticapitalist, antisecular, and antiliberal ideologies, but also racist and xenophobic sentiments. We now turn to these issues.

Ethnic and Civic Aspects of Nationalism

The distinction between civic and ethnic (or cultural) nationalism is a classic one in nationalism studies.[29] At the most basic level, it involves a normative dichotomy between "good" and "bad" nationalism.[30] The good type of nationalism, civic nationalism, is when the nation is defined as a territorial community of laws where membership is conceptualized as an exercise of free will. This nationalism, often associated with France and the French Revolution, is deemed to be liberal, inclusive, progressive, modern, forward looking, and to foster social cohesion. The bad type of nationalism, ethnic nationalism, is when the nation is defined as an organic community where membership is conditional on specific objective criteria such as descent, language, or religion. This nationalism, typically associated with Germany and romantic thinkers such as Herder and Fichte, is said to be illiberal, exclusive, backward, and to lead to conflict and violence.

Two assumptions typically accompany the ethnic-civic distinction. The first assumption is the association of civic nationalism with the developed West and of ethnic nationalism with Eastern Europe and the developing world.[31] This assumption is revealing of the value-laden nature of the ethnic-civic polarity since the good nationalism is linked, almost by definition, to Western societies. Non-Western societies, for their part, seem to be left with the bad nationalism. These connections do not stand up to a close empirical analysis. Using data from a survey where respondents in Western and Eastern European countries were asked to rank various (civic and ethnic) criteria for membership in the nation, Stephen Shulman finds no clear West-East dichotomy.[32] For example, a question on the importance of being born in a country for national membership triggered more positive responses in Spain than in Hungary or Slovakia.[33] The second assumption is that the civic type is the nationalism of states while the ethnic type is substate nationalism. This is also a highly dubious proposition. On the one hand, states often make use of cultural markers to define their identity, sometimes reaching illiberal discourses or policies.[34] On the other hand, some substate nationalisms (for example, Scotland) appear to share few traits of ethnic nationalism.

Considering these criticisms, some authors have suggested dropping the labels of ethnic and civic nationalism completely.[35] However, the distinction can be saved if we accept that nationalisms are neither wholly ethnic nor wholly civic, but always combine the two components.[36] In other words, civic and ethnic nationalisms should be seen as two ends of a continuum rather than discrete categories. Why save these concepts at all? The notion that nationalisms combine ethnic and civic aspects in varying degrees has heuristic value because it tells us something important about nationalist movements. For example, this type of characterization is useful for understanding how nationalist movements structure society and what type of relationship they have with groups other than the one they claim to represent.

Early Basque nationalism was strongly ethnic since it defined the Basque nation in terms of descent and ancestry, thereby erecting firm boundaries between Basques and Spaniards. Basque "blood" and Basque names were the crucial markers of national identity, although the Basque nation was also presented as being more profoundly Catholic and as having stronger moral values. This created strict mechanisms of exclusion toward, for example, migrants from elsewhere in Spain who came to work in the Basque provinces at the end of the nineteenth century. Some scholars have suggested that the degree of ethnic character of a nationalist movement is a function of the sociopolitical dynamic where the elites who articulated it found themselves.[37] From this perspective, threatened or marginalized elites were more likely to build stark and impermeable barriers between their group and others.[38] This hypothesis finds supportive evidence not only in the case of Basque nationalism, but also in the cases of Flanders and Quebec. Early Flemish nationalism, articulated by a Flemish lower middle class and a clergy threatened with marginalization by the *francisation* of Belgium, focused on language (and religious devotion) as the line of demarcation for the Flemish nation. French-Canadian nationalism, projected by a similar type of elite, used a combination of religious (Catholic/Protestant) and linguistic (French/English) markers to define the nations of reference. Both Flemish and French-Canadian nationalism were strongly ethnic during the nineteenth and early twentieth centuries, exhibiting racist and antisemitic tendencies. They consolidated in opposition to a community (Francophone in Belgium and Anglophone in Canada) that held political power at the state level, occupied a prominent socioeconomic position regionally (in Flanders and Quebec), and was deemed to be incompatible in values and spirit. In contrast, the elites spearheading Catalan nationalism in the late nineteenth century, a bourgeoisie not without influence on the Spanish state and in a comfortable position within Cataluña, made only soft use of language as a marker and never insisted on descent as a condition for belonging. Scottish nationalism, for its part, was not built on any "hard" cultural makers and therefore stayed free of ethnic nationalism.

Just as nationalist movements characterized by religious fundamentalism in the late nineteenth century shed the overbearing influence of religion one hundred years later, ethnic nationalism also decreased in intensity. This being said, there has been much historical continuity in the character of the five Western nationalist movements featured in this discussion. Scottish and Catalan nationalism are the most civic. For Scottish nationalism, being civic, at least when it comes to promoting independence from the United Kingdom, is made easier by the lack of linguistic or religious demarcation with England. In the case of Cataluña, the fact that a majority of inhabitants have command of both official languages, combined with a political emphasis on autonomy rather than on independence, helps makes nationalism fairly open. In Quebec, there is greater tension between linguistic considerations and a purely territorial conception of the nation, especially in periods of intense nationalist mobilization such as during referendums on secessions.[39] Flemish nationalism remains the most ethnic of these movements, as it is still guided firmly by language. For example, the Dutch speakers of the Brussels-Capital region are included in the Flemish definition of the nation, while the Francophones on the periphery of Brussels are not, unless they assimilate into the Flemish culture.

In all these cases, as in most Western states, immigration and multiculturalism (as a societal reality) tend to prompt streaks of ethnic nationalism. This is most apparent in Flanders, where the far-right populist nationalist party Vlaams Belang holds strong anti-immigration views.[40] Vlaams Belang has experienced a steady rise (mostly as Vlaams Blok) since its creation in 1979 and is now the second strongest party in Flanders. The racist and xenophobic aspects of the Vlaams Belang/Vlaams Blok program[41] attracted support from a far-right-friendly segment of the Flemish population (dating back to the sympathy shown by some Flemish Movement followers for Nazi Germany), as well as because of new social, economic, and cultural insecurity stemming from growing immigration.

Even in the absence of far-right or conservative ideologies, immigration typically presents dilemmas for nationalist movements, which are seeking to preserve not only a political but also a cultural community. As such, governments of "stateless nations" tend to develop strategies for the rapid and effective integration of immigrants. Quebec, for example, has developed programs to support the learning of French by new immigrants who must, in virtue of existing language legislation, send their children to French schools. Furthermore, the Quebec case shows that here is also a strategic consideration linked to the integration of immigrants into societies where there are strong nationalist movements. Newcomers to Canada who settle in Quebec tend to oppose the independence of the province. However, Quebec's low birth rate makes a severely restrictive immigration policy difficult at best. In response to this dilemma, the Quebec government, especially when led by the PQ, has developed two strategies. First, it chooses immigrants who are likely to "fit" better in Quebec society, that is, with knowledge of French. In this respect, it enjoys the unique position of a substate government having powers over immigration that allows it to select immigrants. Second, the Quebec government seeks to socialize the newcomer.

Where does Basque nationalism fall into this comparative discussion? It represents somewhat of an odd case. To be certain, the dogmatic stress on race, blood, and descent put forward by Sabino Arana is gone. Basque nationalists, for example, are as likely to have Spanish as Basque patronyms. So, what makes a Basque? It cannot be language, since fluency in Basque is not yet widespread, especially in urban centers where both formal and informal communication occurs in Spanish. This is really what differentiates Basque nationalism from Catalan, Flemish, and Quebecois nationalism. Similarly, what makes a Basque cannot be religion, since, apart from immigrant communities, Basques, like Spaniards, are solidly Catholic.[42] From this perspective, it is difficult to say that Basque nationalism is strongly ethnic since newcomers from elsewhere in Spain can integrate without much difficulty. Similarly, immigration from outside Spain is not viewed as posing a particular "threat" to Basque society or culture. In this respect, the Basque Country is more like Scotland than Flanders or Quebec. This does not mean, however, that the Basque Country is a unified society. In fact, Basque society is more badly divided than any of the others discussed here. We now turn toward the cleavages that are most significant in the Basque Country.

Divided Societies

The Basque Country stands out among cases of substate nationalism for its sharp political divisions. A first fault line is the cleavage between moderate and radical nationalism. The Basque Country is not alone in having political parties and popular followings for both autonomist and secessionist options. Cataluña is in similar position with Convergència i Unió (CIU) and Esquerra Republicana de Catalunya (ERC). In Flanders, the language-specific parties, most of which seek greater autonomy within Belgium, coexist with the far-right nationalist party Vlaams Belang (VB) that looks to create an independent Flanders. In Quebec, all three political parties represented in Parliament are nationalist: the Parti Québécois (PQ) supports independence; the Parti Libéral du Québec (PLQ) looks to increase Quebec's autonomy within the Canadian federation and obtain a recognition of the province's distinctiveness; and the Action Démocratique du Québec (ADQ) favors the erection of a "free state" within the Canadian federation. Scotland is a bit different insofar as the Scottish National Party (SNP) is the only major party presenting a resolutely nationalist platform and self-identifying as nationalist first and foremost,[43] although both Scottish Labour and Scottish Liberal Democrat took part in the drive for home rule. Moreover, there have been struggles within the SNP and the PQ (still going on in the latter case) between so-called radicals and moderates.

The peculiarity of the Basque case has been the deeply ambiguous relationship between moderates and radicals. This was in large part the result of political violence. Batasuna (and its predecessors) most often refused to unequivocally condemn ETA violence, which complicated its relationship with the PNV. Before the 2006 cease-fire, every new (failed) attempt at finding political solutions to the conflict soured this relationship between moderate and radical Basque nationalism. This was most clearly the case after the end of the 1998 ETA cease-fire, which triggered reciprocal denunciations and accusations. The PNV had an ambiguous attitude toward radical nationalism throughout the 1980s[44] and, to a lesser extent, in the 1990s until the end of the 1998 cease-fire. It typically denounced the violence of the Basque nationalist family's "lost sons," but attempted to explain or "contextualize" it by invoking the Spanish state's own repression. In sum, Basque nationalist parties have had an uneven, sometimes antagonistic relationship, but the moderate parties never kept Batasuna at arm's length the way, for example, traditional Flemish parties have done with the Vlaams Blok/Vlaams Belang.

A second fault line in the Basque Country is between Basque nationalists and non-Basque nationalists. At the most general level, this is a cleavage found in all the cases discussed in this chapter, although it is less perceptible in Flanders where there is often a (minimalist) consensus on issues relating to the ongoing process of decentralization. What makes the Basque Country stand out when it comes to nationalists and non-Basque nationalists is the particularly tense and adversarial relationship. On the one hand, Basque nationalists often show contempt toward non-nationalists, suggesting that they are "lesser Basques."[45] In fact, there is a strong tendency on the part of Basque nationalists to consider those loyal to Spain as traitors to the Basque Country.[46] On the other hand, non-Basque nationalists typically view Basque nationalism as seeking to impose hegemonic, illegal, and anticonstitutional projects.[47] Therefore, the confrontation between Basque nationalists and non-Basque nationalists is not a standard political rivalry because each side refuses to recognize the legitimacy of the other. On the Basque nationalist side, the result is, at the very least, the conceptualization of two different types of Basques or, from the more radical perspective, the construction of a dichotomy between real/good and false/bad Basques. This dynamic leads to an extreme polarization of Basque politics and, to a lesser degree, of society.[48]

The Basque case stands in sharp contrast to Quebec in this regard. Self-determination has been debated as much in Quebec as in the Basque Country. One could argue that the political debates in Quebec over the political future of the province were given a potentially more heated context since two referendums have been held on secession. Yet, there is an acknowledgment among Quebec politicians that both the "sovereignist" and "federalist" options are legitimate. The legitimacy of sovereignty as a political option has also been widely acknowledged by federal politicians, both Quebeckers and non-Quebeckers. For example, the federal government has participated in both referendums to defend the benefits of Canadian citizenship for Quebeckers. After the 1995 referendum, it formally recognized the legitimacy of the sovereignist option by setting general parameters for the recognition of a referendum outcome favorable to sovereignty, that is, a clear question and a clear result.[49] This contributes to explaining why there really is no such thing as a good and a bad Quebecker. This is certainly the case for Francophones, whose federalist option is always respected. Some sovereignist politicians have a little less patience, especially in tense moments such as referendums, for Anglophones as well as for those whose maternal language is neither French nor English because these groups overwhelmingly favor keeping Quebec in the Canadian federation.

This tolerance for division is also found in Scotland. There, the nationalist option is widely viewed as legitimate, an outcome that is helped by the fact that British politicians take a similar position. Scottish nationalists, for their part, acknowledge the legitimacy of unionism, although they do not agree with it. The scenario is similar in Cataluña, where the autonomist nationalism of the ciu coexists with the secessionist ERC as well as with non-Catalan nationalist positions without accusations of treachery. In Flanders, where there is a variety of political options ranging from the status quo to independence, there is also an implicit assumption that everybody is Flemish, that is, all Dutch speakers. This is notwithstanding the political isolation of the Vlaams Blok/Vlaams Belang by the other Flemish parties, because what is at issue there is its far-right stance on immigration rather than its support for an independent Flemish state.

Above and beyond this social and political polarization between Basque nationalists and non-Basque nationalists is the sociological reality of dual identities.

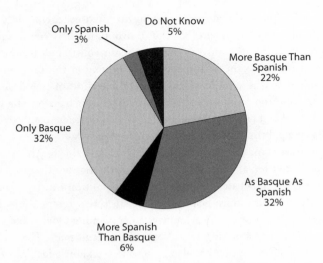

Fig. 7.1. National Identities of the Basques. (Euskobarómetro *November 2005)*

Conventional and academic wisdom has long held that individuals can cumulate multiple nonterritorial identities—for example, reconciling a working class with a youth identity. The possibility of combining territorial identities was for many decades obscured by the orthodoxy of the Jacobin nation-state, which could tolerate only one such identity. In the last decade or so, social scientists have demonstrated, using a wealth of survey data, that a majority of citizens in federal or regional-ized states typically combine state, substate, and, at least in the European context, suprastate identities.[50] This phenomenon of dual, or shared, identities is particularly strong in multinational states.[51] From this perspective, the scenario in the Basque Country is not exceptional. According to the November 2005 *Euskobarómetro*, 60 percent of Basques feel both Spanish and Basque, albeit to different degrees (fig. 7.1). Only 35 percent hold monolithic identities. Not surprisingly, Basques iden-tifying solely as Basque include 90 percent of Batasuna supporters, while those considering themselves only Spanish come primarily from the ranks of the PP and, to a lesser extent, the Socialists. This sociological data explains why mono-identity political projects, such as the PP's promotion of an indivisible Spanish nation and the radical Basque nationalist project of an independent Basque state, are likely to fail. In the long term, such projects can break the dual identity mold, but not always in intended or anticipated ways. The Franco dictatorship is a striking example of a project that sought to impose the state national identity but ended up bolstering substate ones instead. Let us turn toward to the various political and institutional arrangements sought by nationalist movements in the West.

Independence and Other Objectives

The PNV's program with respect to the political future of the Basque Country has been vague since the democratic transition. The PNV never put forward a clear position for independence and appeared at times comfortable working toward increased autonomy within the framework of the system of autonomous communities. At the most general level, the PNV's central struggle was recognition of the Basques' right to self-determination. In practical terms, this meant leaving open the options for political arrangements and institutional configurations. The Ibarretxe plan came therefore somewhat as a surprise since it specified how the PNV wished to actualize self-determination. As we saw, the reactions to the plan were mixed, with Spanish parties denouncing it as disguised independence and Batasuna condemning it for falling short of independence. These contradictory views of the plan stem from the fact that it does not squarely fall within the traditional conception of sovereignty shared by radical Basque nationalists and Spanish nationalists from the PP and, to a lesser extent, the PNV. The Ibarretxe plan's emphasis on co-sovereignty and free association in the context of an asymmetrical and multinational state presents a more nuanced view of sovereignty and how it might be "unpacked."[52]

There are strong strategic and political reasons for nationalist movements to not aim for pure independence. Most certainly, seeking autonomy rather than independence makes it easier to obtain popular support since outright secession is generally considered a radical and risky option. Forgoing pure independence also eliminates several potential problems and sources of conflict, such as the sorting out of populations and citizenship, the sharing of debt and assets, and so on. Hence, choosing a more complex and hybrid formula renders the likelihood of significant political change more probable. Also, nationalist leaders might think that opportunities for transborder, interregional, and multilevel connections afforded by globalization, particularly the process of continental integration in Europe, makes arrangements other than independence more adequate.

The type of program that falls in somewhat of a mysterious zone between straightforward independence and the more common accommodation approaches of federalism or autonomy is not peculiar to Basque nationalism. This has long been the approach of Quebec's PQ, especially as it prepared referendums. The PQ avoids talking about independence or secession, preferring instead the concept of sovereignty. This is purely a rhetorical devise designed to give a progressive twist to its option rather than to have it appear as a breakup. When it puts the question of Quebec's future to a referendum, the PQ also uses the more nuanced concepts of "sovereignty association" (1980) and "sovereignty partnership" (1995). There is a clear strategic reason for using these concepts, since the percentage of Quebeckers supporting outright independence has always fallen well short of 50 percent. In addition, it is possible that some PQ leaders genuinely believe that retaining some form of link with Canada makes most sense in the current global context. The exact nature of these links has always been ill defined. At a minimum, they involve an economic union. At a maximum, they include some common political institutions somehow inspired by the European Union.[53] Quebec's second-most nationalist party, the small Action Démocratique du Québec (ADQ), recently came out with a proposal for making Quebec an autonomous state within Canada. Such a status would involve, according to the ADQ, the elaboration of a Quebec constitution as well as a massive transfer of powers to the Quebec government that could collect all taxes on its territory while compensating Ottawa for the services provided by the federal government.[54]

In Flanders, there is also a nationalist program adopting a position falling somewhere between pure independence and the status quo of decentralized and asymmetrical federalism. The Flemish Christian-Democrats (Christen-Democratisch en Vlaams, CD&V) and Liberals (Vlaamse Liberalen en Democraten, VLD) both see the future of Belgium in terms of a confederation. The confederal model remains ill defined, but seems to rest on the idea of placing virtually every policy field in the control of the regions and communities. In Flanders, the idea of confederation is largely derived from the "problem" of Brussels as an overwhelmingly French-speaking city in "historical" Flemish territory. Flemish parties do not want to abandon Brussels, yet they are not prepared to have Flemish institutions assume authority over several hundred thousands of Francophones who would reject such a notion. The CD&V and VLD prefer some type of shared rule, as exists now, or an "externalized" status such as the "European district." From a theoretical perspective, the confederal model the Flemish Christian Democrats and Liberals seem to conceptualize would feature two mostly sovereign communities linked to Brussels.

A focus of nationalist claims for decentralization in Western states is social policy.[55] This is the case for Quebec, where governments have sought the decentralization of many social programs since the 1960s. They have been successful in many instances (hospital insurance, social assistance, vocational training, and, more recently, parental leave), but in others (for example, unemployment insurance) the federal government has resisted. For Quebec governments, the ability to craft and implement social policy means the opportunity to connect with Quebeckers in meaningful ways by providing such crucial service as health care. Symbolism is also important insofar as seeking the decentralization of social policy is perfectly coherent with the central claim of the Quebec government that the province should have a special status within Canada (or, for the PQ, be independent) because it bears the unique responsibility of overseeing a Francophone majority.

In Belgium, Flemish intellectuals and academics have produced, since the early

1980s, studies showing that Social Security features implicit transfers from wealthier Flanders to poorer Wallonia.[56] These studies have been central to the Flemish project of further decentralizing Belgian federalism. In early 1996, the Christian Democratic-led Flemish government released a document signaling its intention to launch a new round of state reform.[57] This document, while defending interregional solidarity in principle, spoke of the need to end unjustified transfers and to allow each region/community to fashion its social policy according to its preferences and culture.[58] In 1997, the committee on state reform of Flanders' parliament backed up the creation of a Flemish health care and family policy; representatives of all Flemish parties voted in favor, except for those of Agalev (Flemish green party) who abstained.[59] In 1999, the Flemish parliament made a strong statement for more substantial institutional change in Belgium by adopting five resolutions.[60] One of these resolutions, supported by a strong majority of Flemish parliamentarians (Christian Democrats, Liberals, and Volksunie), suggested that health care and family allowances be federalized while Brussels residents would be able to choose which regime they belong to.[61] The arguments brought forward in favor of the federalization revolved around the idea of homogenous competencies, overconsumption of health care in Wallonia, and cultural differences. Since the end of the 1990s, there has been strong backing for a partial federalization of Social Security among Flemish political parties and within Flemish political institutions.

A similar nationalist logic of seeking to decentralize social policy to make the national community congruent with the community of "social redistribution" was at the center of the Scottish drive toward devolution in the late 1980s and the 1990. Indeed, a key argument for devolution was that a Scottish parliament could enact social policies more in tune with the left-leaning preferences of Scots and the specific needs of Scotland. There is some evidence that this argument about developing more suitable social policy for Scotland resonated strongly with voters. For example, in a 1996 poll, 80 percent of Scots agreed (and 12 percent disagreed) with the statement: "Money for Scotland's public services such as schools and hospitals would be spent more wisely if the decisions about it were made by the Scottish Parliament."[62] Policy divergence has materialized to an extent, with the Scottish executive developing, for example, a long-term care program for the elderly not duplicated in Westminster

The Basque case is interesting in this comparative perspective because there has been no *special* attention given to social policy as a target for decentralization.[63] Of course, ETA violence has been a central political focus since the democratic transition of the 1970s and 1980s, which means that an illusive "peace plan" as well as issues such as the fate of political prisoners and reform/decentralization of the judiciary were key concerns for the Basque government. In addition, the almost complete fiscal autonomy enjoyed by the Autonomous Community of the Basque Country limits the potential for grievances over territorial redistribution. Perhaps

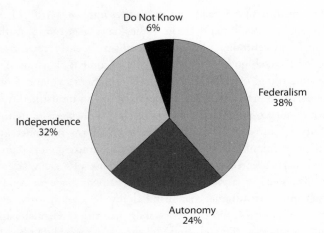

*Fig. 7.2. Preferences for Alternative State Forms. (*Euskobarómetro *November 2005)*

the fact that Basque politics is dominated by a center-right Christian-Democratic party, the Partido Nacionalista Vasco (PNV), does not favor a connection between territorial identity and social policy, although Christian Democratic parties greatly contributed to welfare development after World War II.

The existence of nationalist political projects that fall short of pure independence while going beyond traditional means of accommodation, such as federalism or consociationalism in Quebec and Flanders, gives some perspective to the Ibarretxe plan. Of course, it is important to highlight that nationalist movements in the West also have streams that seek secession: the ERC in Cataluña, the Vlaams Blok/Vlaams Belang in Belgium, and the SNP in Scotland. The SNP, for example, published in 2005 a consultation paper that formally outlines the party's vision of independence, including constitutional arrangements in an independent Scotland and modalities of transition.[64]

At the same time, some parties in these regions also favor the status quo, or a more limited form of change: the Liberals in Quebec, Socialist and Greens in Flanders, and, of course, the Socialists and PP in both Cataluña and the Basque Country. This diversity of preferences also exists in the population at large. In the Basque Country, surveys asking respondents to choose between various political options reveal a definite lack of consensus. Autonomy (defined as the status quo), independence, and federalism (presumably but probably erroneously conceived as something between autonomy and independence) obtain, respectively, 24 percent, 32 percent, and 38 percent support (fig. 7.2). This heterogeneity of political preferences on the territorial organization of the state makes political change really difficult. Not only does it undermine the legitimacy of any particular option, but it places great focus on legal, constitutional, and practical matters that are typically less important when a substantial majority agrees on a specific course for change.

Conclusion: On the Effects of Globalization

In an era when most aspects of politics cannot be analyzed in isolation from the various processes that make up globalization,[65] substate nationalism is certainly no exception. Globalization is not a single process, but rather a series of processes[66] unfolding in different yet interrelated realms: cultural, technological, economic, and political-institutional. The notion that these processes shape substate nationalism is especially convincing if we consider, as is the case in this book, that nationalism is heavily conditioned by the state. Globalization, while not meaning the end of the state, has involved a change in its modes of action. It has, among other things, transformed the state's relationship with territory and community.[67] As a consequence, the dynamic of identity construction and reproduction inherent to a nationalist movement as well as its patterns of territorial mobilization is likely to be shaped by globalization.

The exact effect of globalization on nationalism is still a matter of debate.[68] On the one hand, the argument has been made that processes linked to integration and interdependence are likely to reduce the significance of cultural and national boundaries and perhaps even create cosmopolitan mentalities. On the other hand, it has also been argued that intensified contacts between groups combined with a weakening in the power of the state will serve to exacerbate nationalist sentiments. The first argument was popular when the literature on globalization emerged in the late 1980s and early 1990s, but the second one seems to now be holding greater currency. The reality is, in all likelihood, more complex and ambiguous in the sense that globalization can affect nationalism in many different and sometimes contradictory ways. Not only are different processes of globalization likely to each pull in different way when it comes to political community, but one specific process may at once involve dynamics that spur and discourage nationalism. In addition, the connection between the processes of globalization and substate nationalism is both time and case specific. Different nationalist movements are touched in different ways by globalization, and the impact of global processes may change depending on the evolving domestic context. The next few paragraphs provide some ideas on how globalization is affecting substate nationalism in the Western world.

A first process of globalization features the development of new communication technologies. This process is part of a broader understanding of globalization as the "compression of time and space."[69] At the most general level, this image of spatial and temporal compression suggests the idea of global interdependence, whereby what happens in one part of the globe has consequences elsewhere. From this perspective, global interdependence is not primarily about communications but rather about the transformation of local or national problems into global ones. Environmental issues and economic crises are good examples of this transformation. The compression of time and space also invokes the notion of global interconnectedness, which is best exemplified by the Internet. The Internet offers opportunities of instant communication, information gathering, and political organization. For nationalist movements, this means easier access to the strategies and experiences of their counterparts. The PNV, for example, has looked closely at the Quebec experience and sought advice from Quebecois academics for the preparation of the Ibarretxe proposal. This is certainly easier in the contemporary era of information and rapid communication technologies. So is the nurturing and fostering of close relations with the Basques of France and the diaspora of the Americas, which is central to the Basque identity broadly conceived. The new communication technologies have also facilitated mobilization insofar as information, arguments, and speeches are readily available online. In addition, the Internet provides an infrastructure for coordination and organization. Of course, this is a double-edged sword. In the Basque Country, for example, both the radical nationalists associated with the National Liberation Movement as well as the mostly non-Basque nationalist Peace Movement have taken advantage of the opportunities afforded by the development of communication and information technologies.

A second process of globalization relates to culture. There are two broad components to this process. The first is the global projection of the English language and of American popular culture. A decade or so ago, it seemed that English was becoming the lingua franca and the diffusion of American culture, backed by the economic strength of the United States and facilitated by new communication technologies, would work to marginalize cultural differences, or at least their political significance. It is entirely possible that there is such a force at work. Some authors have used this type of argument to suggest that the new EU member states from Central and Eastern Europe have in fact much in common with the older members from Western Europe.[70] However, there has been a reaction against the perceived homogenizing effects of globalization, just as there has been a reaction against its neoliberal economic character. Nationalist movements such as the Basque one can find new legitimacy for the pursuit of autonomy or independence insofar as they can argue the need for political and institutional tools to protect and promote a cultural community. Another component of the cultural process of globalization is the diffusion of liberal democratic norms.[71] In addition to such things as procedural democracy (elections), an important element of these norms is the notion of rights. Among the many rights that are deemed to be included in the broader liberal democratic norms are minority rights. In Europe, there is a multilayered rights regime stemming from the European Union, the Council of Europe, and the Organization for Security and Cooperation in Europe.[72] The development of this rights regime has involved the construction of a rights culture, which has put nationalist movements on stronger normative footing. These movements can no longer, or at least less easily, be depicted as troublemakers threatening the stability of states and of the overall liberal order. Of course, the rights culture seriously undermines any illiberal nationalist movement. Such is the case for ETA, whose previous legitimization attempts through revolutionary ideologies no longer hold any currency. It is revealing, and indeed striking, that the discourse of human rights is so prevalent in the Basque Country. This is unusual in liberal democracies, and it shows the normative power of a political discourse centered on rights.

A third process of globalization is economic. This is the process often associated with overwhelming effects. Economic globalization, whose centerpiece is the liberalization of international trade, can be argued to bring people closer together by favoring transnational exchanges and contacts. Underpinning the unifying notion behind economic globalization is also a cultural argument, since globalization is said to spread a commitment to liberalism and the market. From this perspective, everybody is likely to share basic principles and values over and above cultural distinctiveness. This may be true, but only partially since there are different understandings of the relationship between societies and the market. Alternate understandings to the neoliberal one have triggered a resistance to globalization that has often taken specific cultural overtones.[73] From this perspective, economic globalization can spur nationalist movements because nationalism involves making statements about cultural, social, and/or political distinctiveness. The case for economic globalization strengthening substate nationalism can also be made by focusing on its effect on the state and its own nationalism. Free trade has destroyed the national economy, which had represented a component of the nationalism of states. In addition, pressures on the state's fiscal policies stemming from neoliberal norms and rules as well as global economic competition have reduced its ability to maintain the cohesion of its national community. Deficit elimination, reduction, and control are constraining the available resources of the state. The policies, often redistributive in nature, that contribute to maintaining citizens' loyalty in multinational societies are not as "automatic" as they were during the heyday of Keynesianism. In addition, the continental economic integration aspect of globalization in Europe and North America offers some measure of discursive protection for nationalist movements with secessionist agendas, since they can argue that independence would not mean isolation or threaten the economic well-being of their community.

A fourth process of globalization is peculiar to Europe: political integration. The European Union influences nationalist movements in different ways. From a discursive perspective, the EU can be presented as being either antithetical to, or coherent with, substate nationalism. The antithetical argument, defended by states, suggests that the logic of nationalism goes against the logic of integration.[74] The coherence position, promoted by substate nationalists, holds that the process of European integration puts a shadow on the prominence of the state and favors instead a system of multilevel governance where regions and self-declared stateless nations could assume agency. The corresponding discourse of a "Europe of regions," or "Europe with the regions" was very popular in the 1990s.[75] At a more practical level, this discourse and the potential agency of regions and self-declared stateless nations in the European framework seemed to be backed up by institutional creations such as the Committee of Regions (COR) and political schemes such as transborder cooperation. More recently, nationalist movements, albeit still solidly behind European integration in principle, have expressed disappointment over treatment of their governments and communities. The COR has been abandoned as a significant political forum for nationalist leaders because this body includes municipal authorities and regions with no or weak legislative power and only has consultative power. The European constitution was considered disappointing because it consecrated a two-level game between the European Union and the state.[76] This document, although it failed to be ratified by all member states, changed the positive view that nationalist movements have had of Europe. These movements tried to shape the constitution, but failed. Basque politicians, for example, proposed that regions be allowed to become associated partners of the EU.[77] As a result, it was difficult for substate nationalists to take a definitive position on the European constitution. On the one hand, they were loath to support a document that ignores their communities. On the other hand, formally rejecting the document would have gone against their pro-European discourse and stance. Of course, European integration, whichever forms it takes and whether it progresses or stalls, is here to stay and, in all likelihood, so is the ambivalence of its effect on substate nationalism. On the one hand, it is true that the EU provides a context that may encourage nationalist movements to favor options other than independence because state sovereignty is clearly not what it used to be. On the other hand, the EU can also cause conflicts between nationalist movements and states. For example, these movements claim for the institutions they control direct participation in EU institutions, a notion typically opposed by states.

On the whole, there is no clear pattern of effect of globalization on nationalist movements. Each of its processes presents potential for stimulating substate nationalism as well as accommodation by the state. This is hardly surprising considering the multifaceted nature of globalization and the multiple forms and dynamics nationalism can assume.

Conclusion

The study of nationalism is permeated by a handful of research questions. At the top of the list is the issue of its modernity: to what extent can the roots of nationalism be located in ancient, or at least premodern, times? This question, which used to be at the center of the debate between "primordialists" and "modernists," is now featured in discussions over the ethno-symbolist approach promoted by Anthony Smith.[1] These types of theoretical debates have framed the investigation of the relationship between nationalism and a variety of sociocultural and economic variables: language, religion, ethnicity, economic development, and also the state.[2] Another erstwhile concern has been to distinguish between different types of nationalism, an effort most often conducted through the concepts of ethnic and civic nationalism. Here, the exercise is more heuristic than theoretical since the idea is to better understand the Janus-faced nature of nationalism.[3] This last image underscores the commonly held view that while nationalism may sometimes represent a force for modernity,[4] progress, and social solidarity, it can also generate exclusion, repression, and violence. In this context, it is hardly surprising that scholarship on nationalism has also featured explicit normative considerations. Political theorists, for example, have evaluated the legitimacy of nationalist claims, from autonomy to secession.[5]

All these research avenues are perfectly legitimate and contribute to the scholarly understanding of nationalism and its manifestation in contemporary politics. What is noticeable, however, is that nationalism has rarely been studied using general theories of comparative politics. This book was a modest attempt at placing nationalism within the framework of historical institutionalism. Such efforts should not involve dismissing the literature specific to nationalism, but rather complementing it by bringing in a variety of insights from the more general scholarship of comparative politics. This scholarship can come from research fields closely connected to nationalism (for example, on citizenship and political community)[6] or from research on basic objects of inquiry in political science (state, civil society) that produce theories pertinent for understanding nationalism.

My own inclination would be to look at the literature on the state. If one accepts that the construction of the state played an important role in the development of nations (a notion no longer accepted solely by modernists), it is likely that research on the state can provide us with insight on nationalism. For example, Hendrik

Spruyt's work explaining the mechanism of the rise of the western European state at the expense of rival forms of political organizations provides a perspective on the contingencies of nation-building.[7] James C. Scott links the state with "high modernist projects" of standardization and "normalization" that speak (in a Gellner-type way) to the construction of nations.[8] The construction of the modern state has been linked to questions relating to resource extraction and conscription that are also crucial for understanding the nation.[9] Timothy Mitchell's work on the colonial state provides insight into nationalism in the developing world.[10] The literature on state-society relations may also prove fertile for thinking about nationalism. For example, distinctions between strong and weak states and civil societies, developed by, among others, Joel Migdal,[11] suggest the possibility of correlations between substate nationalism and particular combinations of state and society types. Also, Peter Evans's notion of the embedded autonomy of the state offers a conceptual framework particularly pertinent for understanding national cohesion.[12] Indeed, states, or regional institutions, are often linked to civil society structures and organizations in a way that creates mutual constraints and limits deviations from nationalist politics.

Another avenue for opening up research on nationalism is to draw from the work of international relations specialists who, especially over the last fifteen years or so, have studied cases of ethnic civil wars and genocide.[13] Although the terminology used by specialists in international relations and comparative politics is different (typically ethnic conflict and nationalism, respectively), these two groups of scholars are really examining the same phenomenon: the mobilization of groups on the basis of identity. It is surprising, considering this common focus, that there exists two fairly distinct literatures not often brought together. For comparative politics scholars of nationalism, the international relations literature on ethnic conflict represents, so to speak, a world to discover. Of course, some aspects of this literature are less useful for studying nationalist movements in stable democracies. The focus on violence, for example, has led to the application of security dilemma perspectives,[14] which only make sense in situations of state breakdown or collapse. This being said, there has been significant research conducted by international relations specialists working on ethnic conflict that can be easily transferred to comparativists studying nationalist movements in stable states. From an institutional perspective, there is a considerable literature on the relationship between specific arrangements and ethnic conflict: federalism, autonomy, electoral systems, and so on.[15] From a behavior-centered perspective, many have made the case for the usefulness of rational choice in explaining ethnic mobilization and violence.[16] Rationalist explanations are problematic for these phenomena because they are unable to incorporate the powerful role played by identity and emotions. In other words, perhaps rational choice is better suited for explaining some political outcomes (for example, coalition government formation or voting in parliament) than others (nationalism and ethnic conflict). The inadequacy of rational choice for tackling identity-related phenomenon has led Roger Petersen to propose an emotions-based approach to ethnic violence, which serves to link the structural context with microlevel outcomes.[17] Petersen's approach theorizes this linkage. The approach is interesting because it proposes a way to confront the arational dimensions of nationalism and ethnic violence by theorizing such emotions as fear, hatred, and resentment, but without resorting to less sophisticated primordialist arguments.

In sum, the danger with becoming a prisoner of the literature on nationalism is getting caught in somewhat sterile debates such as the question of the modern or ancient nature of nations. Theoretical insights useful for explaining mechanisms of identity construction and territorial mobilization may be more plentiful in broader and/or related literatures.

Notes

INTRODUCTION. SUBSTATE NATIONALISM, HISTORICAL INSTITUTIONALISM, AND THE BASQUE COUNTRY

1. One could argue that holding a referendum on a self-determination issue in Spain was already illegal in virtue of the 1978 constitution. However, these types of questions are primarily political as opposed to legal. In Canada, for example, the constitution (as it should be expected) contains no procedure on how to dismantle the federation, but the federal government has nevertheless accepted, in principle, that this could happen by campaigning in two Quebec referendums on independence. The PP legislation was a political assertion of the unity and indivisibility of Spain.

2. Some would suggest that non-Basque nationalists are de facto Spanish nationalists. This may be true in the sense that non-Basque nationalists all support the Spanish political project. However, such terminology would obscure that there are many types of Spanish nationalists just like there are different types of Basque nationalists. Throughout the book, I will therefore refer to "Basque nationalists" and "non-Basque nationalists" unless I specifically discuss Spanish nationalism and its variants.

3. The same message was sent to the Catalan government.

4. See, for example, Rodney Gallop, *A Book of the Basques* (Reno: University of Nevada Press, 1970); Teresa del Valle, *Korrika: Basque Ritual for Ethnic Identity* (Reno: University of Nevada Press, 1993); Mark Kurlansky, *A Basque History of the World* (New York: Penguin Books, 2001).

5. See, for example, William A. Douglass, Carmelo Urza, Linda White, and Joseba Zulaika, eds., *The Basque Diaspora/La diáspora vasca* (Reno, NV: Center for Basque Studies, 2000); Gloria Totoricagüena, *Identity, Culture, and Politics in the Basque Diaspora* (Reno: University of Nevada Press, 2003).

6. There is a long list. See, for example, Javier Corcuera, *Orígenes, ideología y organización del nacionalismo vasco (1876–1904)* (Madrid: Siglo XXI, 1979), and Jean-Claude Larronde, *El nacionalismo vasco: Su origen y su ideología en la obra de Sabino Arana-Goiri* (San Sebastián: Txertoa, 1977).

7. See, for example, Ludger Mees, *Nacionalismo vasco, movimiento obrero y cuestión social (1903–1923)* (Bilbao: Fundación Sabino Arana, 1992); José Luis de la Granja Sainz, *Nacionalismo y II República en el País Vasco* (Madrid: Siglo XXI, 1986).

8. José Luis de la Granja Sainz, *El nacionalismo vasco: Un siglo de historia* (Madrid: Tecnos, 2002).

9. In this category, we have to start with Sabino Arana Goiri himself. See *Obras completas de Arana-Goiri'tar Sabin* (Buenos Aires: Sabindiar-Batza, 1965). Also Francisco Letamendia (Ortzi), *Historia de Euskadi: El nacionalismo vasco y ETA* (Paris: Ruedo Ibérico, 1975); Larronde, *El nacionalismo vasco.*

10. Maximiano García Venero, *Historia del nacionalismo vasco* (Madrid: Editora Nacional, 1968). Granja Sainz places García Venero's work in the "anti-nationalist" category, that is, anti-Basque nationalist. See *El nacionalismo vasco,* 194.

11. Gurutz Jáuregui, *Ideología y estrategia politica de ETA: Análisis de su evolución entre 1959 y 1968* (Madrid: Siglo XXI, 1981); José María Garmendia, *Historia de ETA* (San Sebastián: Haranburu, 1995); John Sullivan, *ETA and Basque Nationalism: The Fight for Euskadi, 1890–1986* (London: Routledge, 1988).

12. Robert P. Clark, *Negotiating with ETA: Obstacles to Peace in the Basque Country, 1975–1988* (Reno: University of Nevada Press, 1990); Ludger Mees, *Nationalism, Violence, and Democracy: The Basque Clash of Identities* (New York: Palgrave Macmillan, 2003). See also Txiki Benegas, *Una propuesta de paz* (Madrid: Espasa Calpe, SA, 2000).

13. Sagrario Morán, *ETA entre España y Francia* (Madrid: Editorial Complutense, 1997).

14. Joseba Zulaika, *Basque Violence: Metaphor and Sacrament* (Reno: University of Nevada Press, 1988); Begoña Aretxaga, "A Hall of Mirrors: On the Spectral Character of Basque Violence," in *Basque Politics and Nationalism on the Eve of the Millenium,* ed. William A. Douglass, Carmelo Urza, Linda White, and Joseba Zulaika, 115–126 (Reno, NV: Center for Basque Studies, 1999).

15. José Manuel Mata López, *El nacionalismo vasco radical: Discurso, organización y expresiones* (Bilbao: Universidad del País Vasco, 1993).

16. Javier Corcuera, *Política y derecho: La construccíon de la autonomía vasca* (Madrid: Centro de Estudios Constitucionales, 1991).

17. Juan Linz, *Conflicto en Euskadi* (Madrid: Espasa-Calpe, 1986).

18. See Barbara Loyer, *Géopolitique du Pays Basque: Nations et nationalismes en Espagne* (Paris: L'Harmattan, 1997); Cyrus Zirakzadeh, *A Rebellious People: Basques, Protests, and Politics* (Reno: University of Nevada Press, 1991). There are, of course, many others. One particularly interesting is Gurutz Jáuregui, *Entre la tragedia y la esperanz: Vasconia ante el nuevo milenio* (Barcelona: Ariel, 1996).

19. Luis Moreno, *The Federalization of Spain* (London: Frank Cass, 2001). Salvador Giner and Luis Moreno, "La dimension éthnica de la sociedad española," in *España: Sociedad y política,* ed. Salvador Giner, 169–197 (Madrid: Espasa-Calpe). See also José Luis de la Granja Sainz, Justo Beramendi, and Pere Anguera, *La España de los nacionalismos y las autonomías* (Madrid: Síntesis, 2001).

20. See, for example, Marianick Ithurralde, *Le Pays basque, la Catalogne et l'Europe: Stratégies politiques des autonomies basque et catalane* (Paris: L'Harmattan, 2002).

21. Daniele Conversi, *The Basque, the Catalans, and Spain: Alternative Routes to Nationalist Mobilisation* (London: Hurst, 1997).

22. Juan Díez Medrano, *Divided Nations: Class Conflict, Politics, and Nationalism in the Basque Country and Catalonia* (Ithaca, NY: Cornell University Press, 1995).

23. Michael Keating, "Northern Ireland and the Basque Country," in *Northern Ireland and the Divided World: Post-Agreement Northern Ireland in Comparative Perspective,* ed. John McGarry, 181–208 (Oxford: Oxford University Press, 2001); Mary Katherine Flynn, *Ideology, Mobilization, and the Nation: The Rise of Irish, Basque, and*

Carlist Nationalist Movements in the Nineteenth and Early Twentieth Centuries (London: MacMillan, 2000).

24. Cyntia L. Irvin, *Militant Nationalism: Between Movement and Party in Ireland and the Basque Country* (Minneapolis: University of Minnesota Press, 1999).

25. Jan Mansvelt Beck, *Territory and Terror: Conflicting Nationalisms in the Basque Country* (London: Routledge, 2005).

26. See Michael Keating, *Plurinational Democracy: Stateless Nations in a Post-Sovereign Era* (Oxford: Oxford University Press, 2001).

27. Many quality books, not to mention articles, had to be left out of this brief survey. Some will be cited in later chapters.

28. In addition to perennialism, ethno-symbolism is another category invoked to qualify scholars of nationalism who give analytical importance to culture. See the discussion in Anthony D. Smith, *Nationalism and Modernism* (London: Routledge, 1998), 145–198.

29. These are the classic arguments put forward by Ernest Gellner and Benedict Anderson. See Gellner, *Nations and Nationalism* (London: Blackwell, 1983) and Anderson, *Imagined Communities*, 2nd ed. (London: Verso, 1991).

30. Eric Hobsbawm, *Nations and Nationalism Since 1780: Programme, Myth, Reality* (Cambridge: Cambridge University Press, 1992)

31. This is the sociobiological approach best represented by the work of Pierre van den Berghe. See *The Ethnic Phenomenon* (New York: Elsevier, 1979).

32. Harold Isaacs, *Idols of the Tribe: Group Identity and Political Change*, 2nd ed. (Cambridge: Harvard University Press, 1989).

33. Clifford Geertz, "The Integrative Revolution: Primordial Sentiments and Civil Politics," in *Old Societies and New States: The Quest for Modernity in Asia and Africa*, ed. Clifford Geertz (London: Free Press of Glencoe, 1963), 109.

34. John Armstrong, *Nations Before Nationalism* (Chapel Hill: University of North Carolina Press, 1982).

35. Smith, *Nationalism and Modernism*, 145–198.

36. See, for example, Adrian Hastings, *The Construction of Nationhood: Ethnicity, Religion, and Nationalism* (Cambridge: Cambridge University Press, 1997).

37. Lois A. West, ed., *Feminist Nationalism* (London: Routledge, 1997); Homi Bhabha, ed., *Nation and Narration* (London: Routlege, 1990).

38. In addition to Harold Isaacs and Clifford Geertz, see Edward Shils, "Primordial, Personal, Sacred, and Civil Ties," *British Journal of Sociology* 8 (1957): 130–145.

39. Will Kymlicka, *Multicultural Citizenship: A Liberal Theory of Minority Rights* (Oxford: Oxford University Press, 1995); Charles Taylor, *Reconciling the Solitudes: Essays on Canadian Nationalism and Federalism* (Montreal: McGill Queen's University Press, 1992); Yael Tamir, *Liberal Nationalism* (Princeton, NJ: Princeton University Press, 1993).

40. Denis Monière, *Pour comprendre le nationalisme au Québec et ailleurs* (Montreal: Les Presses de l'Université de Montréal, 2001).

41. See, for example, Alvin Rabushka and Kenneth A. Shepsle, *Politics in Plural Societies: A Theory of Democratic Instability* (Columbus, OH: Merrill, 1972).

42. Arendt Lijphart, "Consociational Democracy," *World Politics* 21 (1969): 207–225, and *Democracy in Plural Societies* (New Haven, CT: Yale University Press, 1977).

43. Jack Eller and Reed Coughlan, "The Poverty of Primordialism," *Ethnic and Racial Studies* 16 (1993): 183–202.

44. Representative works include scholarship from Anthony D. Smith and Walker Connor. See, respectively, *The Ethnic Origins of Nations* (New York: Blackwell, 1986), and *Ethnonationalism: The Quest for Understanding* (Princeton, NJ: Princeton University Press, 1994).

45. For example, Linda Colley's study on Britishness emphasizes religion but identifies the mechanism of national construction as the antagonistic relationship between Britain and Catholic France. See *Britons: Forging the Nation, 1707–1837* (New Haven, CT: Yale University Press, 1992).

46. James E. Jacobs, *Hills of Conflict: Basque Nationalism in France* (Reno: University of Nevada Press, 1994).

47. Milica Zarcovic Bookman, *The Political Economy of Discontinuous Development: Regional Disparities and Inter-Regional Conflict* (New York: Praeger, 1991).

48. Michael Hechter, *Internal Colonialism: The Celtic Fringe in British National Development, 1536–1966* (Berkeley and Los Angeles: University of California Press, 1975).

49. Ronald Rogowski, Conclusion to *New Nationalism in the Developed West*, ed. Edward A. Tyriakian and Ronald Rogowski, 277–293 (Boston: Allen and Unwin, 1984).

50. Walker Connor, "The Seductive Lure of Economic Explanations," in *Ethnonationalism: The Quest for Understanding*, 144–164.

51. See, for example, Hechter's important contribution *Containing Nationalism* (Oxford: Oxford University Press, 2000).

52. Michael Keating and John McGarry, eds., *Minority Nationalism and the Changing International Order* (Oxford: Oxford University Press, 2001).

53. Jan Aart Scholte, "Globalization and Community," in *Globalization: A Critical Introduction* (London: MacMillan, 2001), 159–181.

54. Stéphane Paquin, *La revanche des petites nations: Le Québec, l'Écosse et la Catalogne face à la mondialisation* (Montreal: VLB Éditeur, 2001).

55. See Manuel Castells, "Globalization, Identity, and the Basque Question," in Douglass et al., *The Basque Diaspora/La diaspora vasca*, 22–33.

56. Paul Brass, *Ethnicity and Nationalism: Theory and Comparison* (London: Sage, 1991).

57. Joseph Rothschild, *Ethnopolitics: A Conceptual Framework* (New York: Columbia University Press, 1981).

58. Rational choice fits this description. See, for example, Antonio Barreto, "Constructing Boundaries: Ethnic Boundaries and Elite Preferences in Puerto Rico," *Nationalism and Ethnic Politics* 7 (2001): 21–40.

59. Gellner, *Nations and Nationalism*.

60. John Breuilly, *Nationalism and the State* (New York: St. Martin's Press, 1982).

61. This is the so-called diffusionist approach. See Karl Deutsch, *Nationalism and Social Communication: An Inquiry Into the Formation of Nationality* (Cambridge: MIT Press, 1966).

62. See, for example, David Brian Robertson, "The Return to History in American Political Science," *Social Science History* 17 (1993): 1–36.

63. This being said, British and other European scholars have also made significant contributions to the literature. See Ellen M. Immergut, *Health Care Politics: Ideas and Institutions in Western Europe* (Cambridge: Cambridge University Press, 1992); Colin Hay and Daniel Wincott, "Structure, Agency, and Historical Institutionalism," *Political Studies* 46 (1998): 951–957. So have Canadian scholars. See André Lecours, ed., *New Institutionalism: Theory and Analysis* (Toronto: University of Toronto Press, 2005); Jane Jenson, "Les réformes des services de garde pour jeunes enfants en France et au Québec: Une analyse historico-institutionnaliste," *Politique et sociétés* 17 (1998): 183–216; Denis Saint-Martin, "The New Managerialism and the Policy Influence of Consultants in Government: An Historical-Institutionalist Analysis of Britain, Canada, and France," *Governance* 11 (1998): 319–356. French researchers, for their part, have used the insight of their sociological tradition to develop a unique institutionalist approach to politics and society. See Bruno Palier and Giuliano Bonoli, "Phénomènes de *path dependence* et réformes des systèmes de protection sociale," *Revue française de science politique* 49 (1999): 399–420; Patrick Hassenteufel and Yves Surel, "Des politiques publiques comme les autres? Construction de l'objet et outils d'analyse des politiques publiques," *Politique européenne*, no. 1 (2000): 8–24; Bruno Théret, "Institutions et institutionnalismes: Vers une convergence des conceptions de l'institution?" in *Innovations, institutionnelles et territoires*, ed. Michèle Tallard, Bruno Théret, and Didier Uri (Paris: L'Harmattan, 2000), 25–58.

64. See, for example, Roy Macridis, *The Study of Comparative Government* (New York: Random, 1955).

65. The best-known collection making this argument at that time was Peter Evans, Dietrich Rueschemeyer, and Theda Skocpol, *Bringing the State Back In* (Cambridge: Cambridge University Press, 1985).

66. Theda Skocpol, *States and Social Revolutions: A Comparative Analysis of France, Russia, and China* (Cambridge: Cambridge University Press, 1979); James March and Johan P. Olsen, *Rediscovering Institutions: The Organizational Basis of Politics* (New York: Free Press, 1989).

67. See Lecours, ed., *New Institutionalism*.

68. Guy Peters, *Institutional Theory in Political Science: The "New Institutionalism"* (London: Continuum, 1999).

69. See, for example, Peter Hall and Rosemary C. R. Taylor, "Political Science and the Three New Institutionalisms," *Political Studies* 44 (1996): 936–957; Ellen M. Immergut, "The Theoretical Core of the New Institutionalism," *Politics and Society* 26 (1998): 4–34.

70. Kathleen Thelen, "Historical Institutionalism in Comparative Politics," *Annual Review of Political Science*, 1999: 369–404.

71. See March and Olsen, *Rediscovering Institutions*.

72. Mark Granovetter, "Economic Action and Social Structures: The Problem of Embeddedness," *American Journal of Sociology* 3 (1985): 481–510.

73. James March and Johan P. Olsen, "The New Institutionalism: Organizational Factors in Political Life," *American Political Science Review* 78 (1984): 734–749.

74. See Walter W. Powell and Paul J. DiMaggio, "The Iron Cage Revisited: Institutional Isomorphism and Collective Rationality in Organizational Fields," *American Sociological Review* 48 (1983): 147–160. Walter W. Powell and Paul J. DiMaggio, eds., *The New Institutionalism in Organizational Analysis* (Chicago: University of Chicago Press, 1991).

75. Elinor Ostrom, "Rational Choice Theory and Institutional Analysis: Toward Complementarity," *American Political Science Review* 85 (1991): 237–243; Keith Dowding, "The Compatibility of Behaviouralism, Rational Choice, and 'New Institutionalism,'" *Journal of Theoretical Politics* 6 (1994): 105–117.

76. Barry R. Weingast, "Rational-Choice Institutionalism," in Katznelson and Milner, *Political Science*, 660–692.

77. Sven Steinmo, Kathleen Thelen, and Frank Longstreth, *Structuring Politics: Historical Institutionalism in Comparative Analysis* (Cambridge: Cambridge University Press, 1992).

78. Peter A. Hall, "Policy Paradigms, Social Learning, and the State: The Case of Economic Policymaking in Britain," *Comparative Politics* 25 (1993): 275–296; Judith Goldstein, *Ideas, Interests, and American Trade Policy* (Ithaca, NY: Cornell University Press, 1993); John L. Campbell, "Institutional Analysis and the Role of Ideas in Political Economy," *Theory and Society* 27 (1998): 377–409.

79. Paul Pierson and Theda Skocpol, "Historical Institutionalism in Contemporary Political Science," in Katznelson and Milner, *Political Science*, 696.

80. Lecours, ed., *New Institutionalism.*

81. Exceptions include Siobhan Harty, "The Institutional Foundations of Sub-state National Movements," *Comparative Politics* 33 (2001): 191–210; André Lecours, "Regionalism, Cultural Diversity, and the State in Spain," *Journal of Multilingual and Multicultural Development* 22 (2001): 210–226; Jacques Bertrand, *Nationalism and Ethnic Conflict in Indonesia* (New York: Cambridge University Press, 2004).

82. Immergut, *Health Care Politics.*

83. See the data in Moreno, *The Federalization of Spain,* 115–116.

84. Serge Govaert, "A Brussels Identity? A Speculative Interpretation," in *Nationalism in Belgium: Shifting Identities, 1780–1995,* ed. Kas Deprez and Louis Vos, 229–239 (New York: St. Martin's Press, 1998).

85. Paul Pierson, "Not Just What, but *When*: Timing and Sequence in Political Processes," *Studies in American Political Development* 14 (2000): 72–92.

86. Ibid., 75.

87. Paul Pierson, "When Effect Becomes Cause: Policy Feedback and Political Change," *World Politics* 45 (1993): 595–628, and "Increasing Returns, Path Dependence, and the Study of Politics," *American Political Science Review* 94 (2000): 251–267.

88. Ruth Berins Collier and David Collier, *Shaping the Political Arena: Critical Junctures, the Labor Movemen, and Regime Dynamics in Latin America* (Princeton, NJ: Princeton University Press, 1991).

89. Pierson, "Not Just What, but *When*," 76.

90. James Mahoney, *The Legacies of Liberalism: Path Dependence and Political Regimes in Central America* (Baltimore: Johns Hopkins University Press, 2001), 7.

91. This being said, historical institutionalism has indeed made progress on the issue of institutional change. See Karen Orren and Stephen Skowronek, "Institutions and Intercurrence: Theory Building in the Fullness of Time," in *Nomos XXXVIII Political Order,* ed. Ian Shapiro and Russell Hardin, 111–146 (New York: New York University Press, 1996); Robert C. Lieberman, "Ideas, Institutions, and Political Order: Explaining Political Change," *American Political Science Review* 96 (2002): 697–712; Kathleen Thelen, "How Institutions Evolve: Insights from Comparative Historical Analysis," in *Comparative Historical Analysis in the Social Sciences,* ed. James Mahoney and Dietrich Rueschemeyer, 208–240 (Cambridge: Cambridge University Press, 2003).

92. For Mahoney, for example, there is one critical juncture in the history of political regimes in Central America, the choices made by liberal elites about how to modernize in the nineteenth and early twentieth centuries. See James Mahoney, *The Legacies of Liberalism.*

93. Peter A. Hall, "Aligning Ontology and Methodology in Comparative Politics," in Mahoney and Rueschemeyer, *Comparative Historical Analysis in the Social Sciences,* 391–395.

94. Evan S. Lieberman, "Causal Inference in Historical Institutional Analysis: A Specification of Periodization Strategies," *Comparative Political Studies* 34 (2001): 1017–1023.

95. See the collection of essays in André Lecours, ed., *New Institutionalism.*

96. Peter Evans et al., *Bringing the State Back In.*

97. The concept of elite is admittedly slippery and can hardly be used in the same manner across historical periods. For the purpose of this study, the "Basque elites" of the nineteenth century are defined sociologically; that is, they are considered as such as a consequence of occupying a prominent social position. For this type of definition of elites, see William Kornhauser, *The Politics of Mass Society* (New York: Free Press, 1959).

CHAPTER ONE. THE EARLY SPANISH STATE

1. Juan Linz, "Early State-Building and Late Peripheral Nationalisms Against the State: The Case of Spain," in *Building States and Nations,* vol. 2, ed. S. N. Eisenstadt and Stein Rokkan (London: Sage 1973), 99.

2. José Ortega y Gasset, *España invertebrada: Bosquejo de algunos pensamientos históricos,* 9th ed. (Madrid: Espasa-Calpe, 1989), 161.

3. Ibid., 142. My translation.

4. It is not always necessary to delve this deeply into history to locate the origins of nationalist movements. The key variable is state construction. For example, the Flemish Movement, and indeed Flanders as it is understood today, is a creature of the Belgian state created in 1830. In this context, the history prior to 1830 that is relevant for explaining Flemish nationalism pertains to the creation of Belgium, and this process is not nearly as long as in the case of Spain.

5. Stanley Payne, *Basque Nationalism* (Reno: University of Nevada Press, 1975), 1–2.

6. Jaume Rossinyol, *Le problème national catalan* (Paris: Mouton, 1974), 121.

7. Moreno, *The Federalization of Spain*, 38.

8. The relationship between Basque and Aquitaine is compared by William H. Jacobsen Jr. to that between Italian and Latin. See "Basque Language Origin Theories," in *Basque Cultural Studies*, ed. William A. Douglass, Carmelo Urza, Linda White, and Josepa Zulaika (Reno: University of Nevada Press, 2000), 27.

9. Gallop, *A Book of the Basques*, 80.

10. Jacobs, *Hills of Conflict*, xiv.

11. Kurlansky, *The Basque History of the World*, 21.

12. Ibid., 48.

13. Barbara Loyer, "Être indépendant ou ne pas être: Le cas basque," *Hérodote* 95 (1999): 47.

14. Letamendia, *Historia de Euskadi*.

15. Salvador de Madariaga, *España: Ensayo de Historia Contemporánea* (Madrid: Espasa-Calpe, SA, 1979), 182.

16. Fernando García de Cortazar, Manuel Montero, Juan M. Betanzos, and Severino Sánchez, *Historia de Alava* (San Sebastián: Txertoa, 1986), 56–58.

17. Fernando García de Cortazar and Manuel Montero, *Historia de Vizcaya: De los orígenes, la Edad Media, el Antiguo Régimen a los siglos XIX y XX* (San Sebastián: Txertoa, 1994), 26.

18. Lola Valverde, *Historia de Guipúzcoa* (San Sebastián: Txertoa, 1984), 45.

19. There is a debate on the level of "Basqueness" of the Kingdom of Navarre. The idea that Navarre was clearly much less Basque than the other provinces is the dominant interpretation. See Rachel Bard, *Navarra: The Durable Kingdom* (Reno: University of Nevada Press, 1982), xiii, and Claudio Sánchez-Albornoz, *Orígenes y destino de Navarra: Trayectoria histórica de Vasconia: Otros escritos* (Barcelona: Planeta, 1974).

20. William A. Douglass, "Sabino's Sin: Racism and the Founding of Basque Nationalism," in *Ethnonationalism in the Contemporary World: Walker Connor and the Study of Nationalism*, ed. Daniele Conversi (London: Routledge, 2002), 99.

21. Ibid., 98. Douglass cites a study of racialist thought in Europe by Léon Poliakov, *The Aryan Myth: A History of Racist and Nationalist Ideas in Europe* (New York: Basic Books, 1974).

22. Marianne Heiberg, *The Making of the Basque Nation* (Cambridge: Cambridge University Press, 1989), 17–19.

23. Joseph Nogaret, *Petite histoire au pays basque français* (Bayonne: Edition de la Société des Sciences, Lettres, Arts et d'Études Régionales de Bayonne, 1928), 23–24.

24. Ibid., 102.

25. Jacob, *Hills of Conflict*, 37.

26. Salvador de Madariaga, *Spain: A Modern History* (New York: Preager, 1958), 228–229. See, in Spanish, de Madariaga's *España: Ensayo de Historia Contemporánea*, 182.

27. One could add Portugal, constituted in 1139.

28. Alberts Balcells, *Catalan Nationalism: Past and Present* (New York: St. Martin's Press, 1996), 5.

29. García Venero, *Historia del nacionalismo vasco*, 61–62.

30. Moreno, *The Federalization of Spain*, 40.

31. See the discussion in García Venero, *Historia del nacionalismo vasco*, 81–82.

32. Of course, the concept of right is somewhat anachronistic in the context of medieval Spain.

33. More on this later in the chapter and in following chapters.

34. The Moors left the Iberian Peninsula after the fall of Grenada in 1492.

35. Although Portugal became an independent kingdom in 1143, it was controlled by Spain between 1580 and 1640.

36. Roger Bigelow Merriman, *The Rise of the Spanish Empire in the Old World and in the New*, vol. 1, *The Middle Ages* (New York: Cooper Square Publishers, 1962), 167.

37. Ibid.

38. Bard, *Navarra*, 82.

39. Ibid., xi.

40. Juan Díez Medrano, *Divided Nations*, 23.

41. On the *juntas, corregidores,* and *pase foral,* see García Venero, *Historia del nacionalismo vasco*, 86–94.

42. Mikel Dorronsoro, Alfredo Herbosa, and Yolanda Orive, *Historia de España y del País Vasco* (Zarautz: Itxaropena, sa, Servicio Editorial de la Universidad del País Vasco, 1998), 41. In the case of Navarre, it was in 1686.

43. Quoted in Douglass, "Sabino's Sin," 99.

44. On collective nobility, see Davydd J. Greeenwood, "Continuity in Change: Spanish Basque Ethnicity as a Historical Process," in *Ethnic Conflict in the Western World*, ed. Milton Esman, 81–102 (Ithaca, NY: Cornell University Press, 1977).

45. On this idea, see Jon Juaristi, *Vestigios de Babel: Para une arqueología de los nacionalismos españoles* (Madrid: Siglo Veintiuno de España Editores, 1992), 9.

46. Heiberg, *The Making of the Basque Nation*, 245n9.

47. Quoted in Heiberg, *The Making of the Basque Nation*, 34. Quoted in Spanish in Letamendia, *Historia de Euskadi*, 37.

48. Bard, *Navarra*, 131.

49. Díez Medrano, *Divided Nations*, 36.

50. This scenario is much different from Cataluña's where the trading patterns barely included the Iberian Peninsula, and where a self-sufficient bourgeoisie who had little contact with the Spanish state was at the forefront of nationalism.

51. It should also be said that the Basque provinces were an isolated, resourceless, and, until the late nineteenth century, poor region. This should most likely be considered when explaining the long life of their fueros, although the relationship of Basque elites with the Spanish state is more important.

52. Moreno, *The Federalization of Spain*, 41.

53. Roger Bigelow Merriman, *The Rise of the Spanish Empire in the Old World and in the New*, vol. 9, *Philip the Prudent* (New York: MacMillan, 1934), 409–422.

54. Claudio Sánchez-Albornoz, *España: Un Enigma Histórico* (Buenos Aires: Sudamericana, 1956), 480.

55. Merriman, *The Rise of the Spanish Empire*, vol. 9, *Philip the Prudent*, 435–444.

56. This last initiative was known as the Unión de Armas.

57. Granja Sainz, *El nacionalismo vasco: Un siglo de historia,* 25.

58. Dorronsoro, Herbosa, and Orive, *Historia de España y del País Vasco,* 39.

59. Richard Herr, "Flow and Ebb, 1700–1833," in *Spain: A History,* ed. Raymond Carr (Oxford: Oxford University Press, 2000), 177.

60. Ibid., 176.

61. Paul Pierson and Theda Skocpol argue that there are three contending approaches to political science: behavioralism, rational choice, and historical institutionalism. See "Historical Institutionalism in Contemporary Political Science," 660–692.

62. The fueros were provincial privileges, but the Carlist struggles and nationalist movement of the late nineteenth century would transform them into a particular status for the Basques.

63. Basque government, *Propuesta de nuevo estatuto político de la Comunidad de Euskadi* (Ajuria-Enea, 2003), 3. My translation and my emphasis.

64. Letamendia, *Historia de Euskadi,* 41.

65. Keating, *Plurinational Democracy,* 44–47.

66. This is mentioned in a critical perspective by Dorronsoro, Herbosa, and Orive, *Historia de España y del País Vasco,* 42.

67. Salvador de Madariaga cites an early-nineteenth-century treatise by Juan Antonio Llorente on the origins of the Basque fueros, which argued that the Basque provinces were never "independent republics" but territories much like the others in Spain. See Madariaga, *España,* 186.

CHAPTER TWO. THE CENTRALIZING STATE

1. Hechter, *Containing Nationalism.*

2. Ortega y Gasset, *España invertebrada,* 61. My translation.

3. Ibid.

4. José Álvarez Junco, "The Nation-Building Process in Nineteenth-Century Spain," in *Nationalism and the Nation in the Iberian Peninsula,* ed. Clare Mar-Molinero and Angel Smith (Oxford: Berg, 1996), 96.

5. Ibid., 91.

6. Dorronsoro, Herbosa, and Orive, *Historia de España y del País Vasco,* 61.

7. Álvarez Junco, "The Nation-Building Process in Nineteenth-Century Spain," 91–93.

8. Madariaga, *Spain,* 56.

9. Reproduced in Dorronsoro, Herbosa, and Orive, *Historia de España y del País Vasco,* 73–74.

10. Ibid., 70–71 and 73.

11. Since this was a period where politics was largely outside the scope of masses, it is difficult to evaluate to what extent this position had societal support. Payne suggests that the decision of Basque representatives to support the new framework did not reflect the preferences of their populations. Payne, *Basque Nationalism,* 37.

12. Ibid.

13. This paragraph draws from Michael Keating, *State and Regional Nationalism* (London: Harvester Wheatsheaf, 1988), 51–52.

14. Mansvelt Beck, *Territory and Terror*, 19–76.

15. Álvarez Junco, "The Nation-Building Process in Nineteenth-Century Spain," 95.

16. Eric Storm, "The Problems of the Spanish Nation-Building Process Around 1900," *National Identities* 6 (2004): 148.

17. Ibid., 147.

18. See, for example, Raymond Carr, *Spain: 1808–1975*, 2nd ed. (Oxford: Clarendon Press, 1982), 369.

19. José Álvarez Junco, *Mater dolorosa: La idea de España en el siglo XIX* (Madrid: Taurus, 2001), 383–432.

20. Sebastian Balfour, "'The Lion and the Pig': Nationalism and National Identity in Fin de Siècle Spain," in Mar-Molinero and Smith, *Nationalism and the Nation in the Iberian Peninsula*, 114.

21. Ibid., 115.

22. Eugen Weber, *Peasants Into Frenchmen: The Modernization of Rural France, 1870–1914* (Stanford, CA: Stanford University Press, 1976).

23. Mansvelt Beck, *Territory and Terror*, 59.

24. Storm, "The Problems of the Spanish Nation-Building Process Around 1900," 144.

25. Mansvelt Beck, *Territory and Terror*, 66; Storm, "The Problems of the Spanish Nation-Building Process Around 1900," 144.

26. Álvarez Junco, "The Nation-Building Process in Nineteenth-Century Spain," 100.

27. Storm, "The Problems of the Spanish Nation-Building Process Around 1900," 144.

28. Carr, *Spain: 1808–1975*, 379.

29. Linz, "Early State-Building and Late Peripheral Nationalism Against the State," 101.

30. Renato Barahona, *Vizcaya on the Eve of Carlism: Politics and Society, 1800–1833* (Reno: University of Nevada Press, 1989), 77. Barahona's comment on the relationship between absolutism and the fueros concerns Bizkaia, but the argument can be applied to the other Basque provinces.

31. Ibid., 79–80.

32. Bard, *Navarra*, 149.

33. The formal contender for the throne was the couple's daughter Isabel, who could have ruled only at her majority. Carlists (*carlistas*) therefore challenged Liberals (*isabelinos* or *cristinos*).

34. Payne, *Basque Nationalism*, 40.

35. See Jeremy MacClancy, *The Decline of Carlism* (Reno: University of Nevada Press, 2000), 4, quoting Vicente Garmendia, *La ideología Carlista (1868–1876): En los orígenes del nacionalismo vasco* (San Sebastián: Diputacíon Foral de Guipúzcoa, 1984).

36. MacClancy, *The Decline of Carlism*, 7.

37. There was another important cleavage in the support for Carlism: the urban-rural divide. As a traditional movement, Carlism was stronger in the countryside, while support for liberalism (and the *isabelinos*) was higher in the cities.

38. Some authors speak of three Carlist wars: 1833–40, 1846–48, 1872–75. The 1846–48 conflict, which featured a Carlist uprising primarily in Cataluña, is otherwise known as the Matiners' War.

39. Payne, *Basque Nationalism*, 44–47.

40. Excerpts of this document are reproduced in Dorronsoro, Herbosa, and Orive, *Historia de España y del País Vasco*, 101–102.

41. Ibid., 97.

42. Payne, *Basque Nationalism*, 54.

43. Conversi, *The Basques, the Catalans, and Spain*, 12.

44. Payne, *Basque Nationalism*, 54.

45. Sabino Arana Goiri, *El partido carlista y los Fueros vasco-navarros* (Buenos Aires, 1912), 61. My translation.

46. Quoted in García Venero, *Historia del nacionalismo vasco*, 166. My translation.

47. Sabino Arana Goiri, "Discurso de Larrazábal," in *Obras completas de Arana-Goiri'tar Sabin*, 157–158. The discourse of Larrazábal is reproduced in its entirety in *Obras completas*, 154–160.

48. Conversi, *The Basques, the Catalans, and Spain*, 56–57; Payne, *Basque Nationalism*, 65–66.

49. Corcuera, *Orígenes, ideología y organización*, 189. My translation.

50. Quoted in ibid., 129. My translation.

51. Or, in its new standardized version, "Euskadi." For more details on Arana's contribution in forging the symbols of Basque nationalism, see Conversi, *The Basques, the Catalans, and Spain*, 53–55.

52. Granja Sainz, *El nacionalismo vasco: Un siglo de historia*, 35.

53. García Venero, *Historia del nacionalismo vasco*, 281.

54. Bard, *Navarra*, 194–195.

55. Ibid.

56. Cyrus Ernesto Zirakzadeh, *A Rebellious People: Basques, Protests, and Politics* (Reno: University of Nevada Press, 1991), 127.

57. Ibid., 125.

58. Ibid., 125–126.

59. Quoted in Pedro de Basaldúa, *El libertador vasco: Sabino de Arana Goiri* (Bilbao: GEU Argitaldaria, 1977), 69. My translation.

60. Ibid.

61. Granja Sainz, *El nacionalismo vasco: Un siglo de historia*, 61–95; Heiberg, *The Making of the Basque Nation*, 45–60.

62. Quoted in Granja Sainz, *El nacionalismo vasco: Un siglo de historia*, 72. My translation.

63. Ibid., 72–73.

64. Ibid., 77–78. My translation.

65. It is unclear if those battled are real or imagined. See Jon Juaristi, *El linaje de Aitor: La invención de la tradición vasca* (Madrid: Taurus, 1987), 201.

66. Arana Goiri, *Bizcaya por su independencia* (Bilbao: GEU Argitaldariak, 1980), 93–94. My translation.

67. Arana Goiri, *Bizcaya por su independencia*, 1892, 135, qtd. in Corcuera, *Orígenes, ideología y organización del nacionalismo vasco 1876–1904*, 203–204. My translation.

68. Arana Goiri "Discurso de Larrazábal," in *Obras completas*, 155. My translation.

69. Sabino Arana Goiri, *Obras escogidas: Antología política* (San Sebastián: L. Haranburu, 1978), 56, qtd. in Douglass, "Sabino's Sin," 106.

70. Sabino Arana Goiri, "El Catalanismo," *Baserritarra*, no. 18, August 29, 1897, qtd. in Larronde, *El nacionalismo vasco*, 165. My translation.

71. Cited in Granja Sainz, *El nacionalismo vasco: Un siglo de historia*, 35. My translation.

72. Sabino Arana Goiri, "Efectos de la invasión," *Baserritarra*, no. 11, July 11, 1897, reproduced partially in Dorronsoro, Herbosa, and Orive, *Historia de España y del País Vasco*, 166–167. My translation.

73. Díez Medrano, *Divided Nations*, 73.

74. Granja Sainz, *El nacionalismo vasco: Un siglo de historia*, 37.

75. Of course, "Catalan nationalism" is no more a monolithic bloc than "Basque nationalism." The Esquerra Republicana de Catalunya (ERC) is more squarely secessionist than the dominant party of Catalan nationalism, Convergència i Unió (CIU).

76. Batasuna was outlawed in 2002 and therefore no longer formally exists.

77. More on this in the following chapter.

78. On Cataluña, see Kenneth McRoberts, *Catalonia: Nation-Building Without a State* (Toronto: Oxford University Press, 2001).

79. As I indicated previously, there is a nationalist party seeking secession in Cataluña, the ERC. However, the ERC advocates independence through nonviolent means only, and typically has not received more than 10 percent of the vote in regional elections, although it is now on the upswing and reached 16 percent in 2003.

80. Díez Medrano, *Divided Nations*.

81. There is solid ground for linking the character of a nationalist movement with the elites initially behind it. See, for example, Liah Greenfeld, *Nationalism: Five Roads to Modernity* (Cambridge: Harvard University Press, 1992).

82. Quoted in Díez Medrano, *Divided Nations*, 1.

83. http://www.ciu.info/portada.html.

CHAPTER THREE. THE AUTHORITARIAN STATE

1. This being said, the PNV enjoyed considerable support in the three provinces during the 1930s. See tables 3.2, 3.3, and 3.4.

2. Francisco J. Romero Salvadó, *Twentieth-Century Spain: Politics and Society in Spain, 1898–1998* (New York: St. Martin's Press, 1998), 44–48.

3. Ibid., 49.

4. Stanley Payne, *Fascism in Spain, 1923–1977* (Madison: University of Wisconsin Press, 1999), 23.

5. Sandie Holguín, *Creating Spaniards: Culture and National Identity in Republican Spain* (Madison: University of Wisconsin Press, 2002), 43–44.

6. Payne, *Fascism in Spain*, 38.

7. He especially admired the Italian fascist regime. Ibid., 28.

8. Payne, *Basque Nationalism*, 102.

9. Ibid.

10. Santiago de Pablo, José Luis de la Granja Sainz, and Ludger Mees, eds., *Documentos para la historia del nacionalismo vasco: De los fueros a nuestros días* (Barcelona: Editorial Ariel, SA, 1998), 87–88.

11. José Luis de la Granja Sainz, *República y Guerra Civil en Euskadi: Del Pacto de San Sebastián al de Santoña* (Bilbao: Oñati, 1990), 36. My translation.

12. Cited in Holguín, *Creating Spaniards*, 48.

13. Ibid., 57–73.

14. The missionaries in the Basque provinces visited villages in the mountains. Ibid., 58.

15. Payne, *Basque Nationalism*, 20.

16. Ibid., 119–121.

17. Sebastian Balfour, "Spain from 1931 to the Present," in Carr, *Spain*, 246.

18. Ibid.

19. Cameron Watson, *Modern Basque History: Eighteenth Century to the Present* (Reno, NV: Center for Basque Studies, 2003), 287.

20. Paul Preston, *The Politics of Revenge: Fascism and the Military in Twentieth-Century Spain* (London: Unwin Hyman, 1990), 1.

21. Juan J. Linz, "The Party System of Spain: Past and Future," in *Party Systems and Voter Alignments: Cross-National Perspectives*, ed. Seymour M. Lipset and Stein Rokkan (New York: Free Press, 1967), 237.

22. Michael Richards, "Constructing the Nationalist State: Self-Sufficiency and Regeneration in the Early Franco Years," in Mar-Molino and Smith, *Nationalism and the Nation in the Iberian Peninsula*, 152–153.

23. Paloma Aguilar, "The Memory of the Civil War in the Transition to Democracy: The Peculiarity of the Basque Case," in *Politics and Policy in Democratic Spain*, ed. Paul Heywood (London: Frank Cass, 1999), 9.

24. Ibid., 16.

25. Paulina Raento and Cameron J. Watson, "Gernika, Guernica, *Guernica*? Contested Meanings of a Basque Place," *Political Geography* 19 (2000): 714.

26. "El Bombardeo de Guernica: 26 de Abril de 1937," in José Antonio Aguirre, *Obras completas de José Antonio Aguirre*, ed. Martin Ugalde (San Sebastián: Sendoa Argitaldaria, 1981), 628. My translation.

27. Cited in Heiberg, *The Making of the Basque Nation*, 88.

28. Raento and Watson, "Gernika, Guernica, *Guernica*?" 715.

29. Ibid.

30. Preston, *The Politics of Revenge*, 32.

31. Giner and Moreno, "La dimension éthnica de la sociedad española."

32. Clark, *The Basques*, 84.

33. Ibid., 81.

34. William A. Douglass and Jon Bilbao, *Amerikanuak: Basques in the New World* (Reno: University of Nevada Press, 1975); Douglass, Urza, White, and Zulaika, *The Basque Diaspora/La diáspora vasca*.

35. José Antonio Aguirre, *De Guernica a Nueva York pasando por Berlin* (Bilbao: Ekin, 1992).

36. José Luis de la Granja Sainz, *El nacionalismo vasco (1876–1975)* (Madrid: Arco/Libros, SL, 2000), 70.

37. Clark, *The Basques*, 90.

38. José Antonio Aguirre, *Veinte años de gestión del gobierno vasco (1936–1956)* (Durango: Leopoldo Zugaza Editor, 1978), 117.

39. Beltza, *El nacionalismo vasco en el exilio 1937–1960* (San Sebastián: Editorial Txertoa, 1977), 15.

40. Granja Sainz, *El nacionalismo vasco (1876–1975)*, 71.

41. Beltza, *El nacionalismo vasco*, 23.

42. Granja Sainz, *El nacionalismo vasco (1876–1975)*, 72–73.

43. Transcripts of the meeting's proceedings printed in Beltza, *El nacionalismo vasco*, 26. My translation.

44. Letter from Marc Lagasse to Juan Antonio Aguirre de Lecube, March 25, 1946, printed in ibid., 112–117 (115). My translation.

45. Conversi, *The Basques, the Catalans, and Spain*, 83.

46. Clark, *The Basques*, 112–113.

47. Ibid., 113.

48. Letter to Unesco delegates from José Antonio Aguirre, November 17, 1952, printed in Beltza, *El nacionalismo vasco*, 133–136 (136). My translation.

49. Conversi, *The Basques, the Catalans and Spain*, 83.

50. Robert P. Clark, *The Basque Insurgents: ETA, 1952–1980* (Madison: University of Wisconsin Press, 1984), 25–26.

51. See Gurutz Jáuregi, "ETA: Orígenes y evolución ideológica y política," in *La Historia de ETA*, ed. Antonio Elorza, José María Garmendia, Gurutz Jáuregui, and Florencio Domínguez Iribarren (Madrid: Temas de Hoy, SA, 2000), 189–195.

52. José Campelo Gutiérrez, *Nacimiento y origen de la violencia etarra* (Madrid: Grupo Libro, SA, 1994), 101.

53. Jáuregi, "ETA: Orígenes y evolución ideológica y política," 191.

54. Ibid., 194.

55. Sullivan, *ETA and Basque Nationalism*, 38.

56. Daniele Conversi, "Language or Race? The Choice of Core Values in the Development of Catalan and Basque Nationalism," *Ethnic and Racial Studies* 13 (1990): 62.

57. Jáuregi, "ETA: Orígenes y evolución ideológica y política," 213.

58. Conversi, "Language or Race?" 62.

59. This was only partially true, since the Basque clergy issued clear denunciations

of the Franco dictatorship (for example, through a petition circulated in 1960), although clerics from elsewhere in Spain did not follow suit. See Conversi, *The Basques, the Catalans, and Spain*, 95.

60. Fernando Sarailh de Ihartza (Frederico Krutwig), *Vasconia* (Buenos Aires: Ediciones Norbait, 1963), 81. My translation.

61. Daniele Conversi, "Domino or Internal Developments? The Influences of International Events and Political Ideologies on Catalan and Basque Nationalism," *West European Politics* 16 (1993): 256.

62. Daniele Conversi, "Ideological Fragmentation, Cultural Nationalism, and State Violence: Euskadi and Catalonia (1939–1968)," *Canadian Review of Studies in Nationalism* 26 (1999): 40.

63. See de Ihartza, *Vasconia*, 327.

64. On the splits within ETA, see Clark, *The Basques*.

65. Ibid., 45.

66. Sullivan, *ETA and Basque Nationalism*, 54.

67. De Ihartza, *Vasconia*, 339.

68. Sullivan, *ETA and Basque Nationalism*, 42–43.

69. Ibid.

70. Conversi, "Ideological Fragmentation, Cultural Nationalism, and State Violence," 40.

71. Jáuregui, *Ideologia y estrategia politica de ETA*, 204–237.

72. Clark, *The Basques*, 35.

73. Ibid., 47–48.

74. Sullivan, *ETA and Basque Nationalism*, 71

75. José María Garmendia, "ETA: Nacimiento, Desarollo y Crisis," in Antonio Elorza et al., *La Historia de ETA* (Madrid: Temas de Hoy, 2000), 143.

76. Ibid.

77. Sullivan, *ETA and Basque Nationalism*, 71.

78. Garmendia, "ETA: Nacimiento, Desarollo y Crisis," 143.

79. Clark, *The Basques*, 51.

80. Conversi, *The Basques, the Catalans and Spain*, 100.

81. Ibid., 100–101.

82. Sagrario Morán, *ETA entre España y Francia*, 92–93.

83. Ibid., 93.

84. De Ihartza, *Vasconia*, 337. My translation.

85. Moreno, *The Federalization of Spain*, 55.

CHAPTER FOUR. THE DEMOCRATIC STATE

1. For a good history of the transition, see Paul Preston, *The Triumph of Democracy in Spain* (London: Methuen, 1986). There are more nuanced, if not critical analyses. See, for example, Elías Díaz, "Ideologies in the Making of the Spanish Transition," *West European Politics* 26 (1998): 26–39, and Lidia Falcón, "Violent Democracy," *Journal of Spanish Cultural Studies* 3 (2002): 15–28.

2. Daniele Conversi, "The Smooth Transition: Spain's 1978 Constitution and the Nationalities Question," *National Identities* 4 (2002): 226–227.

3. Ludger Mees, *Nationalism, Violence, and Democracy: The Basque Clash of Identities* (New York: Palgrave Macmillan, 2003), 35.

4. Clark, *The Basque Insurgents*, 252.

5. Clark, *Negotiating with ETA*, 11–114.

6. Pedro Ibarra Güell, *La evolución estratégica de ETA: De la "Guerra revolucionaria" (1963) a la negociación (1987)* (San Sebastián: Kriselu, 1987), 103.

7. Enric Martínez-Herrera, "From Nation-Building to Building Identification With Political Communities: Consequences of Political Decentralization in Spain, the Basque Country, Catalonia, and Galicia, 1978–2001," *European Journal of Political Research*, 41 (2002): 431.

8. The Senate of the Canadian federation is also ineffective as a house of constituent unit representation in central institutions because senators are appointed by the federal government rather than by the provinces.

9. See Xavier Arbós, "Central versus Peripheral Nationalism in Building Democracy: The Case of Spain," *Canadian Review of Studies in Nationalism* 14 (1987): 149.

10. Ibid., 147.

11. Robert Agranoff, "Inter-Governmental Politics and Policy: Building Federal Arrangements in Spain," *Regional Politics and Policy* 3 (1993): 5.

12. Richard Gunther, Giacomo Sani, and Goldie Shabad, *Spain After Franco: The Making of a Competitive Party System* (Berkeley and Los Angeles: University of California Press, 1988), 342.

13. Iban Bilbao, "The Basque Parliament and Government," *Basque Studies Program Newsletter*, no. 27, 1983. http://basque.unr.edu/09/9.3/9.3.27t/9.3.27.06.bsqparl.htm. Accessed March 25, 2004.

14. In Gipuzkoa and Bizkaia, this rate reached 56.5 percent.

15. Howard R. Penniman and Eusebio M. Mujal-Léon, eds., *Spain at the Polls, 1977, 1979, 1982: A Study of National Elections* (Durham, NC: Duke University Press, 1985), 241.

16. Luis Moreno, "Divided Societies: Electoral Polarization, and the Basque Country," in *Democracy and Ethnic Conflict*, ed. Adrian Guelke (New York: Palgrave Macmillan, 2004), 29–51.

17. HB did not contest the 1977 elections.

18. Navarre enjoys fiscal autonomy also as a result of its historical foral institutions.

19. On the cupo and the common system, see Violeta Ruiz Almendral, "The Asymmetric Distribution of Taxation Powers in the Spanish State of Autonomies: The Common System and the Foral Regimes," *Regional and Federal Studies* 13 (2003): 41–66.

20. Jeremy MacClancy, "Navarra: Historical Realities, Present Myths, Future Possibilities," in Douglass et al., *Basque Politics and Nationalism*, 127–154. As indicated in a previous chapter, no referendum was held in Navarre to find out popular preferences.

21. What the Spanish constitution does not allow, however, is for a federation of autonomous communities (article 145.1).

22. MacClancy, "Navarra," 135.

23. The only other modern precedent was the Statute of Autonomy under the Second Republic, which was very short-lived.

24. Jack Brand, "Andalusia: Nationalism as a Strategy for Autonomy," *Canadian Review of Studies in Nationalism* 15 (1988): 1–9.

25. Josep M. Colomer, "The Spanish 'State of Autonomies,'" in *Politics and Policy in Democratic Spain*, ed. Paul Heywood (London: Frank Cass, 1999), 47.

26. Josep Ma Valles and Montserrat Cuchillo Fox, "Decentralisation in Spain: A Review," *European Journal of Political Research* 16 (1988): 397.

27. More nuances are made in chapter 6.

28. Xosé-Manoel Núñez, "What Is Spanish Nationalism Today? From Legitimacy Crisis to Unfulfilled Renovation (1975–2000), *Ethnic and Racial Studies*, 24 (2001): 737.

29. For a useful chronicle of past Basque governments, see http://cnnenespanol.com/2001/mundo/espana/04/21/especial.vascas.gobiernos.previos/.

30. The pact can be viewed online in English at http://www.euskadi.net/pakea/pacto_i.htm.

31. See Mees, *Nationalism, Violence, and Democracy*, 93.

32. Moreno, *The Federalization of Spain*, 114–115.

33. Ibid., 36.

34. On this, see William A. Douglass and Joseba Zulaika, "On the Interpretation of Terrorist Violence: ETA and the Basque Political Process," *Comparative Studies in Society and History* 32 (1990): 251.

35. Javier Garcia, *Los Gal al descubierto: La trama de la "guerra sucia" contra ETA* (Madrid: El Pais/Aguilar, SA, 1988).

36. Paddy Woodworth, "Why Do They Kill? The Basque Conflict in Spain," *World Policy Journal* 18 (2001): 7.

37. Ibid., 6.

38. See the interview with Christianne Fando, a lawyer who advised ETA during the Algerian talks: http://www.ehj-navarre.org/interviews/ehj_interviews_fando.html.

39. On these agreements, see Florencio Domínguez Iribarren, *De la negociación a la tregua: El final de ETA?* (Madrid: Grupo Santillana de Ediciones, SA, 1998), 71.

40. Mees, *Nationalism, Violence, and Democracy*, 68–71.

41. Richard Gillespie, "The Hour of the Nationalists: Catalan and Basque Parties in the Spanish General Election of 6 June 1993," *Regional Politics and Policy* 3 (1993): 184–185.

42. Ibid., 185.

43. Ibid., 186.

44. Ibid., 187.

45. Sebastian Balfour, "'Bitter Victory, Sweet Defeat': The March 1996 General Elections and the New Government in Spain," *Government and Opposition* 30 (1996): 282–283.

46. Ibid.

47. Edward Moxon-Browne, "Regionalism in Spain: The Basque Elections of 1990," *Regional Politics and Policy* 1 (1990): 191.

48. See http://cnnenespanol.com/2001/mundo/espana/04/21/especial.vascas.gobier-nos.previos/.

49. Granja Sainz, *El nacionalismo vasco: Un siglo de historia*, 58.

50. See Santiago de Pablo and Ludger Mees, *El péndulo patriótico: Historia del Partido Nacionalista Vasco (1895–2005)* (Barcelona: Crítica, 2005).

51. The Declaration can be viewed online at http://www.filosofia.org/his/h1998bar.htm.

52. The Pact of Lizarra can be viewed online at http://www.euskadi.net/pakea/indi-cel_c.htm.

53. Mees, *Nationalism, Violence, and Democracy*, 140.

54. See "Basque Separatists Announce Ceasefire," September 17, 1998, http://www.ict.org.il/spotlight/det.cfm?id=162.

55. Richard Gillespie lists six reasons, but, overall, his analysis is close to mine. See "Peace Moves in the Basque Country," *Journal of Southern Europe and the Balkans* 1 (1999): 119–136.

56. The 76 percent of 1996 represents the categories "total rejection," "before yes, now no," and "fear." Other possible choices were: "total support" (1 percent), "critical support" (5 percent), "aims yes, means no" (11 percent), "indifferent" (2 percent), "no response" (5 percent). Interestingly, it is the "no response" category that had shrunk most from 1986 and 1981 when the figures were 34 percent and 23 percent, respectively. This is reflective, in all likelihood, of the greater social acceptance for being publicly critical toward ETA. Mees, *Nationalism, Violence, and Democracy*, 99.

57. Mees, *Nationalism, Violence, and Democracy*, 134.

58. Gillespie, "Peace Moves in the Basque Country," 123–124.

59. Ludger Mees, "Between Votes and Bullets: The Basque Country," *Ethnic and Racial Studies* 24 (2001): 813.

60. Ibid., 813–814.

61. Mees, *Nationalism, Violence, and Democracy*, 111–112.

62. For an English version of the communiqué, see http://www.basque-red.net/tregua/eng28.htm. See 3.

63. Ibid.

64. Ibid., 3. Section "Reactions to Truce by ETA."

65. "Otegi propone una coalición nacionalista para negociar con el Estado la autode-terminación," *El País*, December 16, 2003.

66. The case hinged on HB having tried to show a video featuring hooded ETA members during the general election campaign.

67. José Manuel Mata López, *El nacionalismo vasco radical: Discurso, organización y expresiones* (Bilbao: Universidad del Pais Vasco, 1993).

68. The closing triggered demonstrations in the Basque Country. See Jorge Sainz, "Decenas de miles de personas marchan en favor de 'Egunkaria,'" *El Correo*, February 23, 2003, 30.

69. See then foreign minister Ana Palacio's response to an *International Herald Tribune* editorial, reprinted in newsletter 4 of the peace organization Elkarri, 2003, 3–4.

70. "Compareció durante cinco horas ante el TSJPV Atutxa declara por no dissolver Batasuna y dice que cuenta con el apoyo de la mayoria," *El Mundo,* December 3, 2003.

71. http://www.transnational.org/forum/power/2004/03.01_Madrid.html.

72. Interview with Iñaki Aguirre, Foreign Action, Autonomous Community of the Basque Country, July 2004.

73. De Pablo and Mees, *El péndulo patriótico,* 459.

74. Andrew Eatwell, "Zapatero and Ibarretxe Begin Talks About Basque Future," *El País* (English ed.), July 27, 2004, 1.

75. "Zapatero e Ibarretxe se limitan a romper la incomunicación," *El Correo,* July 27, 2004, 1.

76. Batasuna, the formal party of radical Basque nationalism, was outlawed for these elections, but the party's leadership urged supporters to vote instead for the little known Partido Comunista de las Tierras Vascas (PCTV).

77. "Mensaje de Euskadi Ta Askatasuna al Pueblo Vasco." My translation.

78. See, for example, the contributors of *Gritos de libertad: 15 voces contra el terror de ETA y la hegemonia nacionalista,* ed. Cayetano González (Madrid: La Esfera de los Libros, 2004).

79. On the idea of "banal nationalism," see Michael Billig, *Banal Nationalism* (London: Sage, 1995).

CHAPTER FIVE. BASQUE PARADIPLOMACY

1. Noé Cornago, "Exploring the Global Dimensions of Paradiplomacy: Functional and Normative Dynamics in the Global Spreading of Subnational Involvement in International Affairs" (paper presented at the Workshop on Constituent Units in International Affairs organized by the Forum of Federations, Hanover, Germany, 2000).

2. Needless to say, many Basques (as well as Quebeckers, Flemings, Scots, and Catalans) see themselves as a nation and their government as a national one. I use the terms "region" and "regional governments" only because my discussion of paradiplomacy is grounded in a broader comparative context.

3. Of course, this is particularly the case for regions with extensive political autonomy and a national identity. For example, see on Quebec, Alain-G. Gagnon, *Québec: State and Society* (Scarborough, ON: Nelson, 1993).

4. Ronald Watts, *Comparing Federal Systems* (Kingston, ON: Institute of Intergovernmental Relations, Queen's University, 1996).

5. See Ivo Duchacek, Daniel Latouche, and Garth Stevenson, eds., *Perforated Sovereignties and International Relations: Trans-Sovereign Contacts of Subnational Governments* (New York: Greenwood Press, 1999), and Hans J. Michelmann and Panayotis Soldatos, eds., *Federalism and International Relations: The Role of Subnational Units* (Oxford: Clarendon Press, 1990). There were some studies on federalism and international relations published in the 1970s. See, in French, Paul Painchaud, "Fédéralisme et politique étrangère," *Études internationales* 5 (1974): 25–44.

6. Éric Philippart and Michaël Van Cutsem, "De l'explication à la prévision: Analyse

des perspectives en matièere de relations internationales des régions d'Europe," *Études internationales* 30 (1999): 789–808.

7. Brian Hocking, *Foreign Relations and Federal States* (London: Leicester University Press, 1993).

8. Brian Hocking, *Localizing Foreign Policy: Non-Central Governments and Multilayered Diplomacy* (London: MacMillan, 1993).

9. For more on regional governments as international negotiators, see André Lecours, "Paradiplomacy: Reflections on the Foreign Policy and International Relations of Regions," *International Negotiation* 7 (2002): 91–114.

10. Louis Balthazar, Louis Bélanger, and Gordon Mace, eds., *Trente ans de politique extérieure du Québec, 1960–1990* (Quebec: Centre Québécois des Relations Internationales, 1993).

11. John Kincaid, "The International Competence of US States and Their Local Governments," in *Paradiplomacy in Action: The Foreign Relations of Subnational Governments,* ed. Francisco Aldecoa and Michael Keating (London: Frank Cass, 1999), 118.

12. This argument, and the reminder of this paragraph, draws from Noé Cornago, "Exploring the Global Dimensions of Paradiplomacy."

13. Liesbet Hooghe and Gary Marks, *Multi-Level Governance and European Integration* (Oxford: Rowan and Littlefield, 2001).

14. The Four Motors is an organization created in 1988 composed of Rhône-Alpes, Lombardy, Cataluña, and Baden-Württemberg to promote political, economic, and cultural cooperation. The Atlantic Arc, created in 1989, involves thirty-two peripheral maritime regions with a common interest in fishing and coastal matters.

15. The Euregio Meuse-Rhin features four partners: the Belgian provinces of Liège and Limburg; the Belgian German-speaking community; the Dutch province of Limburg; and the German region of Aachen.

16. John Ravenhill, "Federal-States Relations in Australian External Affairs," in Aldecoa and Keating, *Paradiplomacy in Action,* 134–152.

17. Martin Nagelschmidt, "Les relations internationales des Länder allemand et l'évolution du système fédéral dans l'Union européenne: Le cas du Bade-Wurtemberg," *Études internationales* 30 (1999): 679–699.

18. See Région Rhône-Alpes, *Rhône-Alpes, actions internationales,* 2000.

19. Stéphane Paquin simply refers to this type of paradiplomacy as "identity paradiplomacy." See *Paradiplomatie identitaire en Catalogne* (Quebec: Les Presses de l'Université Laval, 2003).

20. In addition to processes linked to identity and mobilization, nationalism also tends to involve the issue of interests. See André Lecours, "Ethnonationalism in the West: A Theoretical Exploration," *Nationalism and Ethnic Politics* 6 (2000): 123–124.

21. André Lecours and Luis Moreno, "Paradiplomacy. A Nation-Building Strategy? A Reference to the Basque Country," in *The Conditions of Diversity in Multinational Democracies,* ed. Alain-G. Gagnon, Montserrat Guibernau, and François Rocher (Montreal: Institute for Research on Public Policy, 2003), 267–294.

22. Ibid.

23. Alexander Ugalde Zubiri, *La acción exterior del nacionalismo Vasco (1890–1939):*

Historia, pensamiento y relaciones internacionales (Bilbao: Instituto Vasco de Administración Pública, 1996), 118.

24. Ibid., 123.

25. Ibid.

26. Alexander Ugalde Zubiri, "The International Relations of Basque Nationalism and the First Basque Autonomous Government (1890–1939)," in Aldecoa and Keating, *Paradiplomacy in Action*, 174.

27. Ibid., 175.

28. See chapter 4.

29. Basque government (presidency), *Euskadi: Un pays sans frontières: A Country Without Borders* (Secretary General for Foreign Action of the Basque Government, 1998), 10.

30. José Luis de Castro Ruano, "La acción exterior de la Comunidad Autonoma del Pais Vasco," 6. Unpublished paper.

31. Paquin, *Paradiplomatie identitaire en Catalogne.*

32. Castro Ruano, "La acción exterior de la Comunidad Autonoma del Pais Vasco," 14.

33. Ibid.

34. Ibid., 15.

35. Secretaría General de Acción Exterior, *Presupuestos generales de la Comunidad Autónomas de Euskadi, 2004*, 3.

36. Basque government (presidency), *Euskadi*, 12.

37. Ibid.

38. Basque government (presidency), *Euskadi*, 26.

39. José Luis de Castro Ruano, "La participacion del País Vasco en la Unión Europea de hoy," in *Los Vascos y Europa*, ed. Amado Castilo, Victor Manuel, and Santiago de Pablo (Vitoria-Gasteiz: Fundación Caja Vital Kutxa, 2001), 372.

40. Ibid., 358.

41. Basque government (presidency), *Euskadi*, 31.

42. See http://www.spri.es/aSW/web/cas/ambitos/inter/index.jsp.

43. Iñaki Zabaleta, "The Basques in the International Press: Coverage by the *New York Times* (1950–1996)," in Douglass et al., *Basque Politics and Nationalism on the Eve of the Millenium*, 68–93.

44. "El Gobierno Vasco aumenta un 25% el presupuesto para sus delegaciones exteriores," *El Correo de Alava*, November 14, 2003. See also the interview with Mikel Burzako, Basque director of foreign relations, "Foreign Action Will Promote the Official Centres of the Basque Government," *Euskal Etxeak–Basque Centres Throughout the World*, issue 71 (2005): 6.

45. Secretaría General de Acción Exterior, *Presupuestos generales de la Comunidad Autónomas de Euskadi, 2006*, 5.

46. Basque government (presidency), *Euskadi*, 61.

47. Ibid., 58.

48. Secretaría General de Acción Exterior, *Presupuestos generales de la Comunidad Autónomas de Euskadi, 2006*, 3–4.

49. Basque government (presidency), *Euskadi,* 48.

50. Ibid., 51.

51. Ibid., 35.

52. Francisco Letamendia, "Basque Nationalism and Cross-Border Co-operation Between the Southern and Northern Basque Countries," *Regional and Federal Studies* 7 (1997): 36.

53. Interview with foreign affairs official, Vitoria, February 19, 2003.

54. Castro Ruano, "La acción exterior de la Comunidad Autonoma del Pais Vasco," 23.

55. Ibid.

56. Paquin, *Paradiplomatie identitaire en Catalogne,* 63.

57. Ibid., 72.

58. In the context of a government-in-exile, the leadership of José Antonio Aguirre between 1937 and 1960 very much shaped Basque actions on the world stage.

59. Michael Keating, "Les nationalités minoritaires d'Espagne face à l'Europe," *Études internationales* 30 (1999): 732.

60. On this last point, see Ministère des Relations Internationales, *Répertoire des ententes internationales du Québec, 1964–2000* (Quebec, 2001).

61. See the province's strategic action plan for foreign affairs drafted under a PQ government. Ministère des Relations Internationales, *Le Québec dans un ensemble international en mutation: Plan stratégique, 2001–2004,* 2001, 23–24.

62. Ministère des Relations Internationales, *Québec in International Forums: Exercising Québec's Constitutional Rights at International Organizations and Conferences,* 2005.

63. Norma Greenaway, "Harper Proposes Voice for Quebec," *The Gazette,* December 20, 2005, A1 and A12.

64. On Flemish paradiplomacy, see Stéphane Paquin, "Paradiplomatie identitaire et diplomatie en Belgique fédérale: Le cas de la Flandre," *Canadian Journal of Political Science* 36 (2003): 621–642.

65. Françoise Massart-Piérard, "Politique des relations extérieures et identité politique: La stratégie des entités fédérées de la Belgique," *Études internationales* 30 (1999): 701–727.

66. On Wallonia, see André Lecours, "Diversité culturelle et relations internationales: Les cas du Québec et de la Wallonie/Comunauté française de Belgique," in *Appartenances, institutions et citoyenneté,* ed. Pierre Noreau and José Woerling (Montreal: Wilson and Lafleur, 2005), 207–218.

67. James Rosenau, "Patterned Chaos in Global Life: Structure and Process in the Two Worlds of World Politics," *International Political Science Review* 9 (1988): 327–364.

CHAPTER SIX. THE MANAGEMENT OF BASQUE NATIONALISM IN SPAIN

1. John McGarry and Brendan O'Leary, *The Politics of Ethnic Conflict Regulation* (London: Routledge, 1993).

2. The next few pages draw from Nicola McEwen and André Lecours, "Voice or Recognition? Accommodation Dilemmas in Multinational Societies" (paper presented at the Canadian Political Science Association conference, Halifax, 2003).

3. Ian Lustick, "Stability in Deeply Divided Societies: Consociationalism vs Control," *World Politics* 31 (1979): 325–344.

4. States operating in a mononational context also have their own nationalism, but it is less easily noticed because typically unopposed.

5. For the case of the United Kingdom, see Nicola McEwen, "State Welfare Nationalism: The Territorial Impact of Welfare State Development in Scotland," *Regional and Federal Studies* 12 (2002): 66–90. For a Canada–United Kingdom comparison, see Nicola McEwen, *Nationalism and the State: Welfare and Identity in Scotland and Quebec* (Brussels: Peter Lang, 2006).

6. Jane Jenson, "Fated to Live in Interesting Times: Canada's Changing Citizenship Regimes," *Canadian Journal of Political Science* 30 (1997): 627–644.

7. Daniel Béland and André Lecours, "The Politics of Territorial Solidarity: Sub-State Nationalism and Social Policy Reform in Canada, the United Kingdom, and Belgium," *Comparative Political Studies* 38 (2005): 676–703.

8. On the debate over social security in Belgium, see Johanne Poirier and Steven Vansteenkiste, "Le débat sur la fédéralisation de la sécurité sociale en Belgique: Le miroir du vouloir-vivre ensemble?" *Revue belge de sécurité sociale* 2 (2000): 331–378.

9. Again, this is not only typical of multinational states. For example, the constitution is central to the American national identity.

10. See Kenneth McRoberts, *Misconceiving Canada: The Struggle for Unity* (Toronto: Oxford University Press, 1997).

11. Billig, *Banal Nationalism*.

12. Eric Kaufmann, ed., *Rethinking Ethnicity: Majority Groups and Dominant Minorities* (London: Routledge, 2004).

13. Arendt Lijphart, "Consociational Democracy" and *Democracy in Plural Societies*; Kenneth McRae, "Contrasting Styles of Democratic Decision-Making: Adversarial versus Consensual Politics," *International Political Science Review* 18 (1997): 279–296.

14. On Belgium, see Pascal Delwit, Jean-Michel De Waele, and Paul Magnette, eds., *Gouverner la Belgique: Clivages et compromis dans une société complexe* (Paris: Presses Universitaires de France, 1999).

15. Brass, *Ethnicity and Nationalism*.

16. Brendan O'Leary and John McGarry, eds., *Northern Ireland Conflict: Consociational Engagements* (Oxford: Oxford University Press, 2004).

17. Ronald L. Watts, *Comparing Federal Systems*, 2nd ed. (Montreal: McGill-Queen's University Press, 1999).

18. Henry Hale has recently argued that federations are more likely to collapse when they contain a core ethnic region. See "Divided We Stand: Institutional Sources of Ethnofederal State Survival and Collapse," *World Politics* 56 (2004): 165–193.

19. Federalism also often involves a house for the constituent units at the center, as is the case for the United States and Germany. In this context, approaches of empowerment at the center and territorial autonomy are entirely compatible.

20. This has always been a central debate in the field of federal studies. See, for example, Richard Simeon and Daniel Patrick-Conway, "Federalism and the Management of Conflict in Multinational Societies," in Gagnon and Tully, *Multinational Democracies*, 339–365.

21. An advocate of this approach is Will Kymlicka. See *Multicultural Citizenship*.

22. See Margaret Thatcher quoted in Jo Eric Murkens (with Peter Jones and Michael Keating), *Scottish Independence: A Practical Guide* (Edinburgh: Edinburgh University Press, 2002), 12

23. The Clarity Act has since stipulated (vague) parameters by saying that the question and result must be "clear" for the federal government to recognize both process and outcome.

24. Former prime minister Aznar saw himself as a "convinced Spaniard," not a Spanish nationalist.

25. Joan Ramon Resina, "Post-National Spain? Post-Spanish Spain?" *Nations and Nationalism* 8 (2002): 377–396.

26. This is a relatively new terminology that has replaced the "non-nationalist" versus "nationalist" dichotomy. This being said, not all "constitutionalists" view Spain in a similar manner. There are centralists, federalists, and autonomists.

27. The theory of constitutional patriotism was designed by Habermas with the unification of Germany in mind.

28. See Ángel Castiñeira, "Nations imaginées: Identité personnelle, identité nationale et lieux de mémoire" (paper presented to the Research Group on Multinational Society and Canada Research Chair on Québec and Canadian Studies, UQAM, Montreal, October 2004), 18.

29. For a discussion on this topic, see Xosé-Manoel Núñez, *Los nacionalismos en la España contemporánea (siglos XIX and XX)* (Barcelona: Hipótesis, 1999), and J. Pérez Garzón et al., *La gestión de la memoria: La historia de España al servicio del poder* (Barcelona: Crítica, 2000).

30. This was the case of former prime minister Aznar in his address at Georgetown University in September 2004. Aznar argued that Spain's problem with Islamic terrorism did not begin with the PP government's support of the American military intervention in Iraq, but rather with the Reconquista, described as "a long battle to recover its [Spain's] identity." See "Seven Theses on Today's Terrorism," September 21, 2004, p. 3. http://data.georgetown.edu/president/aznar/inauguraladdress.html.

31. Resina, "Post-National Spain? Post-Spanish Spain?" 382. An independent commission judged that more than the minimal legal requirement of Spanish history was taught in Basque schools.

32. This is slowly changing. For example, the Spanish government produced the European constitution in Catalan, Euskara, and Galician. This has sparked protest from the Valencian PP, which argues that Valencian is different from Catalan.

33. This was the Ley de Calidad de Educación.

34. Núñez, "What Is Spanish Nationalism Today?" 730.

35. The PP's intense focus on ETA led to some bizarre statements. For example, several months after the Madrid attacks and with all evidence pointing toward Islamic fun-

damentalists, former interior minister Ángel Acebes still maintained the possibility of some ETA involvement. See "Acebes insiste en que aún planea 'la sombra de ETA' sobre el 11-M," *El Correo*, July 29, 2004, p. 1.

36. Núñez, "What Is Spanish Nationalism Today?" 740.

37. Ibid.

38. Ibid., 735.

39. The fact that judges are under no obligation to speak the second official language of the autonomous community where they are working (if there is one) does not help.

40. A recent examination of public addresses by Belgian and Spanish monarchs shows, in contrast to Belgium, numerous references to the (qualities of) the Spanish nation and few references to substate communities. Bart Maddens and Kristine vanden Berghe, "The Identity Politics of Multicultural Nationalism: A Comparison Between the Regular Public Addresses of the Belgian and Spanish Monarchs (1990–2000)," *European Journal of Political Research* 42 (2003): 601–627.

41. See Basque government, *Propuesta de Estatuto político de la Comunidad de Euskadi* (Ajuria-Enea, 2003).

42. See, for example, the interview with lehendakari Ibarretxe in *Cita internacional*, "Plan Ibarretxe: Una propuesta abierta al debate," (Madrid: Ediciones Embassy SL, 2004, no. 23), 49–55.

43. See the speech by lehendakari Ibarretxe to the Basque parliament, reproduced in *El Correo*, September 25, 2004, which can be viewed at http://www.bastaya.org/noticias/2004/09/25/Textointegrodiscursolehendakari.htm.

44. See, for example, the most frequently asked questions about the plan Ibarretxe (*Propuesta del Gobierno Vasco para la convivienca en En Euskadi*). Frequently asked questions at http:// www.nuevoestatutodeeuskadi.net/imp_preg.asp?hizk=esp.

45. Interview with Iñaki Aguirre, Foreign Action, Autonomous Community of the Basque Country, July 2004.

46. On this issue, see Enric Martínez-Herrera, "Nationalist Extremism and Outcomes of State Policies in the Basque Country, 1979–2001," *International Journal on Multicultural Societies* 4 (2002). www.unesco.org/most/v14n1martinez.pdf.

47. Carrie Hamilton, "Re-membering the Basque Nationalist Family: Daughters, Fathers, and the Reproduction of the Radical Nationalist Community," *Journal of Spanish Cultural Studies* 1 (2000): 153–171.

48. Sharryn Kasmir, "'More Basque Than You!': Class, Youth, and Identity in an Industrial Basque Town," *Identities: Global Studies in Culture and Power* 9 (2003): 39–68.

49. Paulina Raento, "Political Mobilisation and Place-Specificity: Radical Nationalist Street Campaigning in the Spanish Basque Country," *Space and Polity* 1 (1997): 191–204.

50. See, for example, Jesús Eguiguren Imaz, *La crisis vasca: Entre la rupture y el diáalogo* (Sevilla: Editorial Cambio, 2004).

51. This data is drawn from "Encuesta del grupo vocento: La mitad de los vascos apoyaría el plan Ibarretxe en un referéndum," *El Mundo*, November 30, 2003. http:// www.elmundo.es/elmundo/2003/12/03/espana/1070436545.html.

52. See Basque government (presidency), "La opinión de la sociedad vasca sobre el nuevo pacto político para la convivencia," October 2002. http://www.euskadi.net/estudios_sociologicos.

53. In this context, perhaps the PNV's interest in Quebec and the Parti Québécois's approach is misplaced. I discuss some of the differences between the two situations in the next chapter. On the PNV's interest in the Quebec model, see the reports published in *El País* (international ed.) between July 6 and 10, 2003. http://www.bastaya.org/actualidad/PlanIbarretxe/JoseLuisBarberia_ReportajeQuebec.htm.

54. A survey conducted in the summer of 2004 by Francisco Llera shows that 41 percent of Basques favor PNV-PSOE negotiations over the Ibarretxe proposal, while 26 percent like it as is and 20 percent would like it to be withdrawn completely. See http://www.bastaya.org/actualidad/PlanIbarretxe/Ed_abc_ELPLANNOAVANZA.htm.

55. Flynn, "Constructed Identities and Iberia," 707–713.

56. On the "disappearance" of Spanish nationalism, see Fernando García de Cortázar and José González-Vesga, *Breve historia de España* (Madrid: Alianza, 1993).

57. Núñez, "What Is Spanish Nationalism Today?" 737.

58. Resina, "Post-National Spain? Post-Spanish Spain?"

59. Partido Popular, *Elecciones generales 2000: El compromiso del centro* (Madrid, 2000), 95–111. Half of this chapter discusses European, international, and defense policy.

60. Ibid., 95. My translation.

61. Edurne Uriarte, *España, Patriotismo y Nación* (Madrid: Calpe, SA, 2003).

62. Ibid., 233–253.

63. Núñez, "What Is Spanish Nationalism Today?" 730.

64. Ibid., 737.

CHAPTER SEVEN. BASQUE NATIONALISM IN COMPARATIVE PERSPECTIVE

1. The other major nationalist movement in Spain, the Catalan, has been compared to Basque nationalism in two excellent studies, Daniele Conversi's *The Basques, the Catalans, and Spain,* and Juan Díez Medrano's *Divided Nations.* Michael Keating is one of the few authors who has integrated Basque nationalism into broader research about substate nationalism in Western Europe and Canada. See *Plurinational Democracy: Stateless Nations in a Post-Sovereign Era.*

2. This is partly because a good portion of this literature focuses on ETA.

3. Another one is the Corsican movement, but its level of violence has never been comparable to the Basque. The most comparable case in the West with respect to violence and politics was Northern Ireland. However, the configuration of the political conflict is different since there is no Northern Ireland nationalist movement per se but rather two communities seeking integration into two different states. For a good comparative discussion of the Basque and Northern Ireland cases, see Keating, "Northern Ireland and the Basque Country."

4. There are at least three other nationalist movements in Western Europe: Welsh, Corsican, and Galician. However, they are less politically significant than

the four just enumerated and will not be discussed in any systematic fashion in the present chapter.

5. As indicated in previous chapters, the popularity of the secessionist stream of Catalan nationalism represented by the ERC has grown in recent years.

6. The most similar case here would be the nationalism of certain aboriginal communities such as the Mohawks.

7. Deutsch, *Nationalism and Social Communication*.

8. James C. Scott, *Seeing Like the State* (New Haven, CT: Yale University Press, 1998).

9. A good general book in English on Belgian politics is Kenneth D. McRae, *Conflict and Compromise in Multilingual Societies: Belgium* (Waterloo, ON: Wilfrid Laurier University Press, 1986).

10. Hobsbawm, *Nations and Nationalism since 1780*, 170.

11. Michael Keating, *Nations Against the State: The New Politics of Nationalism in Quebec, Catalonia, and Scotland* (New York: St. Martin's Press, 1996).

12. Pierre Martin, "When Nationalism Meets Continentalism: The Politics of Free Trade in Quebec," *Regional and Federal Studies* 5 (1995): 1–27.

13. The Scottish long-term care for the elderly program actual came out of a Great Britain Royal Commission, the Sutherland report. See Sir Stewart Sutherland, *With Respect to Old Age: Long-Term Care—Rights and Responsibilities: A Report by the Royal Commission on Long-Term Care* (London, March 1999).

14. Helen Fawcett, "The Making of Social Justice Policy in Scotland: Devolution and Social Exclusion," in *Has Devolution Made a Difference? The State of the Nations 2004*, ed. Alan Trench (Exeter: Imprint Academic, 2004), 241.

15. Poirier and Vansteenkiste, "Le débat sur la fédéralisation de la sécurité sociale en Belgique," 345–346.

16. See, for example, the September 2004 speech to the Basque parliament of lehendakari Ibarretxe, 9–10. Available at http://bastaya.org/noticias/2004/09/25/textouintegrodiscursolehendakari.htm.

17. Brian Taylor, *Scotland's Parliament: Triumph and Disaster* (Edinburgh: Edinburgh University Press, 2002), 17.

18. Jan Erk, "From Vlaams Blok to Vlaams Belang: The Belgian Far-Right Renames Itself," *West European Politics* 28 (2005): 493–502.

19. Frédéric Boily, *La pensée nationaliste de Lionel Groulx* (Sillery: Septentrion, 2003).

20. Jeffrey Cormier and Philippe Couton, "The Limits of Québec Nationalism, 1918–39. An Interwar Paradox," *Nationalism and Ethnic Politics* 4 (1998): 47–74.

21. Kenneth McRoberts, *Quebec: Social Change and Political Crisis* (Toronto: McClelland and Stewart, 1993).

22. Kris Deschouwer, "Comprendre le nationalisme flamamd," *Fédéralisme-Régionalisme*, 1999–2000:81–91.

23. On the Flemish Movement, see Louis Vos, "The Flemish National Question," in *Nationalism in Belgium: Shifting Identities, 1780\–1995*, ed. Kas Deprez and Louis Vos (New York: St. Martin's Press, 1998).

24. There is a Lionel-Groulx subway station in Montreal.

25. Louis Balthazar, *Bilan du nationalisme au Québec* (Montreal: L'Hexagone, 1986).

26. On Cataluña, see McRoberts, *Catalonia: Nation-Building Without a State.*

27. On Scottish narratives and self-perceptions, see David McCrone, *Understanding Scotland: The Sociology of a Nation,* 2nd ed. (London: Routledge, 2001).

28. Jocelyn Maclure, *Quebec Identity: The Challenge of Pluralism* (Montreal: McGill-Queen's University Press, 2003).

29. Hans Kohn, *The Idea of Nationalism: A Study of Its Origins and Background* (New York: Macmillan, 1944.)

30. David Brown, "Are There Good and Bad Nationalisms?" *Nations and Nationalism* 5 (1999): 281–303.

31. Kohn, *The Idea of Nationalism.*

32. Steven Shulman, "Challenging the Civic/Ethnic and West/East Dichotomy in the Study of Nationalism," *Comparative Political Studies* 35 (2002): 554–585.

33. Ibid., 571.

34. Rogers Brubaker, *Nationalism Re-Framed: Nationhood and the National Question in the New Europe* (Cambridge: Cambridge University Press, 1996).

35. Bernard Yack, "The Myth of the Civic Nation," in Ronald Beiner, ed., *Theorizing Nationalism* (Albany: State University of New York Press, 1999).

36. Anthony D. Smith, *National Identity* (Reno: University of Nevada Press, 1991), 13.

37. David Brown, *Contemporary Nationalism: Civic, Ethnocultural, and Multicultural Politics* (London: Routledge, 2000), 64–69.

38. Greenfeld, *Nationalism.*

39. Jean-Pierre Derriennic, *Nationalisme et démocratie: Les illusions des indépendantistes Québécois* (Montreal: Boréal, 1995).

40. Marc Swyngedouw and Gilles Ivaldi, "The Extreme Right Utopia in Belgium and France: The Ideology of the Flemish Vlaams Blok and the French Front National," *West European Politics* 24 (2001): 1\–22.

41. See, for example, Vlaams Blok, *Een toekomst voor Vlaanderen,* 2003.

42. As I discussed in chapter 3, Sabino Arana made the argument that the Basques were more Catholic than Spaniards.

43. Two smaller parties, the Scottish Greens and Socialists, also favor independence but find their raison d'être in left-wing progressive politics rather than nationalist politics.

44. The agreement of Ajuria-Enea marked a first change in the PNV's relationship with radical Basque nationalism.

45. This was the attitude of former PNV president Xabier Arzalluz.

46. See Carmelo Urza, "The Election of 30N," *Basque Studies Program Newsletter,* no. 35 (1997). In 2000, reporters Sans Frontières expressed concern that "media outlets and journalists who do not share the radical nationalist ideology are considered 'Basque traitors' or 'Spanish invaders' and are threatened by the armed independence organisation Euskadi ta Askatasuna (ETA)." See http://www.ifex.org/fr/content/view/archivefeatures/1084/.

47. This is best reflected in the denunciations of the Ibarretxe proposal. See, for example, Jesús Eguiguren Imaz, *La crisis vasca*.

48. Social divisions in the Basque Country are not as severe as they were, for example, in Northern Ireland, but the mobilization of civil society in support of or against Basque nationalism makes society in the Basque Country more divided by the "national question" than in Cataluña, Québec, Scotland, or Flanders.

49. For a discussion on this bill, see François Rocher and Nadia Virelli, "Questioning Constitutional Democracy in Canada: From the Canadian Supreme Court Reference to the Clarity Act," in Gagnon, Guibernau, and Rocher, *The Conditions of Diversity in Multinational Democracy*.

50. For example, the Eurobarometer question on national versus European identities measures the relative importance of national and supranational attachments in Europe.

51. See the data presented by Michael Keating in *Plurinational Democracy*, 56–101.

52. Michael Keating in *Plurinational Democracy*.

53. See, for example, Presse Canadienne, "Un modèle pour le BQ, le traité de Maastricht," *Le Devoir*, April 10, 1995, A4.

54. http://www.adq.qc.ca/fr/vision/ADQ_Voie_autonomiste.pdf.

55. Béland and Lecours, "The Politics of Territorial Solidarity."

56. See, for example, Paul van Rompuy, "10 jaar financiële stromen tussen de Gewesten in België," *Leuvense Economische Standpunten*, no. 45, KULeuven, CES, July 1998.

57. Flemish government, "Note de discussion pour une nouvelle étape dans la réforme de l'État," February 29, 1996.

58. Poirier and Vansteenkiste, "Le débat sur la fédéralisation de la sécurité sociale en Belgique," 348–349.

59. Ibid., 349. Agalev changed its name to Groen! in 2003.

60. Guiseppe Pagano, *Les résolutions du Parlement flamand pour une réforme de l'État* (Brussels: CRISP, no. 1670–1671, 2000).

61. Pagano, *Les résolutions du Parlement flamand*, 44.

62. Political Context, *Report on Devolution Poll* (London, 1996), 15.

63. For some comparative perspectives on social policy and nationalism, see the conclusion in Daniel Béland and André Lecours, *Nationalism and Social Policy: The Politics of Territorial Solidarity* (forthcoming).

64. Scottish National Party, *Raising the Standard: There Shall Be an Independent Scottish Parliament*, 2005.

65. A good general work on globalization is Jan Aart Scholte, *Globalization: A Critical Introduction* (London: MacMillan, 2000).

66. David Held, Anthony McGrew, David Goldblatt, and Jonathan Perraton, *Global Transformations: Politics, Economics, Culture* (Stanford, CA: Stanford University Press, 1999), 11–12.

67. Roland Axtmann, "The State of the State: The Model of the Modern State and Its Contemporary Transformation," *International Political Science* 25 (2004): 259–280.

68. See Anthony Smith, *Nations and Nationalism in a Global Era* (Cambridge: Polity Press, 1995).

69. David Harvey, *The Condition of Post-Modernity: An Enquiry into the Origins of Cultural Change* (Oxford: Blackwell, 1989).

70. David Laitin, "Culture and National Identity: The 'East' and European Integration," *West European Politics* 25 (2002): 55–80.

71. Michael Keating and John McGarry, introduction to *Minority Nationalism and the Changing International Order,* ed. Michael Keating and John McGarry (Oxford: Oxford University Press, 2001), 3.

72. Michael Keating, "European Integration and the Nationalities Question," *Politics and Society* 32 (2004): 379.

73. Manuel Castells, *The Power of Identity* (London: Blackwell, 1997).

74. This type of statement is somewhat ironic when it comes from state officials since it assumes that there is no such thing as state nationalism.

75. See, for example, Hooghe and Marks, "'Europe with the Regions.'"

76. Keating, "European Integration and the Nationalities Question."

77. Ibid., 382.

CONCLUSION

1. Montserrat Guibernau and John Hutchinson, eds., *History and National Destiny* (London: Blackwell, 2004).

2. See, for example, Montserrat Guibernau and John Hutchinson, eds., *Understanding Nationalism* (Cambridge, UK: Polity, 2001).

3. Tom Nairn, *Faces of Nationalism: Janus Revisited* (London: Verso, 1997).

4. Greenfeld, *Nationalism.*

5. Joseph Carens, ed., *Is Quebec Nationalism Just? Perspective from Anglophone Canada* (Montreal: McGill-Queen's University Press, 1995); Allen Buchanan, *Secession: The Morality of Political Divorce from Sumter to Lithuania and Quebec* (Boulder, CO: Westview Press, 1991).

6. See, for example, Rogers Brubaker, *Citizenship and Nationhood in France and Germany* (Cambridge: Harvard University Press, 1992).

7. Hendrik Spruyt, *The Sovereign State and Its Competitors: An Analysis of Systems Change* (Princeton, NJ: Princeton University Press, 1994).

8. Scott, *Seeing Like the State.*

9. Margaret Levi, *Of Rule and Revenue* (Berkeley and Los Angeles: University of California Press, 1988), and *Consent, Dissent, and Patriotism* (Cambridge: Cambridge University Press, 1997).

10. Timothy Mitchell, *Colonising Egypt* (Berkeley and Los Angeles: University of California Press, 1991).

11. Joel S. Migdal, *Strong Societies and Weak States: State-Societies Relations and State Capabilities in the Third World* (Princeton, NJ: Princeton University Press, 1988).

12. Peter B. Evans, *Embedded Autonomy: State and Industrial Tranformation* (Princeton, NJ: Princeton University Press, 1995).

13. The literature is too large to cite, but the following is a representative collection. Michael E. Brown et al., eds., *Nationalism and Ethnic Conflict* (Cambridge: MIT Press, 1997).

14. See, for example, Barry R. Posen, "The Security Dilemma and Ethnic Conflict," *Survival* 35 (1993): 27–47.

15. Federalism and autonomy are typically studied as possible remedies for ethnic violence. See, for example, Ruth Lapidoth, *Autonomy: Flexible Solutions to Ethnic Conflict* (Washington, DC: U.S. Institute for Peace, 1996). On the impact of electoral rules, see Steve Saideman et al., "Fixed and Endogenous Elections and Ethnic Conflict: Similar or Different Causal Relationships" (paper presented at the International Studies Association conference, Montreal, February 2004).

16. See John Mueller, "The Banality of 'Ethnic War,'" *International Security* 25 (2000): 42–70. Of course, comparative politics specialists have also put forward rational choice explanations for nationalism.

17. Roger D. Petersen, Understanding Ethnic Violence: Fear, Hatred, and Resentment in Twentieth-Century Eastern Europe (Cambridge: Cambridge University Press, 2002).

Bibliography

Agranoff, Robert. "Inter-Governmental Politics and Policy: Building Federal Arrangements in Spain." *Regional Politics and Policy* 3 (1993): 1–28.

Aguilar, Paloma. "The Memory of the Civil War in the Transition to Democracy: The Peculiarity of the Basque Case." In *Politics and Policy in Democratic Spain*, edited by Paul Heywood, 5–25. London: Frank Cass, 1999.

Aguirre, José Antonio. *De Guernica a Nueva York pasando por Berlin*. Bilbao: Ekin, 1992.

———. *Obras completas de José Antonio Aguirre*. Edited by Martin Ugalde. San Sebastián: Sendoa Argitaldaria, 1981.

———. *Veinte años de gestión del gobierno vasco (1936–1956)*. Durango: Leopoldo Zugaza Editor, 1978.

Aldecoa, Francisco, and Michael Keating, eds. *Paradiplomacy in Action: The Foreign Relations of Subnational Governments*. London: Frank Cass, 1999.

Álvarez Junco, José. *Mater dolorosa: La idea de España en el siglo XIX*. Madrid: Taurus, 2001.

———. "The Nation-Building Process in Nineteenth-Century Spain." In Mar-Molinero and Smith, *Nationalism and the Nation*, 89–106.

Anderson, Benedict. *Imagined Communities*. 2nd ed. London: Verso, 1991.

Arana Goiri, Sabino. *Bizcaya por su independencia*. Bilbao: GEU Argitaldariak, 1980.

———. "El Catalanismo." *Baserritarra*, no. 18, August 29, 1897.

———. "Discurso de Larrazábal." In *Obras completas de Arana-Goiri'tar Sabin*, 154–160.

———. "Efectos de la invasión." *Baserritarra*, no. 11, July 11, 1897.

———. *Obras completas de Arana-Goiri'tar Sabin*. Buenos Aires: Sabindiar-Batza, 1965.

———. *Obras escogidas: Antología politica*. San Sebastián: L. Haranburu, 1978.

———. *El partido carlista y los Fueros vasco-navarros*. Buenos Aires, 1912.

Arbos, Xavier. "Central versus Peripheral Nationalism in Building Democracy: The Case of Spain." *Canadian Review of Studies in Nationalism* 14 (1987): 143–160.

Aretxaga, Begoña. "A Hall of Mirrors: On the Spectral Character of Basque Violence." In Douglass et al., *Basque Politics and Nationalism*, 115–126.

Armstrong, John. *Nations Before Nationalism*. Chapel Hill: University of North Carolina Press, 1982.

Axtmann, Roland. "The State of the State: The Model of the Modern State and Its Contemporary Transformation." *International Political Science Review* 25 (2004): 259–280.

Aznar, José María. "Seven Theses on Today's Terrorism." Inaugural address at Georgetown University, September 21, 2004. http://data.georgetown.edu/president/aznar/inauguraladdress.html.

Balcells, Alberts. *Catalan Nationalism: Past and Present*. New York: St. Martin's Press, 1996.

Balfour, Sebastian. "'Bitter Victory, Sweet Defeat': The March 1996 General Elections and the New Government in Spain." *Government and Opposition* 30 (1996): 275–287.

———. "'The Lion and the Pig': Nationalism and National Identity in Fin-de Siècle Spain." In Mar-Molinero and Smith, *Nationalism and the Nation*, 107–118.

———. "Spain from 1931 to the Present." In Carr, *Spain: A History*, 243–282.

Balthazar, Louis. *Bilan du nationalisme au Québec*. Montreal: L'Hexagone, 1986.

Balthazar, Louis, Louis Bélanger, and Gordon Mace, eds. *Trente ans de politique extérieure du Québec, 1960–1990*. Quebec: Centre québécois des relations internationales, 1993.

Barahona, Renato. *Vizcaya on the Eve of Carlism: Politics and Society, 1800–1833*. Reno: University of Nevada Press, 1989.

Bard, Rachel. *Navarra: The Durable Kingdom*. Reno: University of Nevada Press, 1982.

Barreto, Antonio. "Constructing Boundaries: Ethnic Boundaries and Elite Preferences in Puerto Rico." *Nationalism and Ethnic Politics* 7 (2001): 21–40.

Basaldúa, Pedro de. *El libertador vasco: Sabino de Arana Goiri*. Bilbao: GEU Argitaldaria, 1977.

Basque government (presidency). *Euskadi: Un pays sans frontières: A Country Without Borders*. Secretary General for Foreign Action of the Basque Government, 1998.

———. "La opinion de la sociedad vasca sobre el nuevo pacto político para la convivencia," October 2002. http://www.euskadi.net/estudios_sociologicos.

———. *Propuesta de nuevo estatuto político de la Comunidad de Euskadi*. Ajuria-Enea, 2003.

Beiner, Ronald, ed. *Theorizing Nationalism*. Albany: State University of New York Press, 1999.

Béland, Daniel, and André Lecours. *Nationalism and Social Policy: The Politics of Territorial Solidarity*. Place: Publisher, forthcoming.

———. "The Politics of Territorial Solidarity: Sub-state Nationalism and Social Policy Reform in Canada, the United Kingdom, and Belgium." *Comparative Political Studies* 38 (2005): 676–703.

Beltza. *El nacionalismo vasco en el exilio 1937–1960*. San Sebastián: Editorial Txertoa, 1977.

Benegas, Txiki. *Una propuesta de paz*. Madrid: Espasa Calpe, SA, 2000.

Bertrand, Jacques. *Nationalism and Ethnic Conflict in Indonesia*. New York: Cambridge University Press, 2004.

Bhabha, Homi, ed. *Nation and Narration*. London: Routledge, 1990.

Bilbao, Iban. "The Basque Parliament and Government." *Basque Studies Program Newsletter*, no. 27, 1983. http://basque.unr.edu/09/9.3/9.3.27t/9.3.27.06.bsqparl.htm.

Billig, Michael. *Banal Nationalism*. London: Sage, 1995.

Boily, Frédéric. *La pensée nationaliste de Lionel Groulx*. Sillery, QC: Septentrion, 2003.

Bookman, Milica Zarcovic. *The Political Economy of Discontinuous Development: Regional Disparities and Inter-Regional Conflict*. New York: Praeger, 1991.

Brand, Jack. "Andalusia: Nationalism as a Strategy for Autonomy." *Canadian Review of Studies in Nationalism* 15 (1988): 1–9.

Brass, Paul. *Ethnicity and Nationalism: Theory and Comparison*. London: Sage, 1991.

Breuilly, John. *Nationalism and the State*. New York: St. Martin's Press, 1982.

Brown, David. "Are There Good and Bad Nationalisms?" *Nations and Nationalism* 5 (1999): 281–303.

———. *Contemporary Nationalism: Civic, Ethnocultural, and Multicultural Politics*. London: Routledge, 2000.

Brown, Michael E., et al., eds. *Nationalism and Ethnic Conflict*. Cambridge: MIT Press, 1997.

Brubaker, Rogers. *Citizenship and Nationhood in France and Germany*. Cambridge: Harvard University Press, 1992.

———. *Nationalism Re-Framed: Nationhood and the National Question in the New Europe*. Cambridge: Cambridge University Press, 1996.

Buchanan, Allen. *Secession: The Morality of Political Divorce from Sumter to Lithuania and Quebec*. Boulder, CO: Westview Press, 1991.

Campbell, John L. "Institutional Analysis and the Role of Ideas in Political Economy." *Theory and Society* 27 (1998): 377–409.

Campelo Gutiérrez, José. *Nacimiento y origen de la violencia etarra*. Madrid: Grupo Libro, SA, 1994.

Carens, Joseph, ed. *Is Quebec Nationalism Just? Perspective from Anglophone Canada*. Montreal: McGill-Queen's University Press, 1995.

Carr, Raymond. *Spain: 1808–1975*. 2nd ed. Oxford: Clarendon Press, 1982.

———, ed. *Spain: A History*. Oxford: Oxford University, 2000.

Castells, Manuel. "Globalization, Identity, and the Basque Question." In Douglass et al., *The Basque Diaspora/La diaspora vasca*, 22–33

Castells, Manuel. *The Power of Identity*. London: Blackwell, 1997.

Castiñeira, Ángel. "Nations imaginées: Identité personnelle, identité nationale et lieux de mémoire." Paper presented to the Research Group on Multinational Society and Canada Research Chair on Québec and Canadian Studies, UQAM, Montreal, October 2004.

Castro Ruano, José Luis de. "La accion exterior de la Comunidad Autonoma del Pais Vasco." Unpublished paper.

———. "La participacion del Pais Vasco en la Union Europea de hoy." In *Los Vascos y Europa*, edited by Amado Castilo and Victor Manuel. Vitoria-Gasteiz: Fundación Caja Vital Kutxa, 2001.

Clark, Robert P. *The Basque Insurgents: ETA, 1952–1980*. Madison: University of Wisconsin Press, 1984.

———. *The Basques: The Franco Years and Beyond*. Reno: University of Nevada Press, 1979.

———. *Negotiating with ETA: Obstacles to Peace in the Basque Country, 1975–1988.* Reno: University of Nevada Press, 1990.

Colley, Linda. *Britons: Forging the Nation, 1707–1837.* New Haven, CT: Yale University Press, 1992.

Collier, Ruth Berins, and David Collier. *Shaping the Political Arenas: Critical Junctures, the Labor Movement, and Regime Dynamics in Latin America.* Princeton, NJ: Princeton University Press, 1991.

Colomer, Josep M. "The Spanish 'State of Autonomies.'" In *Politics and Policy in Democratic Spain,* edited by Paul Heywood, 40–52. London: Frank Cass, 1999.

Connor, Walker. *Ethnonationalism: The Quest for Understanding.* Princeton, NJ: Princeton University Press, 1994.

———. "The Seductive Lure of Economic Explanations." In *Ethnonationalism,* by Walker Connor, 144–164.

Conversi, Daniele. *The Basque, the Catalans, and Spain: Alternative Routes to Nationalist Mobilization.* London: Hurst, 1997.

———. "Domino or Internal Developments? The Influences of International Events and Political Ideologies on Catalan and Basque Nationalism." *West European Politics* 16 (1993): 245–269.

———. "Ideological Fragmentation, Cultural Nationalism, and State Violence: Euskadi and Catalonia (1939–1968)." *Canadian Review of Studies in Nationalism* 26 (1999): 37–51.

———. "Language or Race? The Choice of Core Values in the Development of Catalan and Basque Nationalism." *Ethnic and Racial Studies* 13 (1990): 50–69.

———. "The Smooth Transition: Spain's 1978 Constitution and the Nationalities Question." *National Identities* 4 (2002): 223–244.

Corcuera, Javier. *Orígenes, ideología y organización del nacionalismo vasco (1876–1904).* Madrid: Siglo XXI, 1979.

———. *Politica y derecho: La construcción de la autonomía vasca.* Madrid: Centro de Estudios Constitucionales, 1991.

Cormier, Jeffrey, and Philippe Couton. "The Limits of Québec Nationalism, 1918–39: An Interwar Paradox." *Nationalism and Ethnic Politics* 4 (1998): 47–74.

Cornago Prieto, Noé. "Exploring the Global Dimensions of Paradiplomacy: Functional and Normative Dynamics in the Global Spreading of Subnational Involvement in International Affairs." Presented at the Workshop on Constituent Units in International Affairs organized by the Forum of Federations, Hanover, Germany, 2000.

Del Valle, Teresa. *Korrika: Basque Ritual for Ethnic Identity.* Reno: University of Nevada Press, 1993.

Delwit, Pascal, Jean-Michel De Waele, and Paul Magnette, eds. *Gouverner la Belgique: Clivages et compromis dans une société complexe.* Paris: Presses Universitaires de France, 1999.

Deprez, Kas, and Louis Vos, eds. *Nationalism in Belgium: Shifting Identities, 1780–1995.* New York: St. Martin's Press, 1998.

Derriennic, Jean-Pierre. *Nationalisme et démocratie: Les illusions des indépendantistes Québécois.* Montreal: Boréal, 1995.

Deschouwer, Kris. "Comprendre le nationalisme flamamd." *Fédéralisme-Régionalisme*, 1999–2000:81–91.

Deutsch, Karl. *Nationalism and Social Communication: An Inquiry into the Formation of Nationality.* Cambridge: MIT Press, 1966.

Díaz, Elías. "Ideologies in the Making of the Spanish Transition." *West European Politics* 26 (1998): 26–39.

Díez Medrano, Juan. *Divided Nations: Class Conflict, Politics, and Nationalism in the Basque Country and Catalonia.* Ithaca, NY: Cornell University Press, 1995.

Domínguez Iribarren, Florencio. *De la negociación a la tregua: ¿El final de ETA?* Madrid: Grupo Santillana de Ediciones, SA, 1998.

Dorronsoro, Mikel, Alfredo Herbosa, and Yolanda Orive. *Historia de España y del País Vasco.* Zarautz: Itxaropena, SA, Servicio Editorial de la Universidad del País Vasco, 1998.

Douglass, William A. "Sabino's Sin: Racism and the Founding of Basque Nationalism." In *Ethnonationalism in the Contemporary World: Walker Connor and the Study of Nationalism,* edited by Daniele Conversi. London: Routledge, 2002.

Douglass, William A., and Jon Bilbao. *Amerikanuak: Basques in the New World.* Reno: University of Nevada Press, 1975.

Douglass, William A., Carmelo Urza, Linda White, and Joseba Zulaika, eds. *The Basque Diaspora/La diáspora vasca.* Reno, NV: Center for Basque Studies, 2000.

———, eds. *Basque Politics and Nationalism on the Eve of the Millenium.* Reno, NV: Center for Basque Studies, 1999.

Douglass, William A., and Pedro Ibarra Güell. "A Basque Referendum: Resolution of Political Conflict or the Promised Land of Error." Unpublished paper.

Douglass, William A., and Joseba Zulaika. "On the Interpretation of Terrorist Violence: ETA and the Basque Political Process." *Comparative Studies in Society and History* 32 (1990): 238–257.

Dowding, Keith. "The Compatibility of Behaviouralism, Rational Choice, and 'New Institutionalism.'" *Journal of Theoretical Politics* 6 (1994): 105–117.

Duchacek, Ivo, Daniel Latouche, and Garth Stevenson, eds. *Perforated Sovereignties and International Relations: Trans-Sovereign Contacts of Subnational Governments.* New York: Greenwood Press, 1999.

Eatwell, Andrew. "Zapatero and Ibarretxe Begin Talks About Basque Future." *El País* (English edition), July 27, 2004.

Eguiguren Imaz, Jesús. *La crisis vasca: Entre la ruptura y el diálogo.* Sevilla: Editorial Cambio, 2004.

Eller, Jack, and Reed Coughlan. "The Poverty of Primordialism." *Ethnic and Racial Studies* 16 (1993): 183–202.

Erk, Jan. "From Vlaams Blok to Vlaams Belang: The Belgian Far Right Renames Itself." *West European Politics* 28 (2005): 493–502.

Evans, Peter. *Embedded Autonomy: State and Industrial Tranformation.* Princeton, NJ: Princeton University Press, 1995.

Evans, Peter, Dietrich Rueschemeyer, and Theda Skocpol. *Bringing the State Back In.* Cambridge: Cambridge University Press, 1985.

Falcón, Lidia. "Violent Democracy." *Journal of Spanish Cultural Studies* 3 (2002): 15–28.

Fawcett, Helen. "The Making of Social Justice Policy in Scotland: Devolution and Social Exclusion." In *Has Devolution Made a Difference? The State of the Nations 2004*, edited by Alan Trench. Exeter: Imprint Academic, 2004.

Flynn, Mary Katherine. "Constructed Identities and Iberia." *Ethnic and Racial Studies* 24 (2001): 703–718.

———. *Ideology, Mobilization and the Nation: The Rise of Irish, Basque, and Carlist Nationalist Movements in the Nineteenth and Early Twentieth Centuries*. London: MacMillan, 2000.

Gagnon, Alain-G. *Québec: State and Society*. Scarborough, ON: Nelson, 1993.

Gallop, Rodney. *A Book of the Basques*. Reno: University of Nevada Press, 1970.

García, Javier. *Los Gal al descubierto: La trama de la "guerra sucia" contra ETA*. Madrid: El País/Aguilar, SA, 1988.

García de Cortázar, Fernando, and José González-Vesga. *Breve historia de España*. Madrid: Alianza, 1993.

García de Cortazar, Fernando, and Manuel Montero. *Historia de Vizcaya: Los orígenes, la Edad Media, el Antiguo Régimen a los siglos XIX y XX*. San Sebastián: Txertoa, 1994.

García de Cortazar, Fernando, Manuel Montero, Juan M. Betanzos, and Severino Sanchez. *Historia de Alava*. San Sebastián: Txertoa, 1986.

García Venero, Maximiano. *Historia del nacionalismo vasco*. Madrid: Editora Nacional, 1968.

Garmendia, José María. *Historia de ETA*. San Sebastián: Haranburu, 1995.

———. "ETA: Nacimiento, Desarollo y Crisis." In Antonio Elorza et al., *La Historia de ETA*, 77–168. Madrid: Temas de Hoy, 2000.

Garmendia, Vicente. *La ideologia Carlista (1868–1876): En los orígenes del nacionalismo vasco*. San Sebastián: Diputación Foral de Guipúzcoa, 1984.

Geertz, Clifford. "The Integrative Revolution: Primordial Sentiments and Civil Politics." In *Old Societies and New States: The Quest for Modernity in Asia and Africa*, edited by Clifford Geertz, 255–310. London: Free Press of Glencoe, 1963.

Gellner, Ernest. *Nations and Nationalism*. London: Blackwell, 1983.

Gillespie, Richard. "The Hour of the Nationalists: Catalan and Basque Parties in the Spanish General Election of 6 June 1993." *Regional Politics and Policy* 3 (1993): 177–191.

———. "Peace Moves in the Basque Country." *Journal of Southern Europe and the Balkans* 1 (1999): 119–136.

Giner, Salvador, and Luis Moreno. "La dimension éthnica de la sociedad española." In *España: Sociedad y política*, edited by Salvador Giner, 169–197. Madrid: Espasa-Calpe, 1990.

Goldstein, Judith. *Ideas, Interests, and American Trade Policy*. Ithaca, NY: Cornell University Press, 1993.

González, Cayetano, ed. *Gritos de libertad: 15 voces contra el terror de ETA y la hegemonía nacionalista*. Madrid: La Esfera de los Libros, 2004.

Govaert, Serge. "A Brussels Identity? A Speculative Interpretation." In *Nationalism in Belgium: Shifting Identities, 1780–1995,* edited by Kas Deprez and Louis Vos, 229–239. New York: St. Martin's Press, 1998.

Granja Sainz, José Luis de la. *El nacionalismo vasco (1876–1975).* Madrid: Arco/Libros, SL, 2000.

———. *El nacionalismo vasco: Un siglo de historia.* Madrid: Tecnos, 2002.

———. *Nacionalismo y II República en el País Vasco.* Madrid: Siglo XXI, 1986.

———. *República y Guerra Civil en Euskadi: Del Pacto de San Sebastián al de Santoña.* Bilbao: Oñati, 1990.

Granja Sainz, José Luis de la, Justo Beramendi, and Pere Anguera. *La España de los nacionalismos y las autonomías.* Madrid: Síntesis, 2001.

Granovetter, Mark. "Economic Action and Social Structures: The Problem of Embeddedness." *American Journal of Sociology* 3 (1985): 481–510.

Greenaway, Norma. "Harper Proposes Voice for Quebec." *The Gazette,* December 20, 2005, A1, A12.

Greenfeld, Liah. *Nationalism: Five Roads to Modernity.* Cambridge: Harvard University Press, 1992.

Greenwood, Davydd J. "Continuity in Change: Spanish Basque Ethnicity as a Historical Process." In *Ethnic Conflict in the Western World,* edited by Milton Esman, 81–102. Ithaca, NY: Cornell University Press, 1977.

Ibarra Güell, Pedro. *La evolución estratégica de ETA: De la "Guerra revolucionaria" (1963) a la negociación (1987).* San Sebastián: Kriselu, 1987.

Guibernau, Montserrat, and John Hutchinson, eds. *History and National Destiny.* London: Blackwell, 2004.

———. *Understanding Nationalism.* Cambridge, UK: Polity, 2001.

Gunther, Richard, Giacomo Sani, and Goldie Shabad. *Spain After Franco: The Making of a Competitive Party System.* Berkeley and Los Angeles: University of California Press, 1988.

Hale, Henry. "Divided We Stand: Institutional Sources of Ethnofederal State Survival and Collapse." *World Politics* 56 (2004): 165–193.

Hall, Peter A. "Aligning Ontology and Methodology in Comparative Politics." In Mahoney and Rueschemeyer, *Comparative Historical Analysis in the Social Sciences,* 391–395.

———. "Policy Paradigms, Social Learning, and the State: The Case of Economic Policymaking in Britain." *Comparative Politics* 25 (1993): 275–296.

Hall, Peter A., and Rosemary C. R Taylor. "Political Science and the Three New Institutionalisms." *Political Studies* 44 (1996): 936–957.

Hamilton, Carrie. "Re-membering the Basque Nationalist Family: Daughters, Fathers, and the Reproduction of the Radical Nationalist Community." *Journal of Spanish Cultural Studies* 1 (2000): 153–171.

Harty, Siobhan. "The Institutional Foundations of Sub-state National Movements." *Comparative Politics* 33 (2001): 191–210.

Harvey, David. *The Condition of Post-Modernity: An Enquiry into the Origins of Cultural Change.* Oxford: Blackwell, 1989.

Hassenteufel, Patrick, and Yves Surel. "Des politiques publiques comme les autres? Construction de l'objet et outils d'analyse des politiques publiques." *Politique européenne* no. 1 (2000): 8–24.

Hastings, Adrian. *The Construction of Nationhood: Ethnicity, Religion, and Nationalism.* Cambridge: Cambridge University Press, 1997.

Hay, Colin, and Daniel Wincott. "Structure, Agency, and Historical Institutionalism." *Political Studies* 46 (1998): 951–957.

Hechter, Michael. *Containing Nationalism.* Oxford: Oxford University Press, 2000.

———. *Internal Colonialism: The Celtic Fringe in British National Development, 1536–1966.* Berkeley and Los Angeles: University of California Press, 1975.

Heiberg, Marianne. *The Making of the Basque Nation.* Cambridge: Cambridge University Press, 1987.

Held, David, Anthony McGrew, David Goldblatt, and Jonathan Perraton. *Global Transformations: Politics, Economics, Culture.* Stanford, CA: Stanford University Press, 1999.

Herr, Richard. "Flow and Ebb, 1700–1833." In Carr, *Spain: A History.*

Hobsbawm, Eric. *Nations and Nationalism Since 1780: Programme, Myth, Reality.* Cambridge: Cambridge University Press, 1992.

Hocking, Brian. *Foreign Relations and Federal States.* London: Leicester University Press, 1993.

———. *Localizing Foreign Policy: Non-Central Governments and Multilayered Diplomacy.* London: MacMillan, 1993.

Holguín, Sandie. *Creating Spaniards: Culture and National Identity in Republican Spain.* Madison: University of Wisconsin Press, 2002.

Hooghe, Liesbet, and Gary Marks. "'Europe with the Regions': Channels of Regional Representation Within the European Union." *Publius* 26 (1996): 73–91.

———. *Multi-Level Governance and European Integration.* Oxford: Rowan and Littlefield, 2001.

Ibarra Güell, Pedro. *La evolución estratégica de ETA: De la "Guerra revolucionaria" (1963) a la negociación (1987).* San Sebastián: Kriselu, 1987.

Immergut, Ellen M. *Health Care Politics: Ideas and Institutions in Western Europe.* Cambridge: Cambridge University Press, 1992.

———. "The Theoretical Core of the New Institutionalism." *Politics and Society* 26 (1998): 4–34.

Irvin, Cynthia L. *Militant Nationalism: Between Movement and Party in Ireland and the Basque Country.* Minneapolis: University of Minnesota Press, 1999.

Isaacs, Harold. *Idols of the Tribe: Group Identity and Political Change.* 2nd ed. Cambridge: Harvard University Press, 1989.

Ithurralde, Marianick. *Le Pays basque, la Catalogne et l'Europe: Stratégies politiques des autonomies basque et catalane.* Paris: L'Harmattan, 2002.

Jacobs, James E. *Hills of Conflict: Basque Nationalism in France.* Reno: University of Nevada Press, 1994.

Jacobsen, William H., Jr. "Basque Language Origin Theories." In *Basque Cultural*

Studies, edited by William A. Douglass, Carmelo Urza, Linda White, and Josepa Zulaika, 27–43. Reno: University of Nevada Press, 2000.

Jáuregui, Gurutz. *Entre la tragedia y la esperanz: Vasconia ante el nuevo milenio.* Barcelona: Ariel, 1996.

———. "ETA: Origenes y evolucion ideologica y politica." In *La Historia de ETA,* edited by Antonio Elorza, José María Garmendia, Gurutz Jáuregui, and Florencio Domínguez Iribarren, 189–195. Madrid: Temas de Hoy, SA, 2000.

———. *Ideología y estrategia política de ETA: Análisis de su evolución entre 1959 y 1968.* Madrid: Siglo XXI, 1981.

Jenson, Jane. "Fated to Live in Interesting Times: Canada's Changing Citizenship Regimes." *Canadian Journal of Political Science* 30 (1997): 627–644.

———. "Les réformes des services de garde pour jeunes enfants en France et au Québec: Une analyse historico-institutionnaliste." *Politique et sociétés* 17 (1998): 183–216.

Juaristi, Jon. *El linaje de Aitor: La invención de la tradición vasca.* Madrid: Taurus, 1987.

———. *Vestigios de Babel: Para une arqueología de los nacionalismos españoles.* Madrid: Siglo Veintiuno de España Editores, 1992.

Kasmir, Sharryn. "'More Basque Than You!': Class, Youth, and Identity in an Industrial Basque Town." *Identities: Global Studies in Culture and Power* 9 (2003): 39–68.

Katznelson, Ira, and Helen V. Milner, eds. *Political Science: State of the Discipline.* New York: Norton, 2002.

Kaufmann, Eric, ed. *Rethinking Ethnicity: Majority Groups and Dominant Minorities.* London: Routledge, 2004.

Keating, Michael. "European Integration and the Nationalities Question." *Politics and Society* 32 (2004): 367–388.

———. "Les nationalités minoritaires d'Espagne face à l'Europe." *Études internationales* 30 (1999): 729–743.

———. *Nations Against the State: The New Politics of Nationalism in Quebec, Catalonia, and Scotland.* New York: St. Martin's Press, 1996.

———. "Northern Ireland and the Basque Country." In *Northern Ireland and the Divided World: Post-Agreement Northern Ireland in Comparative Perspective,* edited by John McGarry, 181–208. Oxford: Oxford University Press, 2001.

———. *Plurinational Democracy: Stateless Nations in a Post-Sovereign Era.* Oxford: Oxford University Press, 2001.

———. *State and Regional Nationalism.* London: Harvester Wheatsheaf, 1988.

Keating, Michael, and John McGarry, eds. *Minority Nationalism and the Changing International Order.* Oxford: Oxford University Press, 2001.

Kincaid, John. "The International Competence of US States and Their Local Governments." In Aldecoa and Keating, *Paradiplomacy in Action,* 111–133.

Kohn, Hans. *The Idea of Nationalism: A Study of Its Origins and Background.* New York: Macmillan, 1944.

Kornhauser, William. *The Politics of Mass Society.* New York: Free Press, 1959.

Kurlansky, Mark. *A Basque History of the World.* New York: Penguin Books, 2001.

Kymlicka, Will. *Multicultural Citizenship: A Liberal Theory of Minority Rights.* Oxford: Oxford University Press, 1995.

Laitin, David. "Culture and National Identity: The 'East' and European Integration." *West European Politics* 25 (2002): 55–80.

Lapidoth, Ruth. *Autonomy: Flexible Solutions to Ethnic Conflict.* Washington, DC: U.S. Institute for Peace, 1996.

Larronde, Jean-Claude. *El nacionalismo vasco: Su origen y su ideología en la obra de Sabino Arana-Goiri.* San Sebastián: Txertoa, 1977.

Lecours, André. "Diversité culturelle et relations internationales: Les cas du Québec et de la Wallonie/Comunauté française de Belgique." In *Appartenances, institutions et citoyenneté,* edited by Pierre Noreau and José Woerlhing, 207–218. Montreal: Wilson and Lafleur, 2005.

———. "Ethnonationalism in the West: A Theoretical Exploration." *Nationalism and Ethnic Politics* 6 (2000): 103–124.

———. "Paradiplomacy: Reflections on the Foreign Policy and International Relations of Regions." *International Negotiation* 7 (2002): 91–114.

———. "Regionalism, Cultural Diversity, and the State in Spain." *Journal of Multilingual and Multicultural Development* 22 (2001): 210–226.

———, ed. *New Institutionalism: Theory and Analysis.* Toronto: University of Toronto Press, 2005.

Lecours, André, and Luis Moreno. "Paradiplomacy: A Nation-Building Strategy? A Reference to the Basque Country." In *The Conditions of Diversity in Multinational Democracies,* edited by Alain-G. Gagnon, Montserrat Guibernau, and François Rocher, 267–294. Montreal: Institute for Research on Public Policy, 2003.

Letamendia, Francisco (Ortzi). "Basque Nationalism and Cross-Border Co-operation between the Southern and Northern Basque Countries." *Regional and Federal Studies* 7 (1997): 25–41.

———. *Historia de Euskadi: El nacionalismo vasco y ETA.* Paris: Ruedo Ibérico, 1975.

Levi, Margaret. *Consent, Dissent, and Patriotism.* Cambridge: Cambridge University Press, 1997.

———. *Of Rule and Revenue.* Berkeley and Los Angeles: University of California Press, 1988.

Lieberman, Evan S. "Causal Inference in Historical Institutional Analysis: A Specification of Periodization Strategies." *Comparative Political Studies* 34 (2001): 1017–1023.

Lieberman, Robert C. "Ideas, Institutions, and Political Order: Explaining Political Change." *American Political Science Review* 96 (2002): 697–712.

Lijphart, Arendt. "Consociational Democracy." *World Politics* 21 (1969): 207–225

———. *Democracy in Plural Societies.* New Haven, CT: Yale University Press, 1977.

Linz, Juan J. *Conflicto en Euskadi.* Madrid: Espasa-Calpe, 1986.

———. "Early State-Building and Late Peripheral Nationalism Against the State: The Case of Spain." In *Building States and Nations,* vol. 2, edited by S. N. Eisenstadt and Stein Rokkan, 32–116. London: Sage, 1973.

———. "The Party System of Spain: Past and Future." In *Party Systems and Voter Alignments: Cross-National Perspectives,* edited by Seymour M. Lipset and Stein Rokkan, 197–282. New York: Free Press, 1967.

Loyer, Barbara. "Être indépendant ou ne pas être: Le cas basque." *Hérodote* 95 (1999): 47–62.

———. *Géopolitique du Pays Basque: Nations et nationalismes en Espagne.* Paris: L'Harmattan, 1997.

Lustick, Ian. "Stability in Deeply Divided Societies: Consociationalism vs Control." *World Politics* 31 (1979): 325–344.

MacClancy, Jeremy. *The Decline of Carlism.* Reno: University of Nevada Press, 2000.

———. "Navarra: Historical Realities, Present Myths, Future Possibilities." In Douglass et al., *Basque Politics and Nationalism,* 127–154.

Maclure, Jocelyn. *Quebec Identity: The Challenge of Pluralism.* Montreal: McGill-Queen's University Press, 2003.

Macridis, Roy. *The Study of Comparative Government.* New York: Random, 1955.

Madariaga, Salvador de. *España: Ensayo de Historia Contemporánea.* Madrid: Espasa-Calpe, SA, 1979.

———. *Spain: A Modern History.* New York: Praeger, 1958.

Maddens, Bart, and Kristine vanden Berghe. "The Identity Politics of Multicultural Nationalism: A Comparison Between the Regular Public Addresses of the Belgian and Spanish Monarchs (1990–2000)." *European Journal of Political Research* 42 (2003): 601–627.

Mahoney, James. *The Legacies of Liberalism: Path Dependence and Political Regimes in Central America.* Baltimore: Johns Hopkins University Press, 2001.

Mahoney, James, and Dietrich Rueschemeyer, eds. *Comparative Historical Analysis in the Social Sciences.* Cambridge: Cambridge University Press, 2003.

Mansvelt Beck, Jan. *Territory and Terror: Conflicting Nationalisms in the Basque Country.* London: Routledge, 2005.

March, James, and Johan P. Olsen. "The New Institutionalism: Organizational Factors in Political Life." *American Political Science Review* 78 (1984): 734–749.

———. *Rediscovering Institutions: The Organizational Basis of Politics.* New York: Free Press, 1989.

Mar-Molinero, Clare, and Angel Smith, eds. *Nationalism and the Nation in the Iberian Peninsula.* Oxford: Berg, 1996.

Martin, Pierre. "When Nationalism Meets Continentalism: The Politics of Free Trade in Quebec." *Regional and Federal Studies* 5 (1995): 1–27.

Martínez-Herrera, Enric. "From Nation-Building to Building Identification With Political Communities: Consequences of Political Decentralization in Spain, the Basque Country, Catalonia, and Galicia, 1978–2001." *European Journal of Political Research* 41 (2002): 421–453.

———. "Nationalist Extremism and Outcomes of State Policies in the Basque Country, 1979–2001," *International Journal on Multicultural Societies* 4 (2002). www.unesco.org/most/v14n1martinez.pdf.

Massart-Piérard, Françoise. "Politique des relations extérieures et identité politique:

La stratégie des entités fédérées de la Belgique." *Études internationales* 30 (1999): 701–727.

Mata López, José Manuel. *El nacionalismo vasco radical: Discurso, organización y expresiones.* Bilbao: Universidad del País Vasco, 1993.

Ma Valles, Josep, and Montserrat Cuchillo Fox. "Decentralisation in Spain: A Review." *European Journal of Political Research* 16 (1988): 395–407.

McCrone, David. *Understanding Scotland: The Sociology of a Nation.* 2nd ed. London: Routledge, 2001.

McEwen, Nicola. *Nationalism and the State: Welfare and Identity in Scotland and Quebec.* Brussels: Peter Lang, 2006.

———. "State Welfare Nationalism: The Territorial Impact of Welfare State Development in Scotland." *Regional and Federal Studies* 12 (2002): 66–90.

McEwen, Nicola, and André Lecours. "Voice or Recognition? Accommodation Dilemmas in Multinational Societies." Paper presented at the Canadian Political Science Association conference, Halifax, 2003.

McGarry, John, and Brendan O'Leary. *The Politics of Ethnic Conflict Regulation.* London: Routledge, 1993.

McRae, Kenneth D. *Conflict and Compromise in Multilingual Societies: Belgium.* Waterloo, ON: Wilfrid Laurier University Press, 1986.

———. "Contrasting Styles of Democratic Decision-making: Adversarial versus Consensual Politics." *International Political Science Review* 18 (1997): 279–296.

McRoberts, Kenneth. *Catalonia: Nation-Building Without a State.* Toronto: Oxford University Press, 2001.

———. *Misconceiving Canada: The Struggle for Unity.* Toronto: Oxford University Press, 1997.

———. *Quebec: Social Change and Political Crisis.* Toronto: McClelland and Stewart, 1993.

Mees, Ludger. "Between Votes and Bullets: The Basque Country." *Ethnic and Racial Studies* 24 (2001): 798–827.

———. *Nacionalismo vasco, movimiento obrero y cuestión social (1903–1923).* Bilbao: Fundación Sabino Arana, 1992.

———. *Nationalism, Violence, and Democracy: The Basque Clash of Identities.* New York: Palgrave MacMillan, 2003.

Merriman, Roger Bigelow. 1918. *The Rise of the Spanish Empire in the Old World and in the New.* Vol. 1, *The Middle Ages.* New York: Cooper Square Publishers, 1962.

———. *The Rise of the Spanish Empire in the Old World and in the New.* Vol. 9, *Philip the Prudent.* New York: Macmillan, 1934.

Michelmann, Hans J., and Panayotis Soldatos, eds. *Federalism and International Relations: The Role of Subnational Units.* Oxford: Clarendon Press, 1990.

Migdal, Joel S. *Strong Societies and Weak States: State-Societies Relations and State Capabilities in the Third World.* Princeton, NJ: Princeton University Press, 1988.

Ministère des Relations Internationales. *Le Québec dans un ensemble international en mutation: Plan stratégique, 2001–2004.* Quebec: 2001.

———. *Québec in International Forums: Exercising Québec's Constitutional Rights at International Organization and Conference.* 2005.

———. *Répertoire des ententes internationales du Québec, 1964–2000.* 2001.

Mitchell, Timothy. *Colonising Egypt.* Berkeley and Los Angeles: University of California Press, 1991.

Monière, Denis. *Pour comprendre le nationalisme au Québec et ailleurs.* Montreal: Les Presses de l'Université de Montréal, 2001.

Morán, Sagrario. *ETA entre España y Francia.* Madrid: Editorial Complutense, 1997.

Moreno, Luis. "Divided Societies: Electoral Polarization and the Basque Country." In *Democracy and Ethnic Conflict,* edited by Adrian Guelke, 29–51. New York: Palgrave MacMillan, 2004.

———. *The Federalization of Spain.* London: Frank Cass, 2001.

Moxon-Browne, Edward. "Regionalism in Spain: The Basque Elections of 1990." *Regional Politics and Policy* 1 (1990): 191–197.

Mueller, John. "The Banality of 'Ethnic War.'" *International Security* 25 (2000): 42–70.

Murkens, Jo Eric (with Peter Jones and Michael Keating. *Scottish Independence: A Practical Guide.* Edinburgh: Edinburgh University Press, 2002.

Nagelschmidt, Martin. "Les relations internationales des Länder allemand et l'évolution du système fédéral dans l'Union européenne: Le cas du Bade-Wurtemberg." *Études internationales* 30 (1999): 679–699.

Nairn, Tom. *Faces of Nationalism: Janus Revisited.* London: Verso, 1997.

Nogaret, Joseph. *Petite histoire au pays basque français.* Bayonne: Edition de la Société des Sciences, Lettres, Arts et d'Études Régionales de Bayonne, 1928.

Noreau, Pierre, and José Woerling, eds. *Appartenances, institutions et citoyenneté.* Montreal: Wilson and Lafleur, 2005.

Núñez, Xosé-Manoel. *Los nacionalismos en la España contemporánea (siglos XIX and XX).* Barcelona: Hipótesis, 1999.

———. "What Is Spanish Nationalism Today? From Legitimacy Crisis to Unfulfilled Renovation (1975–2000)." *Ethnic and Racial Studies* 24 (2001): 719–752.

O'Leary, Brendan, and John McGarry, eds. *Northern Ireland Conflict: Consociational Engagements.* Oxford: Oxford University Press, 2004.

Orren, Karen, and Stephen Skowronek. "Institutions and Intercurrence: Theory Building in the Fullness of Time." In *Nomos XXXVIII Political Order,* edited by Ian Shapiro and Russell Hardin, 111–146. New York: New York University Press, 1996.

Ortega y Gasset, José. *España invertebrada: Bosquejo de algunos pensamientos históricos.* 9th ed. Madrid: Espasa-Calpe, 1989.

Ostrom, Elinor. "Rational Choice Theory and Institutional Analysis: Toward Complementarity." *American Political Science Review* 85 (1991): 237–243.

Pablo, Santiago de, José Luis de la Granja Sainz, and Ludger Mees, eds. *Documentos para la historia del nacionalismo vasco: De los Fueros a nuestros días.* Barcelona: Editorial Ariel, SA, 1998.

Pablo, Santiago de, and Ludger Mees. *El péndulo patriótico: Historia del Partido Nacionalista Vasco (1895–2005).* Barcelona: Crítica, 2005.

Pagano, Guiseppe. *Les résolutions du Parlement flamand pour une réforme de l'État.* Brussels: CRISP, no. 1670–1671, 2000.

Painchaud, Paul. "Fédéralisme et politique étrangère." *Études internationales* 5 (1974): 25–44.

Palier, Bruno, and Giuliano Bonoli. "Phénomènes de *path dependence* et réformes des systèmes de protection sociale." *Revue française de science politique* 49 (1999): 399–420.

Paquin, Stéphane. *Paradiplomatie identitaire en Catalogne.* Quebec: Les Presses de l'Université Laval, 2003.

———. "Paradiplomatie identitaire et diplomatie en Belgique fédérale: Le cas de la Flandre." *Canadian Journal of Political Science* 36 (2003): 621–642.

———. *La revanche des petites nations: Le Québec, l'Écosse et la Catalogne face à la mondialisation.* Montreal: VLB Éditeur, 2001.

Partido Popular. *Elecciones generales 2000: El compromiso del centro.* Madrid, 2000. 95–111.

Payne, Stanley. *Basque Nationalism.* Reno: University of Nevada Press, 1975.

———. *Fascism in Spain, 1923–1977.* Madison: University of Wisconsin Press, 1999.

Penniman, Howard R., and Eusebio M. Mujal-Léon, eds. *Spain at the Polls, 1977, 1979, 1982: A Study of National Elections.* Durham, NC: Duke University Press, 1985.

Pérez Garzón, J., et al. *La gestión de la memoria: La historia de España al servicio del poder.* Barcelona: Crítica, 2000.

Peters, Guy. *Institutional Theory in Political Science: The "New Institutionalism."* London: Continuum, 1999.

Petersen, Roger D. *Understanding Ethnic Violence: Fear, Hatred, and Resentment in Twentieth-Century Eastern Europe.* Cambridge: Cambridge University Press, 2002.

Philippart, Éric, and Michaël Van Cutsem. "De l'explication à la prévision: Analyse des perspectives en matièere de relations internationales des régions d'Europe." *Études internationales* 30 (1999): 789–808.

Pierson, Paul. "Increasing Returns, Path Dependence, and the Study of Politics." *American Political Science Review* 94 (2000): 251–267.

———. "Not Just What, but *When*: Timing and Sequence in Political Processes." *Studies in American Political Development* 14 (2000): 72–92.

———. "When Effect Becomes Cause: Policy Feedback and Political Change." *World Politics* 45 (1993): 595–628.

Pierson, Paul, and Theda Skocpol. "Historical Institutionalism in Contemporary Political Science." In Katznelson and Milner, *Political Science,* 693–721.

Poirier, Johanne, and Steven Vansteenkiste. "Le débat sur la fédéralisation de la sécurité sociale en Belgique: Le miroir du vouloir-vivre ensemble?" *Revue belge de sécurité sociale* 2 (2000): 331–378.

Poliakov, Léon. *The Aryan Myth: A History of Racist and Nationalist Ideas in Europe.* New York: Basic Books, 1974.

Political Context. *Report on Devolution Poll.* London, 1996.

Posen, Barry R. "The Security Dilemma and Ethnic Conflict." *Survival* 35 (1993): 27–47.

Powell, Walter W., and Paul J. DiMaggio. "The Iron Cage Revisited: Institutional Isomorphism and Collective Rationality in Organizational Fields." *American Sociological Review* 48 (1983): 147–160.

———, eds. *The New Institutionalism in Organizational Analysis.* Chicago: University of Chicago Press, 1991.

Presse Canadienne. "Un modèle pour le BQ, le traité de Maastricht." *Le Devoir,* April 10, 1995, A4.

Preston, Paul. *The Politics of Revenge: Fascism and the Military in Twentieth-Century Spain.* London: Unwin Hyman, 1990.

———. *The Triumph of Democracy in Spain.* London: Methuen, 1986.

Rabushka, Alvin, and Kenneth A. Shepsle. *Politics in Plural Societies: A Theory of Democratic Instability.* Columbus, OH: Merrill, 1972.

Raento, Paulina. "Political Mobilisation and Place-Specificity: Radical Nationalist Street Campaigning in the Spanish Basque Country." *Space and Polity* 1 (1997): 191–204.

Raento, Paulina, and Cameron J. Watson. "Gernika, Guernica, *Guernica?* Contested Meanings of a Basque Place." *Political Geography* 19 (2000): 707–736.

Ravenhill, John. "Federal-States Relations in Australian External Affairs." In Aldecoa and Keating, *Paradiplomacy in Action,* 134–152.

Région Rhône-Alpes. *Rhône-Alpes, actions internationales.* 2000.

Resina, Joan Ramon. "Post-National Spain? Post-Spanish Spain?" *Nations and Nationalism* 8 (2002): 377–396.

Richards, Michael. "Constructing the Nationalist State: Self-Sufficiency and Regeneration in the Early Franco Years." In Mar-Molino and Smith, *Nationalism and the Nation in the Iberian Peninsula,* 149–170.

Robertson, David Brian. "The Return to History in American Political Science." *Social Science History* 17 (1993): 1–36.

Rocher, Francois, and Nadia Virelli. "Questioning Constitutional Democracy in Canada: From the Canadian Supreme Court Reference to the Clarity Act." In *The Conditions of Diversity in Multinational Democracy,* edited by Alain-G. Gagnon, Montserrat Guibernau, and François Rocher, 207–237. Montreal: IRPP, 2003.

Rogowski, Ronald. Conclusion to *New Nationalism in the Developed West,* edited by Edward A. Tyriakian and Ronald Rogowski, 277–293. Boston: Allen and Unwin, 1984.

Romero Salvado, Francisco J. *Twentieth-Century Spain: Politics and Society in Spain, 1898–1998.* New York: St. Martin's Press, 1998.

Rosenau, James. "Patterned Chaos in Global Life: Structure and Process in the Two Worlds of World Politics." *International Political Science Review* 9 (1988): 327–364.

Rossinyol, Jaume. *Le problème national catalan.* Paris: Mouton, 1974.

Rothschild, Joseph. *Ethnopolitics: A Conceptual Framework.* New York: Columbia University Press, 1981.

Ruiz Almendral, Violeta. "The Asymmetric Distribution of Taxation Powers in the Spanish State of Autonomies: The Common System and the Foral Regimes." *Regional and Federal Studies* 13 (2003): 41–66.

Saideman, Steve, et al. "Fixed and Endogenous Elections and Ethnic Conflict: Similar or Different Causal Relationships." Paper presented at the International Studies Association conference, Montreal, February 2004.

Saint-Martin, Denis. "The New Managerialism and the Policy Influence of Consultants in Government: An Historical-Institutionalist Analysis of Britain, Canada, and France." *Governance* 11 (1998): 319–356.

Sainz, Jorge. "Decenas de miles de personas marchan en favor de 'Egunkaria.'" *El Correo*, February 23 2003, 30.

Sánchez-Albornoz, Claudio. *España: Un enigma histórico.* Buenos Aires: Sudamericana, 1956.

———. *Orígenes y destino de Navarra: Trayectoria histórica de Vasconia: Otros escritos.* Barcelona: Planeta, 1974.

Sarailh de Ihartza, Fernando (Frederico Krutwig). *Vasconia.* Buenos Aires: Ediciones Norbait, 1963.

Scholte, Jan Aart. *Globalization: A Critical Introduction.* London: MacMillan, 2001.

Scott, James C. *Seeing Like the State.* New Haven, CT: Yale University Press, 1998.

Scottish National Party. *Raising the Standard: There Shall Be an Independent Scottish Parliament.* 2005.

Secretaría General de Acción Exterior. *Presupuestos generales de la Comunidad Autónomas de Euskadi.* 2004.

———. *Presupuestos generales de la Comunidad Autónomas de Euskadi.* 2006.

Shils, Edward. "Primordial, Personal, Sacred, and Civil Ties." *British Journal of Sociology* 8 (1957): 130–145.

Shulman, Steven. "Challenging the Civic/Ethnic and West/East Dichotomy in the Study of Nationalism." *Comparative Political Studies* 35 (2002): 554–585.

Simeon, Richard, and Daniel Patrick-Conway. "Federalism and the Management of Conflict in Multinational Societies." In *Multinational Democracies*, edited by Alain-G. Gagnon and James Tully, 339–365. Cambridge: Cambridge University Press, 2001.

Skocpol, Theda. *States and Social Revolutions: A Comparative Analysis of France, Russia, and China.* Cambridge: Cambridge University Press, 1979.

Smith, Anthony D. *The Ethnic Origins of Nations.* New York: Blackwell, 1986.

———. *National Identity.* Reno: University of Nevada Press, 1991.

———. *Nationalism and Modernism: A Critical Survey of Recent Theories of Nations and Nationalism.* London: Routledge, 1998.

———. *Nations and Nationalism in a Global Era.* Cambridge: Polity Press, 1995.

Spruyt, Hendrik. *The Sovereign State and Its Competitors: An Analysis of Systems Change.* Princeton, NJ: Princeton University Press, 1994.

Steinmo, Sven, Kathleen Thelen, and Frank Longstreth. *Structuring Politics: Historical Institutionalism in Comparative Analysis.* Cambridge: Cambridge University Press, 1992.

Storm, Eric. "The Problems of the Spanish Nation-Building Process around 1900." *National Identities* 6 (2004): 143–156.

Sullivan, John. *ETA and Basque Nationalism: The Fight for Euskadi, 1890–1986.* London: Routledge, 1988.

Sutherland, Stewart. *With Respect to Old Age: Long Term Care—Rights and Responsibilities: A Report by the Royal Commission on Long-Term Care.* London, March 1999.

Swyngedouw, Marc, and Gilles Ivaldi. "The Extreme Right Utopia in Belgium and France: The Ideology of the Flemish Vlaams Blok and the French Front National." *West European Politics* 24 (2001): 1–22.

Tamir, Yael. *Liberal Nationalism.* Princeton, NJ: Princeton University Press, 1993.

Taylor, Brian. *Scotland's Parliament: Triumph and Disaster.* Edinburgh: Edinburgh University Press, 2002.

Taylor, Charles. *Reconciling the Solitudes: Essays on Canadian Nationalism and Federalism.* Montreal: McGill Queen's University Press, 1992.

Thelen, Kathleen. "Historical Institutionalism in Comparative Politics." *Annual Review of Political Science,* 1999, 369–404.

———. "How Institutions Evolve: Insights from Comparative Historical Analysis." In Mahoney and Rueschemeyer, *Comparative Historical Analysis in the Social Sciences,* 208–240.

Théret, Bruno. "Institutions et institutionnalismes: Vers une convergence des conceptions de l'institution?" In *Innovations institutionnelles et territoires,* edited by Michèle Tallard, Bruno Théret, and Didier Uri, 25–58. Paris: L'Harmattan, 2000.

Totoricagüena, Gloria. *Identity, Culture, and Politics in the Basque Diaspora.* Reno: University of Nevada Press, 2003.

Trench, Alan, ed. *Has Devolution Made a Difference? The State of the Nations 2004.* Exeter: Imprint Academic, 2004.

Ugalde Zubiri, Alexander. *La acción exterior del nacionalismo vasco (1890–1939): Historia, pensamiento y relaciones internacionales.* Bilbao: Instituto Vasco de Adminstracion Pública, 1996.

———. "The International Relations of Basque Nationalism and the First Basque Autonomous Government (1890–1939)." In Aldecoa and Keating, *Paradiplomacy in Action,* 170–184.

Uriarte, Edurne. *España, patriotismo y nación.* Madrid: Calpe, SA, 2003.

Urza, Carmelo. "The Election of 30N." *Basque Studies Program Newsletter,* no. 35 (1997). http://basque.unr.edu/09/9.3/9.3.35t/9.3.35.05.election.htm.

Valverde, Lola. *Historia de Guipúzcoa.* San Sebastián: Txertoa, 1984.

Van den Berghe, Pierre. *The Ethnic Phenomenon.* New York: Elsevier, 1979.

Van Rompuy, Paul. "10 jaar financiële stromen tussen de Gewesten in België." *Leuvense Economische Standpunten,* no. 45, KULeuven, CES, July 1998.

Vlaams Blok. *Een toekomst voor Vlaanderen.* 2003.

Vos, Louis. "The Flemish National Question." In *Nationalism in Belgium: Shifting Identities, 1780\–1995,* edited by Kas Deprez and Louis Vos, 83–95. New York: St. Martin's Press, 1998.

Watson, Cameron. *Modern Basque History: Eighteenth Century to the Present.* Reno: Center for Basque Studies, 2003.

Watts, Ronald. *Comparing Federal Systems.* Kingston, ON: Institute of Intergovernmental Relations, Queen's University, 1996.

———. *Comparing Federal Systems.* 2nd ed. Montreal: McGill-Queen's University Press, 1999.

Weber, Eugen. *Peasants Into Frenchmen: The Modernization of Rural France, 1870–1914.* Stanford, CA: Stanford University Press, 1976.

Weingast, Barry R. "Rational-Choice Institutionalism." In Katznelson and Milner, *Political Science,* 660–692.

West, Lois A., ed. *Feminist Nationalism.* London: Routledge, 1997.

Woodworth, Paddy. "Why Do They Kill? The Basque Conflict in Spain." *World Policy Journal* 18 (2001): 1–12.

Yack, Bernard. "The Myth of the Civic Nation." In *Theorizing Nationalism,* edited by Ronald Beiner, 103–118. Albany: State University of New York Press, 1999.

Zabaleta, Iñaki. "The Basques in the International Press: Coverage by the New York Times (1950–1996)." In Douglass et al., *Basque Politics and Nationalism on the Eve of the Millenium,* 68–93.

Zirakzadeh, Cyrus Ernesto. *A Rebellious People: Basques, Protests, and Politics.* Reno: University of Nevada Press, 1991.

Zulaika, Joseba. *Basque Violence: Metaphor and Sacrament.* Reno: University of Nevada Press, 1988.

Index

Page numbers in italics refer to figures.